Chinese Family Businesses in Malaysia

Lee focuses on the historical and cultural journey of Chinese family businesses (CFBs) in Malaysia, uncovering the dynamic interplay of ethnic resources, generational knowledge, and state-led development policies that have shaped their survival and success.

With one of the largest Chinese communities in Southeast Asia, Malaysia offers a rich landscape to explore the evolution of CFBs. Through analyzing 12 small and medium-sized enterprises (SMEs) across key economic sectors, the book examines how Chinese family businesses have adapted to a shifting landscape, from leveraging deep-rooted networks and ethnic heritage to navigating government policies that have both challenged and shaped their growth. It uncovers key factors such as tacit knowledge, innovation, and generational transitions that have driven the evolution of these enterprises in Malaysia's competitive business environment. Drawing on detailed case studies, Lee demonstrates how tradition, innovation, and strategic decision-making converge to sustain business longevity across generations.

An essential read for researchers, students, family business practitioners and business historians, and anyone interested in understanding the resilience and adaptability of Chinese family businesses.

Lee Kean Yew is an associate researcher at the department of Chinese Studies, Faculty of Arts and Social Sciences, University of Malaya. He also serves as the academic director at the Centre for Malaysia Chinese Studies, focusing on Chinese family business and innovation management.

Chinese Family Businesses in Malaysia

Fostering Tacit Knowledge Innovation

Lee Kean Yew

Routledge
Taylor & Francis Group
LONDON AND NEW YORK

First published 2025
by Routledge
4 Park Square, Milton Park, Abingdon, Oxon OX14 4RN

and by Routledge
605 Third Avenue, New York, NY 10158

Routledge is an imprint of the Taylor & Francis Group, an informa business

British Library Cataloguing-in-Publication Data
A catalogue record for this book is available from the British Library

ISBN: 9781032705781 (hbk)
ISBN: 9781032705866 (pbk)
ISBN: 9781032705842 (ebk)

DOI: 10.4324/9781032705842

Typeset in Times New Roman
by Newgen Publishing UK

With deepest love and gratitude to my beloved parents, Lee Kid Seong and Chong Siew Thai, whose exemplary lives left an indelible impact on my life.

Contents

Figures

Tables

Foreword

I would like to congratulate Dr. Lee Kean Yew on the publication of this book, and I sincerely hope that readers will gain many useful insights from it. As this book points out, Chinese business people have been driving economic and industrial activities in many Asian countries, and the role that innovation plays in their sustainable growth is extremely important. I have been working with long-lived firms for 25 years, and have discovered more than 100,000 long- lived companies in 170 countries and regions around the world that have been in business for more than 100 years since their founding. As of 2013, I have discovered 10 companies surviving over a hundred years in Malaysia, of which 4 are long-lived companies by overseas Chinese. In addition, at that time, there existed 20 other overseas Chinese companies that had been in business for more than three generations in Malaysia. Considering the fact that many companies have emerged since the 1940s, it would not be surprising if a great number of companies are going to celebrate their 100th anniversary in the coming two decades. In order to achieve sustainable growth, it is important to adhere to the founders spirit and, as emphasized by Dr. Lee Kean Yew in this book, to engage in innovative activities that respond to changes in the business environment and customer preferences. In particular, the use of tacit knowledge, and its conversion to explicit knowledge, and sharing among all members involved, are crucial keys to success. I sincerely hope that many executives, managers in corporate planning, marketing and engineering will read this book carefully and use it effectively.

Toshio Goto, Research Professor, Japan University of Economics

Foreword

A novel and insightful assessment of family-owned SMEs through the interlocking themes of tacit knowledge, generational change and innovation. Since family firms constitute about 80% of enterprises globally, this book is a vital business and policy guide to how the skills and entrepreneurial capacity of the founding generation can be codified and nurtured to create resourceful companies.

Edmund Terence Gomez, Emeritus Professor, Universiti Malaya

Preface

Chinese family businesses (CFBs) represent a significant portion of Malaysia's corporate sector and have played a key role in the nation's economic development. These firms are built upon a unique foundation of Chinese tradition and family values, making them renowned for their embedded networks, habitual ownership practices, and strong family alliances. However, the success of these firms is not merely the result of their founding principles. Rather, it hinges on the effective transfer and development of tacit knowledge, the unspoken insights and skills that are passed down through generations.

This book explores how tacit knowledge is preserved, developed, and transformed as CFBs navigate generational changes, focusing on the food, plastic, and rubber industries. By adopting a business history approach, examining CFBs from their startup phases through to the first quarter of 2024. Drawing on Alfred Chandler's theory of organizational development, this book focuses on the "3M" framework: Manufacturing, Management, and Marketing. By tracing their historical development, we can better understand how these businesses have evolved over multiple generations. The study particularly highlights how second and third generations, often equipped with higher education and professional qualifications, bring fresh insights into their family businesses. These successors leverage their knowledge and enhance tacit knowledge to modernize operations, streamline processes, and expand market reach.

Through comparative longitudinal case studies, this book illustrates how different generations of CFB leaders codify tacit knowledge, adapt to new challenges, and embrace innovation. These firms have successfully transformed unspoken practices into structured knowledge and embraced innovation to remain competitive. The book also reveals how different generations adopt new techniques and technologies while preserving core family values. By examining the evolution of these businesses, we gain insights into how successors harness their professional skills to introduce modern practices.

The journey of these CFBs is marked by sacrifices, challenges, and transformative learning. Yet, their ability to transfer and adapt tacit knowledge has allowed them to emerge as globally competitive enterprises. This transformative learning process where tacit knowledge evolves with each generation is key to achieving innovation and sustainability, particularly during leadership transitions.

Finally, this book offers a set of policy recommendations to support the growth of CFBs in Malaysia. By understanding the pivotal role of tacit knowledge in fostering innovation and strategic development, we can better appreciate the enduring legacy and adaptability of Chinese family businesses, ensuring their continued success in an ever-changing economic environment.

Acknowledgements

I would like to extend my gratitude to Professor Chin Yee Whah, Associate Professor Jacob Donald Tan, Professor Wong Heung Wah, and Associate Professor Chen Tsung-Yuan for sharing their vast knowledge and experience, especially involving the subjects of business history and ethnic enterprise.

I am deeply grateful to Miss Wong Sau Man, my research assistant, for her valuable assistance and support. Recognizing the volume of research required for such a project, that involves a multi-dimensional assessment of firms operating over an exceptionally long time, sometimes up to three generations, I was worried that it would take me and Miss Wong Sau Man a lengthy period to complete this book. However, she proved to be a most enterprising student. From the outset, she has worked extremely diligently to re-arranging data on ethnic Chinese family-based manufacturing firms in different dialect groups now controlled by the second generation and beyond. This was quickly followed up with my previous in-depth interviews with the stakeholders of the firms identified for research. Further research was carried out at the Companies Commission of Malaysia (CCM) where I spent a great deal of time reviewing the company records of these enterprises. This primary research led to the accumulation of a considerable volume of data. Both of us have spent much time analyzing this database to determine the most effective manner to systematically present these empirical findings. Her ability to process large volumes of information and distil them into clear, insightful, and well-structured narratives has been an invaluable asset to this project. She demonstrates remarkable composure under pressure, efficiently managing her workload while navigating unforeseen challenges with grace and precision. Moreover, her capacity to engage in thoughtful discussions with objectivity, free from personal bias, reflects a deep intellectual maturity. In these moments, a genuine passion for knowledge shines in her eyes. These qualities embody the essence of a true scholar. With her keen intellect, determination, and curiosity, I have no doubt that she will reach even greater heights in her academic and professional journey.

I take this opportunity to express my deepest appreciation and gratitude to the Malaysian government's Mybrain 15 PHD program (KPT(B) 810710145269), and to the University of Malaya's PPP Research Grant (No.: PS010/2011A) in sponsoring me . Without these sponsorships, this book would not be made possible and have received praise for embarking on this area of research. The support from the Asia Europe Institute, Department of Chinese Studies and Malaysian Chinese Research Centre (MCRC), and the University of Malaya also merit a mention for the quality of what has been produced.

Not to be forgotten, I dedicated my heartiest appreciation to all members, friends and colleagues of my Alma Mater, University of Malaya since I started my postgraduate journey there. Words cannot describe my sincerest gratitude to my family members including my parents, wife Lim Joan Ann, and my daughter Joey Lee Min Wei for their unending affection and encouragement. I also appreciate the interviewees who have been willing to openly share their ideas on how ethnic enterprises, such as Chinese family businesses, function in Malaysia.

I would like to thank the anonymous reviewers for their carefully reading my monograph, and for their many insightful comments and suggestions. Finally, any flaws or mistakes seen in this work are solely my responsibility.

Symbols and Abbreviations

ACA	Accelerated Capital Allowance
ACCCIM	Associated Chinese Chambers of Commerce and Industry of Malaysia
AFTA	ASEAN Free Trade Area
ASB	Amanah Saham Bumiputera
ASN	Amanah Saham Nasional
CCB	Central Cooperative Bank
CEPT	Common Effective Preferential Treatment
CFBs	Chinese family businesses
DISF	Domestic Investment Strategic Fund
EPF	Employees Provident Fund
FDI	Foreign Direct Investment
FIMA	Food Industries of Malaysia
FMM	Federation of Malaysian Manufacturers
GDP	Gross Domestic Produce
GLCs	Government-linked Companies
HICOM	Heavy Industries Corporation of Malaysia
JAKIM	Department of Islamic Development Malaysia
LEP	Look East Policy
MARDEC	Malaysian Rubber Development Corporation
MATRADE	Malaysia External Trade Development Corporation
MREPC	Malaysian Rubber Export Promotion Council
MIDA	Malaysian Industrial Development Authority
NEP	New Economic Policy
SSM	Companies Commission of Malaysia
OBM	Original Brand Manufacturing
OEM	Original Equipment Manufacturing
ODM	Original Design Manufacturing
PERNAS	Perbadanan Nasional Berhad
PETRONAS	Petroliam Nasional Berhad
PNB	Permodalan Nasional Berhad
R&D	Research and Development
SMEs	Small and Medium scale enterprises

1 The Making of Family-Owned Chinese Businesses in Malaysia

Although ethnic Chinese constitute only about 23% of Malaysia's population, this minority group has significantly contributed to the country's economic development since the beginning of the 20th century. Despite their substantial impact, research on Chinese family businesses in Malaysia remains scarce, particularly regarding how these businesses have leveraged their ethnic and class resources to grow and sustain their businesses. Furthermore, there is a notable gap in understanding the intra-ethnic and inter-ethnic networks established by the Chinese community in their business endeavors. Crucially, many of these family businesses have seen ownership and control pass to the second, third, and even fourth generations. Despite the long-standing presence of Chinese businesses in Malaysia, limited research has been conducted in exploring the impacts of these generational transitions. Additionally, the challenges and opportunities faced by Chinese entrepreneurs in the Malaysian economy have not been thoroughly examined.

1.1 Ethnic Chinese in Malaysian Business and Family Business

In Malaysia, family businesses account for about 70% of listed companies and contribute 67.2% to the national gross domestic product (GDP) (Amran, 2010). This diverse minority group has played a vital role in the country's economic growth since the early 20th century (Yew, 2021). However, there is a notable gap in research concerning Chinese family-owned businesses, especially regarding their use of tacit knowledge and Chinese networks for enterprise growth (Yew, 2020). Additionally, studies on the intra-ethnic and inter-ethnic networks formed by these businesses are lacking. Ownership and tacit knowledge have often been passed down through multiple generations, yet the implications and outcomes of these transitions remain unexamined, as do the obstacles and opportunities faced by this ethnic group.

Historically, Chinese business owners have maintained significant ownership in public listed companies, with their share capital nearly doubling from 27.2% in 1970 to 45.5% in 1990. This growth primarily came at the expense of declining foreign ownership, which fell from 63.4% to 25.4%. Concurrently, Bumiputera

DOI: 10.4324/9781032705842-1

(a term that refers to indigenous Malaysians) capital ownership rose dramatically, driven by government policies designed to elevate the economic status of the Malay population (Whah, 2008).

In 1970, the low percentage of Malay share capital ownership highlighted stark wealth disparities, prompting the introduction of the New Economic Policy (NEP) aimed at addressing these inequalities. During this period, Chinese ownership was particularly notable in construction and transportation, although their presence was less significant in larger sectors like agriculture and manufacturing. From 1970 to 2004, trends in Chinese corporate ownership varied across sectors. The mining and quarrying sectors saw a significant increase in Chinese ownership from 1.8% to 39.5%. In agriculture, forestry, and fisheries, ownership surged from 22.4% to 52.9%. The wholesale and retail sectors also saw growth with Chinese ownership rising from 30.4% to 50.7%. However, in manufacturing, ownership remained stable, while it declined by 10% in construction.

In contrast, Bumiputera ownership expanded across all sectors during the same period, particularly in construction and agriculture, where ownership increased significantly. Their stake in commerce, and in the transportation and communication sectors, also saw substantial growth. Additionally, Bumiputera gained notable shares in banking and insurance, traditionally dominated by foreign capital, reflecting shifts in the ownership landscape within the Malaysian economy (Whah & Lim, 2018). Refer to Table 1.1.

In Table 1.2, the limited corporate presence of Chinese businesses in Malaysia raises two key concerns. Historically, Chinese Malaysians have shown strong entrepreneurial spirit across various sectors. The early post-independence era emphasized *laissez-faire* policies that encouraged foreign direct investment (FDI). This included import substitution industrialization (ISI) strategies in the early 1960s, aimed at creating domestic business opportunities. This was followed by export-oriented industrialization (EOI) supported by government incentives to foster employment and investment. These policies helped multinational subsidiaries create skilled job opportunities and facilitated knowledge transfer in modern manufacturing, especially in the plastics and semiconductor industries, thereby paving the way for future Chinese entrepreneurs to accumulate financial and human capital (Lim, 1983).

Research indicates that Chinese manufacturing enterprises in Malaysia evolved from cottage industries in colonial times to larger manufacturing activities, notably in rubber, food, wood-based industries, and plastics (Tan, 1982). However, many Chinese entrepreneurs, primarily family firms in the manufacturing sector, faced challenges in accessing capital, technical expertise, and managerial skills for large-scale operations. Insufficient government support further hindered local firms from expanding production or reducing dependency on foreign technology (Khor, 1983). Although business opportunities were booming, the government's initial ISI policy offered little incentive for local companies. During this time, trust agencies held shares for Bumiputera interests, increasing capital ownership from 0.8% to 5.1% (see Table 1.1). By the mid-1980s, Bumiputera equity stock grew at approximately 32% per annum, outpacing trust agency holdings, driven by private

Table 1.1 Ownership of Share Capital (at Par Value) of Limited Companies by Ethnic Group, Malaysia, 1970–2008 (RM million)

Ownership Group	*1970*		*1980*		*1990*		*2004*		*2008*	
	RM	*%*	*RM*	*%*	*RM*	*%*	*RM*	*%*	*RM*	*%*
Bumiputera	122,0	2,4	4,050,5	12,5	20,877,5	19,3	100,037,2	18,9	127,407,6	21,9
Individual And Institutions	81,3	1,6	1,880,1	5,8	15,322,0	14,2	-	-	-	-
Individual	-	-	-	-	-	-	79,449,9	15,0	109,982,6	18,9
Institution	-	-	-	-	-	-	11,890,7	2,2	10,811,0	1,9
Trust Agencies	40,7	0,8	2,170,4	6,7	5,555,5	5,1	8,696,6	1,7	6,614,1	1,1
Non-Bumiputera	1,438,9	28,3	14,442,9	44,6	50,754,0	46,8	214,972,8	40,6	213,355,5	36,7
Chinese	1,382,9	27,2	w.i.	w.i.	49,296,5	45,5	206,682,9	39,0	203,092,1	34,9
Indians	55,9	1,1	w.i.	w.i.	1,068,0	1,0	6,392,6	1,2	9,564,6	1,6
Others	0,0	0,0	w.i.	w.i.	389,5	0,3	1,897,3	0,4	698,8	0,1
Foreigners	3,218,4	63,4	13,92720	42,9	27,525,5	25,4	172,279,6	32,5	220,530,8	37,9
Nominee	305,1	6,0	w.i.	w.i.	9,220,4	8,5	42,479,1	8,0	20,547,2	3,5
Total	5,084,4	100,0	2,420,4	100,0	108,377,4	100,0	529,768,7	100,0	581,841,2	100,0

Source: Malaysia 1976: 99; 1984: 112; 1986: 125; 1993: 67; 1996: 86; 2010: 403.

Table 1.2 Share Capital Ownership (at Par Value) of Listed Companies by Ethnic Groups and Sectors, Peninsular Malaysia, 1970 and Malaysia, 2004

Sectors	*Ethnic Group*										*Total**	
	Malay (%)		*Chinese (%)*		*Indian (%)*		*Foreigners (%)*		*Nominee Companies*		*RM Million*	*RM Million*
	1970	*2004*	*1970*	*2004*	*1970*	*2004*	*1970*	*2004*	*1970*	*2004*	*1970*	*2004*
Agriculture, forestry and fisheries	0.9	16.4	22.4	52.9	0.1	0.8	75.3	23	-	6.6	1,432	-
Mining and quarrying	0,7	12,3	1,8	39,5	0,4	0,2	72,4	22,5	-	25,4	544	-
Manufacturing	2,5	8,1	22	24,5	0,7	0,6	59,6	64,7	-	1,9	1,348	-
Construction	2,2	35,2	52,8	42,6	0,8	1,1	24,1	14,9	-	5,9	58	-
Transportation and communications	2,5	26,7	43,4	27,7	2,3	2,5	12	31,3	-	11,4	82	-
Commerce (retail and wholesale)	2,2	20,4	30,4	50,7	0,7	2	63,5	25,6	-	0,7	605	-
Banking and insurance	3,3	12,5	24,3	10,2	0,6	0,3	52,2	59,5	-	17,5	637	-
Services	-	18,7	-	39,5	-	1,1	-	29,5	-	10,9	-	-
Utility	-	6,3	-	8,9	-	02	-	67,3	-	17,2	-	-
Others	2,3	24,3	37,8	45,7	2,3	1,2	31,4	23,2	-	3,9	583	-
Total	1,9	18,9	22,5	39,0	1,00	1,2	60,7	32,5	-	8,0	5,289	529,769

Note: * The total included share capital ownership by Federal and State Government and Statutory Bodies. Source: Malaysia, 1973: 83; 2006: 338 and 357.

Bumiputera enterprises and the National Trust Scheme (ASN) of the National Equity Corporation (PNB) (Malaysia, 1986).

Puthucheary (1960) highlighted that the manufacturing sector, predominantly made up of Chinese family firms, had a significant presence. During British colonial rule, these firms relied heavily on unskilled labor (Tan, 1982). A comparison of the top 100 companies in 1970 and 2001 revealed that only the foreign-owned Rothmans maintained its leading position in manufacturing (Lim, 1981; Gomez, 2007), suggesting that family firms in this sector under-invested in research and development (R&D) and neglected the advancement of innovative tacit knowledge.

Gomez (1999) attributed the declining wealth of Malaysian manufacturing firms to inefficiencies due to entrenched corporate control, difficult access to external investment, and minimal investment toward innovation. After the 1997 Asian financial crisis, the Malaysian government recognized the importance of integrating local firms into the global supply chains of multinational corporations (MNCs) to diversify the economy (Dosi et al., 1992). Among the successful manufacturing firms, three of the 20 family-owned firms were part of the Hong Leong Group, including Malaysian Pacific Industries (MPI) in electronics, OYL Industries in air-conditioning, and Hong Leong Industries, a tiles manufacturer.

According to numerous previous works (Lim, 1981; Sieh, 1982; Tan, 1982), government-linked companies dominated the industry as the leading manufacturing firms during the era of 'New Wealth', while several family firms emerged as significant publicly listed entities. Noteworthy among these were firms owned by the Lim, Yeoh, Quek, Kuok, Tan, and Lee families[1]. However, Gomez (2004) pointed out that many prominent family firms struggled to maintain their status, as founders often preferred their heirs to pursue professional careers, which hindered the firms' growth. Discriminatory public policies and insufficient government support for ethnic Chinese family firms further exacerbated these challenges (Gomez, 2004; Gomez, 2009). These issues remain underexplored, with a notable lack of theoretical and empirical studies on family firms in Malaysia.

Western literature on ethnically-based family businesses characterizes these enterprises as encompassing "family firms, trade guilds, and extensive intra-ethnic business transactions" (Ward & Jenkins, 1984; Ward, 1991). In the early 1990s, immigrant entrepreneurs often viewed their ethnic group through a monolithic lens, believing that these connections are necessary to achieve success in the global economy. However, in Southeast Asia, non-indigenous communities tend to identify more with their birthplace than their ancestral homelands (Yew & Tan, 2022). Concepts of pan-ethnic identity can obscure the resilience and agency of entrepreneurs in developing their businesses.

Currently, many ethnic-based family businesses are managed by second or third-generation descendants of migrants (Gomez & Hsiao, 2013). First-generation migrants typically engage in business to secure economic stability while preserving cultural traditions (Benton & Gomez, 2000; Suddaby & Jaskiewicz, 2020; Yew, 2019). These businesses often emerge from religious beliefs and family values, fostering competitive enterprises within local contexts (Light & Bonacich, 1988).

In contrast, subsequent generations may need external incentives to adapt to local markets and sustain their businesses.

According to the World Bank, family firms own 67.2% of the equity listed on Bursa Malaysia, the country's stock exchange. Of these, second-generation managers oversee 30% of SMEs and publicly listed companies (Jasani, 2002), with the remaining 70% expected to undergo generational transitions soon. Chinese entrepreneurs have a history of forming intra-ethnic partnerships, with some colonial-era firms evolving into successful family businesses.

This book focuses on the cultural dimensions of ethnic businesses, particularly the roles of networks and tacit knowledge within local markets established by Chinese family businesses (CFBs). Ward and Jenkins (1984) argue that historical concepts may not always be empirically valid, while other scholars contend that ethnicity, including the 'Chineseness' of tacit knowledge, plays a minimal role in enterprise development (Yew, 2020). Others also suggest that the concept of 'networks' is often overused in ethnic business literature (Yew & Tan, 2022). According to Benton and Gomez (2000, 2008), attributing the dynamism of ethnic minority enterprises solely to intra-ethnic business networks misrepresents the historical context, as these networks are multidimensional rather than homogeneous.

The book aims to explore how CFBs in Malaysia sustain themselves across three generations by developing tacit knowledge and adapting to local markets. Employing a stage model theory of development, the study compares the evolutionary progress of founding generations with subsequent generations in 12 SMEs across three economic sectors. Research methods included analysis of the Companies Commission of Malaysia (SSM) records, annual reports, and in-depth interviews. This study introduces a new evolutionary model for CFBs in the manufacturing sector, revealing that tacit knowledge and innovation are dynamic processes involving knowledge creation, evolution, transfer, and application. This process is essential for the sustainability of CFBs in the food, plastic, and rubber manufacturing sectors, contributing to improved self-realization, thinking structures, and competitive advantage within the industry.

1.2 Defining Malaysian Chinese Family Business

Malaysia is home to three primary ethnic groups: Malays, Chinese, and Indians[2]. Despite Malays being the majority and holding most of the political positions, Chinese businesses play a pivotal role in the economy. By the early 21st century, Malaysian Chinese controlled about 65% of the country's private sector assets and 44% of large firms, even though they comprised only approximately 23% of the population in 2018 (Carney et al., 2002; Mosbah et al., 2018). Over generations since independence, these culturally and ethnically Chinese family businesses have become Malaysian in identity, now referred to as Malaysian Chinese family businesses.

Redding (1993) and Yeung (2004) emphasize that the success of these businesses often stems from effective practices adopted by hardworking and practical founders. The term *Huaqiao*[3] (Chinese nationals abroad) has been criticized for suggesting ongoing loyalty to China; thus, *huaren*[4] (ethnic Chinese) is now preferred. The initial wave of ethnic Chinese brought to colonial Malaya were generally poor and uneducated, often adopting the mindset of "*gong-zibu-chu-tou*"[5] (working under someone else has no future), leading many to seek self-employment (Chan, 1980; Omohundro, 1983).

Due to limited capital, early Chinese entrepreneurs typically operated small businesses like confectionery shops and street vending. As these enterprises grew, they utilized "bamboo networks," establishing a global web of Chinese businesses across borders[6]. Despite their minority status, this network allowed them to exert significant economic influence throughout Southeast Asia, taking advantage of their position within Asian production networks (Hodder, 1996).

With the rise of China and globalization, enduring CFBs in Malaysia leverage historical knowledge and innovation. They often use traditional practices to create new products and brands, utilizing founder's tacit knowledge and unique marketing strategies to strengthen their ethnic Chinese identity. This identity acts as a resource for expanding their market presence locally and internationally, with "Chinese-type" products reflecting a rich heritage that aids in their ongoing success.

Different generations within these businesses introduce distinct characteristics, management styles, and goals (Okorofo, 1999). Each generation builds upon past experiences to foster innovation (Drozdow, 1989; Ward, 1987). Research indicates that founders are less likely to convert tacit knowledge (personal experience) into codified knowledge (knowledge not readily available in the market) (Aoki, 2001; Polanyi, 1962, 1966). This transformation is essential for creating "learning organizations," where knowledge extends beyond explicit explanations[7]. As newer generations enter the business, these transformations drive innovation and become apparent through branding, product offerings, packaging, and marketing strategies.

Codifying knowledge into innovative practices is seen as a long-term investment for CFBs. Additionally, literature suggests that family-owned SMEs are often more efficient than larger firms in certain sectors (Cortes et al., 1987; Liedholm & Mead, 1987; Little et al., 1987). For example, in Malaysia, successful family SMEs leverage improved access to technology, engage in joint ventures with foreign partners, and establish international networks, facilitating growth opportunities (Tan & Batra, 1995). The next generation of CFBs in Malaysia has evolved from traditional Chinese companies into globally recognized brands, demonstrating the potential for growth and adaptation in a changing economic landscape.

1.3 Tacit Knowledge Innovation and the Concept of Chinese Family Business Model

Tacit knowledge innovation in CFBs is a key topic in knowledge management, as it reflects the idea that individuals often possess knowledge that is difficult to articulate (Yew, 2023). Polanyi distinguishes between tacit and codified knowledge, noting that the latter can be tested and utilized by others (Polanyi, 1958, 1966). CFBs leverage tacit knowledge—similar to venture capitalists—creating a competitive advantage that drives growth (Aoki, 2001). Polanyi (1966) notes that:

"Tacit knowledge is defined as knowledge that cannot be obtained by a mere sum of codified (digitalized) information. It can be generated through intimate 'indwelling' within a relevant local domain, or as personal knowledge through particular experiences, personal qualities and competence; therefore, it cannot become immediately available in open markets."

The expansion of Chinese family businesses (CFBs) is significantly influenced by social networks, or *guanxi*[8]. Gomez and Benton (2004) highlight that intra-ethnic relations and transnational networks, rooted in Confucian ethics, are pivotal in formation and accumulation of capital. While the idea that ties among ethnic Chinese migrants naturally evolve into business networks is prevalent, the evidence supporting the notion that these ties primarily stem from common ethnic identity is limited[9].

Over the years, it has become more noticeable that innovation in products and processes is essential for economic development, and for stimulating growth regardless of external economic conditions (Craig & Moores, 2006; Porter, 1990). This innovation involves adopting new ideas, behaviors, or systems within organizations (Daft, 1982; Schumpeter, 1934). Steier (2001) argues that planned actions to transfer tacit knowledge across generations is crucial for introducing innovation and enhancing organizational capabilities. In Malaysia, CFBs are predominantly controlled by founders and their next generations (Claessens et al., 2000). However, transferring this tacit knowledge varies significantly depending on access to resources and the expectations of various sectors (Brush et al., 2004). Storey (1994) identifies former management experience, family history, and relevant sector knowledge as key factors that work together to influence business growth.

Globally, 85% of companies are SMEs, with many having family control on the board. In Malaysia, 59% of family businesses are CFBs, 65% of which are linked to SMEs. While 30% are managed by the second generation, 70% still remain under founder control. Wong (1985) proposed a four-phase development model for CFBs, tracing their evolution from emergence through various centralized phases of family involvement.

Initially, family businesses exhibit informal structures and owner-manager control, typically focusing on a single product (Tagiuri & Davis, 1996). As they grow, professionalization and diversification become necessary (Dyer, 1986). The resource-based view states that resources, including tacit and codified knowledge gained through innovation, create competitive advantages (Graves & Thomas, 2008). Intangible resources, particularly tacit knowledge, are critical for achieving sustainable competitive advantages (Barney, 1991; Hall, 1992).

CFBs navigate multiple cycles—family, ownership, and business—simultaneously (Carlock & Ward, 2001; Gersick et al., 1997; Neubauer & Lank, 1998). Research demonstrates the need for a conceptual framework that links the evolutionary development of family businesses with the family business model, emphasizing the role of tacit knowledge and innovation in their progression from founders to subsequent generations (see Figure 1.1).

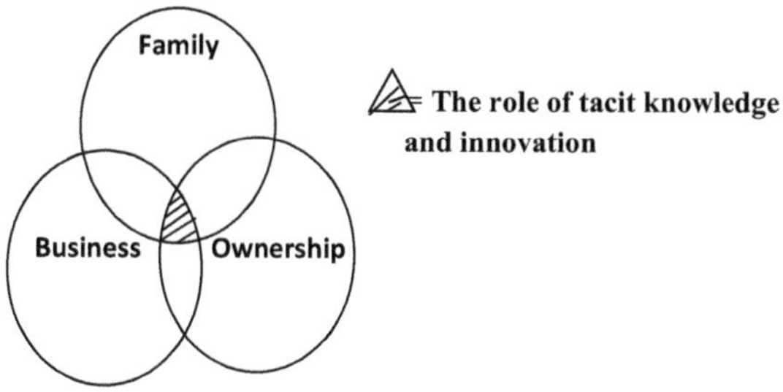

Figure 1.1 The Revised Version of the Three-Circle Model of Tacit Knowledge and Innovation Based on Gersick et al. (1997).

1.4 Role of the State

The role of the state in the economy is often overlooked in discussions about CFBs, yet it is important in the emergence of new enterprises. State intervention is particularly relevant in Southeast Asia (Robison et al., 1987), including Malaysia, where public policy planning has focused on the development of domestic enterprises, including those owned by ethnic minorities. The expansion of these businesses is highly influenced by the socioeconomic context in which they operate. In contrast to more industrialized economies, where state influence may be less direct, the Malaysian state actively promotes enterprise development.

Engelen (2001) posits that entrepreneurs operate within institutional frameworks that can either empower or constrain them. Kloosterman (2010) highlights how national institutional structures affect opportunity, with some regimes pushing unemployed migrants toward self-employment while limiting the potential for high-growth businesses. The "invisibility of migrant entrepreneurs" complicates the policy-making landscape, as noted by various researchers (Kloosterman & Rath, 2003; Kontos, 2003; Ng & Ng, 2003; Ram & Smallbone, 2001).

Government policies can significantly impact on small businesses through direct support, such as financial assistance, and softer measures, like information and training (Hadjimanolis, 2000). The outcomes of these policies can vary, particularly for ethnic enterprises. For instance, immigration policies can shape the supply of ethnic minority entrepreneurs (Waldinger et al., 1990; Rath & Kloosterman, 1999; Waldinger, 1986, 1989, 1995), while sector-specific policies may channel ethnic businesses into certain economic activities, as seen in the UK (Reynolds et al., 1994). In Britain, the government acknowledged the importance of small firms for job creation during the recession of 1979, leading to increased support for self-employment, particularly among minorities (Atkinson & Storey, 1994). The 1980s saw a surge in new firm formation, driven by rising unemployment and civil unrest impacting ethnic minorities.

Collins (2003) argues that the policy environment influences the formation, advancement, and survival of ethnic enterprises. Both macro- and micro-level policies, including migration and taxation, impact immigrant entrepreneurship. Collins suggests that policies should not only encourage entrepreneurship among unemployed immigrants but also improve communication with ethnic entrepreneurs, advocating for tailored strategies rather than a generalized approach. Language barriers and unique community networks necessitate customized policies for ethnic entrepreneurs.

In Malaysia, the NEP introduced in 1971 was a pivotal policy aimed at addressing issues of ethnic disparity following the riot incident in May 1969. The NEP sought to eradicate poverty across ethnic lines while restructuring a more united society, facilitating greater state intervention through trust agencies and public enterprises that accumulated capital for the Bumiputera (Mehmet, 1986). From 1971 to 1981, the state significantly increased its presence in the corporate sector, with trust agencies acquiring substantial equity in companies. Government-linked companies (GLCs) became key players, acting as "distributional coalitions" to concentrate wealth and compete with large businesses controlled by ethnic minorities, particularly the Chinese (Yew & Tan, 2022).

The NEP promised that no particular group would suffer deprivation during its implementation, asserting that asset redistribution would occur through economic growth and preferential access to credit for Malays. However, when public enterprises encroached upon sectors like banking and construction—areas with significant minority presence—Chinese business owners expressed dissatisfaction with state intervention[10]. The NEP significantly altered Malaysia's corporate landscape, leading to a decline in Chinese ownership across various sectors. From 1990 to 2008, Chinese corporate ownership fell from 45.5% to an estimated 34.9%. Meanwhile, Bumiputera capital ownership increased marginally, reaching 21.9% by 2008. Notably, among Malaysia's top 100 publicly listed firms in 2001, only about 20 were in manufacturing, most of which were foreign-owned, illustrating the challenges faced by local firms in scaling up during Malaysia's economic transformation[11].

1.5 Structural Shifts and Wealth Typologies in Malaysian Chinese Businesses under the NEP

The NEP, significantly transformed the landscape of Chinese business in Malaysia, resulting in Sino-Malay alliances often labeled as 'Ali-Baba' partnerships, where Chinese entrepreneurs maintained ownership while Malays served as silent partners (Koon, 1997; Whah, 2017). The challenges faced by subsequent generations of CFBs were heavily influenced by shifts in government public policy, particularly the NEP, which varied by sector.

Heng and Sieh (2000) identify three categories of Chinese business structures in Malaysia: 'old wealth,' 'new wealth,' and 'declining wealth.' Old wealth refers to CFBs established prior to the NEP, typically as conglomerates and often run by founders lacking technological expertise. Early successes in rubber plantations and tin mining allowed these businesses to diversify into manufacturing sectors like food, plastics, and rubber in the 1960s. However, few of these conglomerates have emerged as significant publicly listed firms, as most struggle to compete with better-capitalized and technologically advanced foreign firms, remaining relatively small-scale (Chin & Lim, 2018; Khor, 1983).

The old wealth category often suffers from entrenched poor management and control structures. Founders' focus on preserving existing capital can stifle creativity and innovation. In contrast, new wealth began to flourish in the 1990s, as Chinese businesses adapted successfully to the NEP, and were increasingly managed by a well-educated second generation. This new generation has formed connections with government agencies and foreign investors, exemplified by Sweetco's partnership with Korean investors and the Perlis State Economic Planning Corporation to establish Malaysia's first PVC flooring factory.

New wealth businesses are pivotal in Malaysia's rapid industrialization, facilitated by public-private partnerships under the Malaysia Incorporated Policy (Malaysia Inc) (Gomez, 1994). This collaboration is evident in the motor vehicle assembly and distribution sectors, involving family firms like Oriental Holdings and the Lion Group. Companies such as YTL Corporation, led by the Yeoh family, have demonstrated significant growth, reporting a 55% increase since their public listing in 1986. YTL operates in multiple sectors, including property development, construction, technology, power generation, and cement production. Another notable example is IOI Corporation, which is currently being led by the Lee family's second generation.

The declining wealth category encompasses Chinese businesses that are unable to adapt to the NEP, resulting in stagnation or decline (Heng & Sieh, 2000). The struggle is due to entrenched corporate control, poor access to external investment, and limited effort toward innovation. A prominent case is Yeo Hiap Seng (YHS), where third-generation family members were pushed to step down from directorships due to poor company performance.

In the aftermath of the 1997 Asian financial crisis, the Malaysian government realized that it was necessary to integrate Malaysian enterprises, particularly those owned by ethnic Chinese, into global supply chains established by multinational corporations (MNCs). To facilitate this integration, the government launched initiatives like the Global Supplier Program (GSP) and the Industrial Linkage Program (ILP), aimed at diversifying the economy and enhancing the competitiveness of local businesses (Dosi et al., 1992).

1.6 Problem Statement

An ethnic enclave economy is prominently defined by the ethnic identity of the community. During the colonial and immediate post-colonial period, businesses that belonged to ethnic enclave economies had the tendency to be involved in products which had a strong co-identity bias. In conducting their businesses, ethnic-related business ties were important for migrants and those who only spoke their own dialect or a Chinese language. As a result, such businesses grew among individuals from the same background.

Nevertheless, this changed by the turn of the century as the way these Chinese businesses operate evolved following massive transformations in opportunity structures and resources due to modernization. Therefore, considering the obvious evolution in society, the economy, and among Chinese businesses, this begs the question on the validity of the concept of a Chinese family business. Furthermore, this raises the concerns on whether the concept of tacit knowledge innovation can be applied to family business and managed by the following generation.

1.6.1 Research Questions

While the changes, opportunities and challenges faced by the Chinese businesses in Malaysia have been documented by previous scholars (Brown, 1994; Gomez, 1999; Jesudason, 1989; 1997), no detailed research has been conducted on the evolution of the Chinese family businesses, specifically the SMEs. Considering this research gap, the current work serves as an attempt to investigate the evolution of Chinese SMEs and the changes, opportunities, and challenges that they have faced in the economy by examining their advancement and growth.
The main questions that will be evaluated are as follows:

(1) How have Malaysian Chinese family businesses that have undergone generational shifts retain a prominent presence in their respective industries?
(2) Was the conversion of tacit knowledge to a codified form, through tacit knowledge innovation, a crucial factor that sustain large, medium, and small-scale in Chinese family businesses?
(3) Were there changes in class, ethnic resources, and Chinese networks of such Chinese family businesses through the generations? Did it influence the growth and evolution of Chinese SMEs in Malaysia?

1.6.2 Research Objectives

The objectives of this study are as follows:

1. Determine how Malaysian Chinese family businesses achieved a competitive advantage in their respective industries, aligned with changes in the market.
2. Find reasons why little emphasis is given on the conversion of tacit knowledge into R&D in certain Malaysian Chinese SMEs based on their respective industries.
3. Identify other factors besides the class, ethnic resources, and Chinese networks that have enabled Malaysian Chinese family businesses to expand family firms.

1.7 Significance of the Study

This study is significant for several reasons. Firstly, it reviews and analyzes key theoretical arguments about Chinese family businesses, with particular attention to the historical background of Malaysian Chinese, themes of generational change, and tacit knowledge innovation. This includes an analysis of family business and tacit knowledge innovation from four perspectives: converting tacit to codified knowledge, resource management, opportunity structure, and Chinese networks. The focus on tacit knowledge innovation sheds light on the enterprise development of Chinese family SMEs in Malaysia.

Secondly, the book provides detailed information on the research methodology, conceptual model, and case study sampling among Malaysian family SMEs. The research methodology emphasizes the use of in-depth longitudinal case studies to examine the generational change and innovation milestones of these Chinese family SMEs across different industries.

Thirdly, the book navigates the history of manufacturing firms and the transformation of tacit knowledge in the food, plastic, and rubber industries. This historical perspective offers insights into how Chinese family businesses in these industries produce various types of products, ranging from highly sophisticated to less complex ones. The case studies illustrate the significant challenges faced by Chinese family firms in retaining tacit knowledge.

Lastly, the study emphasizes the impact of cultural factors on Chinese family businesses. While family businesses are often discussed from economic and business perspectives, cultural influences are equally important. This book reviews and discusses these cultural factors from a historical perspective, thus highlighting their foundational role in business practices. The emphasis on culture and environment, which has become increasingly important in Western business management, is equally relevant to Chinese family businesses. Understanding these cultural dimensions provides a comprehensive foundation for academics to explore this topic further.

1.8 Structure of the Book

This book is structured into nine comprehensive chapters. The first chapter provides an introduction, outlining the study's aims and significance. The second chapter traces the history of business development by the Chinese in Malaysia. Chapter 3 presents a literature review on Chinese family businesses, with a specific focus on generational change and stages of business growth in Southeast Asian countries.

Chapter 4 discusses the conceptual framework and research methodologies used in this study. It details the sampling method, data collection processes, and appropriate data analysis techniques. Chapters 5, 6, and 7 present in-depth case studies of Chinese businesses in the food, plastic, and rubber industries, respectively. Each case is explored historically, capturing the essence of the business through concepts such as class resources, ethnic resources, knowledge factors, Chinese networks, local markets, and the role of the state.

The first part of Chapter 8 discusses the study's findings thematically, while the latter part analyzes additional themes that emerged from the case studies. The final chapter summarizes the study's theoretical and empirical contributions and discusses its limitations.

Notes

1 See Whah (2017).
2 The Indian community, making up around 6.9% of Malaysia's population, largely consists of descendants of laborers brought from South India during British colonial rule (Kaur, 2006). They have contributed significantly to sectors such as plantations, education, and healthcare.
3 The term *Huaqiao* (华侨) refers to Chinese nationals residing abroad, particularly those who maintain Chinese citizenship or identify strongly with their Chinese heritage. Historically, Huaqiao were seen as an important extension of China's global influence, often maintaining close ties with their homeland while contributing economically and culturally to their host countries.
4 The term *Huaren* (华人) refers to ethnic Chinese who live outside of China, distinguishing them from *Huaqiao*, who are Chinese nationals abroad. Unlike *Huaqiao*, *Huaren* typically hold citizenship in their host countries, identifying with their Chinese heritage while integrating into the local society.
5 The Chinese phrase *gong-zibu-chu-tou* (工字不出头) translates to 'working under someone else has no future.' It reflects a traditional Chinese entrepreneurial mindset, emphasizing self-reliance and the belief that true success and upward mobility can only be achieved through independent business ownership, rather than working as an employee for others.
6 See Weidenbaum & Hughes (1996) and Menkhoff (1993).
7 See Polanyi (1966).
8 See Tong & Yong (2014).
9 See Gomez (2007).
10 See Gomez (2003).
11 See Gomez (2007).

2 From China to Rooting Innovation in Malaysia

The *Merriam-Webster Dictionary* defines a dynasty as: "a succession of rulers of the same line of descent" or "a powerful group or family that maintains its position for a considerable time." In Malaysia, as in other East and Southeast Asian countries, the Chinese community has historically controlled and continues to significantly influence the economy. Focused on economic advancement, many Malaysian Chinese reside in major urban centers and have adopted the English language, a legacy of British colonization and Western cultural influence in Southeast Asia. Malaysian Chinese family businesses are often seen as dynastic enterprises, aimed at building, maintaining, and expanding family power and resources over generations. Numerous well-established Malaysian Chinese family businesses aim to expand their empire beyond ethnocentrically governed Malaysia, where policies tend to offer certain privileges to Muslim-Malays. Similarities that these countries share in history, structure, culture, practices, and familial linkages across East and Southeast Asia support the view of Malaysian Chinese family businesses as part of a broader sociological grouping of overseas Chinese family businesses.

2.1 Arrival of Chinese in the Malay Archipelago

The Malay Archipelago is a testament to centuries of cultural exchange and historical significance (Bowring, 2018; Heng, 2009; McAmis, 2002). One of the most pivotal moments in this history is the arrival of the Chinese, which profoundly reshaped the region's socio-economic and cultural landscape. This migration showcases a complex tapestry of influences that have had a lasting impact on the archipelago.

Chinese migration to Malacca began in the early 15th century with the establishment of the Sultanate (Yen, 2006). *Zhangzhou* Hokkiens were among the first Chinese pioneers, motivated by the prominence of the *Yue Gang* (Port of Moon) in *Zhangzhou*, a crucial trading hub between 1465 and 1505. During this time, *Zhangzhou* traders engaged in maritime commerce with Southeast Asia, which led them to Malacca, where some adopted local customs and intermarried with indigenous women, marking the beginnings of the Peranakan Chinese[1] in the region (Chen, 1983; Cheng, 1983; Tan, 1988).

DOI: 10.4324/9781032705842-2

The 18th century witnessed a surge in Chinese migration, which continued until the 1920s (Kuhn, 2008; Tan, 2011). Most of these migrants were laborers rather than traders. Following the Opium War, the Qing government opened five ports to British trade, facilitating the recruitment of workers for overseas labor (Reid & Rodgers, 2001; Trocki, 2012). The economic boom in Malaya, driven by labor demands in the rubber and tin industries, further attracted many Chinese migrants (Blythe, 1947; Campbell, 1970). While some were coerced into contract labor, many migrated voluntarily, supported by kinship networks and religious organizations (Wu, 2009).

The influx of Chinese immigrants enriched the cultural fabric of Malaya, fostering strong community bonds characterized by mutual support. This led to the formation of secret societies like *Ghee Hin*, *Hai San*, and *Toa Peh Kong*, as well as dialect groups and *'huiguan'* (Goodrich, 1959; Mak, 1993; Peng, 1977). These organizations provided personal security, economic support, and social development, often under the leadership of Chinese *kapitans*. The diverse Chinese population included dialect groups such as Hokkien, Hakka, Cantonese, and Teochew (Mak & Him, 1992).

Under British colonial rule, occupational roles were strategically allocated among ethnic groups to achieve administrative objectives (Keong, 2007). This resulted in distinct economic roles organized by dialect identity, allowing wealthy Chinese to thrive in sectors like sugar plantations, tin mining, and retail (Freedman, 1960). Despite their settlement, the Chinese maintained strong cultural ties through schools, associations, and language newspapers, which became central to preserving their heritage (Wang, 1993). However, the ethnic-based political system reinforced divides between Malays and non-Malays, restricting full assimilation (Freedman, 2001).

Suryadinata (1993) noted the limited political participation of the Malaysian Chinese population contrasted with their significant economic influence, which could not be overlooked by the government. In response, the Malaysian government implemented the New Economic Policy (NEP), adversely impacting the social status and business growth of the Chinese community. Yeung (2006) observed that while the economic upturn of the 1990s eased racial tensions, the 1997 Asian financial crisis revived hostility toward the Chinese.

Understanding the migration narratives in the Malay Archipelago, particularly the arrival of the Chinese, highlights more than mere population movement; it underscores cultural blending, economic transformation, and societal adaptation. These histories illustrate how communities integrate diverse influences, emphasizing the connections between civilizations. By studying these migration stories, we acknowledge the diversity that formed the region's identity and provide insights into the evolution of Chinese family businesses.

2.2 The Indentured System and Immigration Act 1959

The Indentured System and the Immigration Act of 1959 significantly shaped Chinese migration to Malaya, influencing both social and economic structures within the Chinese community and beyond. A closer examination of these historical events reveals how the Chinese adapted to changing regulations and settled in the region.

British intervention in the Malay States during the 1870s created a demand for migrant labor, linking India, China, and Malaya (Amrith, 2015; Sai, 2021). Colonial Malaya's economy became part of the Old International Division of Labour, producing goods for industrializing Britain and other northern hemisphere countries (Drabble, 2003). The British government facilitated migration through an open border policy, encouraging the influx of Chinese and Indian workers. Between 1881 and 1939, Malaya experienced the highest immigration rate globally, reflecting its vigorous economic activity (Huff & Caggiano, 2008).

The late 19th century saw significant growth in tin mining, driven by merchant capital in the Straits Settlements and Malay leaders inviting Straits Chinese merchants to develop the industry (Blythe, 1947; Reid, 2011). Initially, Chinese merchants sourced labor from the Straits Settlements, but as demand grew, private labor brokers were authorized to recruit migrants from southern China (Kaur, 2004; Hooker, 2002). Migration patterns were often linked to kinship networks, with brokers recruiting relatives and friends, covering passage and travel costs (Kaur, 2012). Upon arrival, migrants entered a credit-ticket system, where labor contracts facilitated the repayment of these costs. This system characterized the labor trade and primarily supplied Chinese labor migrants. They were housed in Singapore receiving depots until their travel expenses were settled by employers, after which they negotiated labor terms to repay debts. Unemployed migrants could be sold to other employers, often lacking regulatory protections (Trocki, 2019; Yen, 1986). This historical practice underscores the lasting influence of kinship networks on the prevalence of family-owned Chinese businesses in Malaysia.

Before 1927, there were no restrictions on migrant workers from China, India, and Indonesia. However, as the British enforced the Immigration Restriction Ordinance in 1930, permanent entry was limited (Bashford, 2014). By late 1932, quotas reduced the entry to 1,000 men monthly, although no restrictions applied to Chinese women and children under the age of 12 (Saw, 1988). Although these restrictions were initially minor, their significance grew after Malaya's independence. The unrestricted entry of Chinese women facilitated ethnic intermarriage and permanent settlement, allowing for the transfer of tacit knowledge to future generations.

Colonial migration policies contributed to a plural society, with Chinese and Indian populations surpassing Malays by 1947 (Del Tufo, 1949). This demographic shift raised concerns among Malay nationalists and influenced post-independence policies regarding citizenship, labor migration, and Malay privileges. As a result, immigration laws indirectly affected the growth of Chinese businesses from both political and social angles. In 1957, the new national government enacted the Immigration Act of 1959 to regulate non-citizen entry, particularly targeting illegal workers (Kassim & Zin, 2011; Low & Mokhtar, 2017). This legislation aimed to protect the employment of Malaya's residents and promote national integration, imposing stricter controls on family reunification and limiting non-citizen immigration (Kaur, 2004). The Employment Restriction Act of 1968 further tightened these measures, restricting immigration to skilled non-citizens (Kassim, 2001; Kaur, 2012).

These migration acts significantly impacted the Chinese population's inflow and outflow, shaping the dynamics of Chinese businesses and their ethnic markets. Furthermore, migration patterns influenced the formation of the Chinese community in Malaya, organizing them into sub-dialect groups linked to their dialectal origins[2], reflecting patterns seen in their ancestral regions in China.

2.3 Sub-Ethnic Chinese in Malaya and their Contribution to the Economy

Chinese Malaysians can be categorized into "dialect groups," also known as *fangyanqun* (方言群)[3], namely Hokkien (福建), Hakka (客家), Cantonese (广府), Teochew (潮州), Hainanese (海南), Foochow (福州), Kwongsai (广西), and Henghua (兴化). During the era of British rule, the development of ports and mining activities by the British government brought in Chinese immigrants who participated in trade, work, and settlement. Consequently, hundreds of thousands of Chinese migrants from various dialect groups arrived in Malaya from China. These groups brought with them distinct cultural practices, varying significantly between each dialect group (Mak, 1985). These practices are often influenced by geographical origins, reflecting their ancestral beliefs. The colonial period also witnessed a rise in Chinese-based culinary businesses such as sesame oil shops, pastry houses, and restaurants (Salobir, 2011; Yen, 2000). Due to the contributions of diverse groups to Malaysia's rich culinary tradition, the Nanyang heritage became a pivotal cultural melting pot (Zainal & Kassim, 2010).

Nowadays, some of these tacit knowledge and customs are still commonly practiced and integrated into other cultures. These fact that these practices and Chinese traditions are able to withstand the test of time demonstrate the dynamic nature of Malaysian Chinese (Yen, 1995; Yew & Tan, 2022). Regardless of dialect group, Malaysian Chinese family businesses are rooted in the concept of *"jia"* (family)[4]. These businesses serve as instruments to advance family interests and can be relinquished when they no longer fulfill that purpose (Wong & Chau, 2019).

Chinese were crucial to colonial strategies, with their role in Western-Chinese business relations becoming formalized (Skinner, 1951). They increasingly served Western import-export companies by gathering local products for export and distributing European goods in local markets. Consequently, Western capital increasingly supported Chinese credit systems. Western merchants needed to establish the trustworthiness of collaborating Chinese traders, and creolized Chinese traders often had an advantage over their China-born counterparts in this regard. A local Chinese trader with a local family and property within the colony was more likely to be trusted not to abscond (Lee, 1978).

In the Straits Settlements, the British soon abandoned the indirect rule system through Chinese officers as unworkable for such a heterogeneous society (内部多籍贯的华人社会). Despite the diverse and complex nature of the Chinese community, the Baba business elite managed to maintain prominence throughout the 19th century. However, their position was more precarious compared to the Peranakan oligarchy, with less absolute power and less direct control. By the 1840s, sinkheh[5] (immigrant Chinese) had already outnumbered Babas (Straits-born Chinese). Different productive sectors were categorized based on semi-autonomous hierarchies of credit and patronage, managed by various sub-ethnic groups of sinkheh Chinese. Although the Babas played a crucial role in linking these patronage structures to the British and channeling British capital into Chinese businesses, they needed allies within the community. Consequently, they aligned with Hokkien merchants, and from the 1840s, leading Baba and Hokkien merchants often worked together (Lee, 1978).

2.3.1 Hokkien Chinese

The Hokkiens were among the earliest Chinese immigrants to Nanyang, with their migration from Fujian Province, southern China, dating back centuries. Renowned for their business acumen and adaptability, Hokkien traders established significant business institutions and formed diverse ethnic networks abroad (Chin, 2010). During the Qing period (1644–1670), many southern Chinese, particularly from Xiamen (Amoy), Quanzhou, and Zhangzhou, migrated to Southeast Asia, seeking refuge from the Manchu conquest, with some settling in Malacca.

In Malaysia, the Hokkiens primarily settled in Malacca, Sarawak, Penang, and parts of Johor and Selangor, replicating their Chinese living environment by organizing into dialect-based groups. This organization was crucial for establishing social connections within the early Chinese community. For example, in Kuching, Sarawak, where Hokkiens are predominant, Hokkien has emerged as a "powerful lingua franca" (Hsiao & Lim, 2007). The significant influx of Hokkiens increased their numbers and solidified their dominant role within the early Chinese community, giving them advantages in economic ventures.

Over time, Hokkiens were drawn to opportunities in trading, agriculture, and manufacturing, contributing substantially to these sectors. They also dominated the banking and finance sectors. During British colonization, Batu Pahat Bank Ltd. was established by Hokkiens in Batu Pahat, Johor, in 1920. Similarly, Ban Hin Lee Bank Ltd. (BHL) was founded in 1935 by a prominent Hokkien figure Yeap Chor Ee in Penang, serving the local business community (Tan, 1953). In Sarawak, a Hokkien businessman Wee Kheng Chiang established Bian Chiang Bank in Kuching in 1924, focusing on business financing for the local Chinese community. Following Malaysia's independence, Hokkiens dominated the rubber plantation job market and led the trading sector, with many Chinese traders and wholesalers of Hokkien descent. Their dialect became the lingua franca of trade, facilitating business transactions and the transfer of tacit knowledge, preserving and passing down cultural heritage across generations.

Though relatively unknown outside Malaysia, YTL Corporation exemplifies a local success story, demonstrating sustained growth through three generations of the Yeoh family (Kennedy, 2002). Yeoh Tiong Lay expanded a timber business inherited from his father into a major construction company. In 1988, his son,

Francis Yeoh Sock Ping, took over as managing director, transforming YTL Corporation into a diversified conglomerate with six listed entities.

The Hong Leong Group, founded by Kwek Hong Png and his brothers in Singapore in 1941, began in hardware trading and expanded into manufacturing construction materials such as steel pipes and tiles (Tan, 1982; Yoshihara, 1988). Over 50 years, it evolved into a legendary conglomerate with interests in finance and property, controlled by over 15 family members from the second and third generations of the Kwek family.

Loh Boon Siew, known for Kah Motor, pioneered the motorcycle and motor vehicle assembly industry in Malaysia, acquiring the sole distributorship for Honda motorbikes in 1957. He established Malaysia's first motorcycle manufacturing company in 1968 and the Kah Motor Assembly Plant in 1969 (Flower & Lim, 2006). His legacy continues under the leadership of his son, Loh Kian Chong.

Lim Goh Tong, founder of the Genting Group, expanded the company from a single gaming and leisure enterprise into a diversified conglomerate. Starting with plantations in 1980, Genting Group ventured into various industries, including paper milling and power supply. Lim passed the leadership baton to his second son, Lim Kok Thay, who joined the Group in 1976, continuing its legacy of innovation and growth (Lim, 2004).

2.3.2 Cantonese Chinese

The Cantonese, hailing from Guangdong Province in China, especially Guangzhou, have a rich history of maritime trade through the Pearl River Delta, near Hong Kong and Macau (Tan, 1990). Their culture emphasizes diligence and bravery, attracting them to the burgeoning tin industry in the Malay Peninsula. However, from the 1840s to the 1870s, Cantonese migrants comprised only 23% of the total Chinese migration to the region, partly due to the lure of the American gold rush (Gong, 2003).

Upon arriving in the Malay Peninsula, many Cantonese migrants were often under the authority of Penang Hokkien and Hakka towkays in Perak and Negeri Sembilan, respectively (Wen & Wong, 2020). This economic necessity led them to temporarily set aside their dialect identity for survival, mirroring the experience of Cantonese in Canada, who subsumed their identity within dominant communities (Barth, 1969). This adaptability highlights the resilience of the Cantonese character.

Migration surged in the late 1880s, with Cantonese numbers increasing from fewer than 300 in 1880 to over 2,000 by 1887 (Tan, 1997). This influx prompted the establishment of the Selangor Kwong Siew Association by prominent figures such as Chiew Yeok, Chan Sow Lin, and Loke Yew, alongside the Hakka elite Yap Kwan Seng from Chih Xi district in Guangzhou.

After the Kapitan era, the Cantonese became a dominant group in the development of towns like Kuala Lumpur, Ipoh, Seremban, and Sandakan. Known for their urbanization, Cantonese predominantly reside in principal towns and their dialect is widely spoken in regions such as Klang Valley, Seremban, and Sandakan (Ember et al., 2004). Unlike the entrepreneurial Hokkiens and Teochews, the Cantonese often took a more measured approach, waiting for opportune moments to engage in business. Their contributions span various sectors of Malaysia's economy, from small businesses to larger enterprises.

Prominent figures such as Loke Yew emerged during the colonial period, amassing wealth through tin mining and revenue farming, ultimately becoming one of Malaya's richest men (Tregonning, 1963). Born in 1845 in Xinhui, Guangdong (Butcher, 1993), Loke immigrated to Singapore in 1858, later moving to Perak to invest in tin mines. After the Larut Wars, he relocated to Kuala Lumpur, establishing his own enterprises in tin mining, rubber, and revenue farming (Yong, 2015). His business empire spanned the Malay Peninsula and Singapore, and in 1936, his son Loke Wan Tho founded Associated Theatres Ltd., later known as Cathay Organization (Chung, 2002).

Chan Sow Lin, supported by Loke Yew, founded Chan Sow Lin & Co. Ltd., which became the first Chinese iron foundry in Selangor. His efforts in ironworks advanced local mining and construction industries, leading to significant technological progress. In recognition of his contributions, the colonial government honored him by naming a principal thoroughfare "Jalan Chan Sow Lin." (Lynelle Tham, 2022)

Eu Yan Sang, established by Eu Kong from Foshan, Guangdong, in 1879, began as a Chinese herbal remedies store aimed at treating laborers suffering from opium addiction (Yew, 2020). The name "仁生" (Rén Shēng), meaning "caring for mankind,"[6] reflects his mission. Under the leadership of Richard Eu Yee Ming, the business transformed into a global provider of integrated traditional Chinese medicine products (Yeung, 2004). In April 2024, Eu Yan Sang was acquired by Mitsui & Co. and Rohto Pharmaceutical. This acquisition signals their recognition of the future value and potential of TCM.

2.3.3 Hakka Chinese

Hakka history is marked by a rich cultural heritage. The term "Hakka," meaning "guest people," refers to Han Chinese originating from northern China. They migrated to southeastern China's mountainous regions, such as Guangdong, Fujian, Guangxi, and Hainan, before arriving in Malaya. Unique geographical features contributed to the development of Hakka mountain songs (山歌)[7], which became a significant part of their culture. Despite facing lower social status compared to other Chinese groups, the Hakkas were recognized for their resilience and diligence, with Hakka women particularly noted for their strong will (Campbell, 1912).

By the late Ming and early Qing periods, a group of Hakkas from Wuhua established a gold mine in Galas, south-central Kelantan. The mid-19th century discovery of tin in Malaysia prompted a significant influx of Hakkas from Huizhou and Meixian into Negeri Sembilan, Selangor, and Perak to develop tin mines. Many Hakkas worked in the mining regions of Larut, Perak, during the 1860s and 1870s (Wong, 2009). The early 20th century saw a peak in Hakka migration, driven by poverty and the search for better opportunities.

As Hakka numbers grew, they began forming communities and associations like those of other Chinese sub-dialects. Notable early Hakka communities in Penang and Malacca established groups like the *Kaying*, *Huizhou*, and *Zenglong* associations, which provided protection, support, and financial assistance (Seng, 2015). Over time, these associations evolved from maintaining connections with their hometowns in China to fostering relationships among Hakka people abroad (Cohen, 1968; Hsiao, 2020; Leong et al., 1997).

As the second-largest subgroup within the Malaysian Chinese population, early Hakka settlers migrated to gold and tin mines and established businesses such as Chinese medicine shops and tailoring. With the decline of the mining industry, many transitioned to rubber plantations in Kedah and Johor, especially in Kulai and Kluang. In Sabah, Hakkas focused on agriculture, becoming cash crop farmers. Those from *Dabu* and *Kaying* often ran low-capital businesses like stores selling Western clothing, dry goods, fabric, Chinese medicines, eyeglasses, clocks, pawnshops, and smithies (Wong, 2000; 2007). Such enterprises became characteristic of Hakka businesses in both Singapore and Malaysia.

One prominent Hakka figure was Yap Ah Loy, the Chinese Kapitan of Kuala Lumpur in the late 19th century. His efforts were instrumental in transforming Kuala Lumpur from a mining settlement into a commercial hub following the Larut Wars (Carstens, 1988). Other notable Hakka Kapitans included Cheong Fatt Tze, Chung Keng Quee, and Chin Ah Yam.

Jeffrey Cheah, a Hakka entrepreneur with a mining background, has significantly impacted education and sustainable development (Woo et al., 2020). Since 1974, he transformed his family business, Sunway Group, into a diversified conglomerate with interests spanning construction, property development, hospitality, healthcare, and education, expanding operations beyond Southeast Asia to China, India, and the Caribbean (Asgari et al., 2010). His daughter, Sarena Cheah, has been a part of Sunway Group since 1995 and currently holds various directorships.

Similarly, the late Lee Loy Seng's family controls two listed companies, Batu Kawan Berhad and Kuala Lumpur Kepong Berhad (KLK) (Gomez & Hsiao, 2012). Lee Loy Seng was a prominent miner and plantation owner in Ipoh, and under his family's leadership, the companies have become key players in the oil palm industry. The Lee family's business interests have expanded into chemicals and stock brokerage (Bany-Ariffin et al., 2010), with the third generation represented by Lee Jia Zhang serving as an Executive Director at KLK.

2.3.4 Teochew Chinese

The Teochews hail from the Chaoshan region in eastern Guangdong, particularly Shantou (Tan, 2018). Their migration to the Malay Peninsula began in the 18th century, with initial settlements in Province Wellesley (Seberang Perai) in Penang and around Kuala Muda in Kedah. Notably, Thailand attracted more Teochews than the Malay Peninsula (Lee, 2014).

The signing of the Treaty of Tientsin in 1858, which ended the Second Opium War, opened Chinese ports like Shantou for foreign trade and legalized Chinese emigration, prompting many Teochews to seek better opportunities abroad (Nield, 2015). During the 19th century, a significant number settled in Johor and Singapore, primarily working in plantation agriculture (Kuhn, 2008). They were instrumental in establishing pepper and gambier plantations, while those in Kedah and northern Perak often worked as fishermen.

Teochews constitute a substantial segment of the Chinese community in Johor Bahru and other coastal towns in Western Johor, such as Pontian, Muar, and Batu Pahat. They also reside in Kedah, north Perak, Selangor, and Malacca, particularly in Ayer Salak, one of Malaysia's oldest predominantly Teochew villages (Lee, 2019). Despite their numbers, the Teochew dialect has become less commonly spoken, having been the lingua franca among Chinese in Johor Bahru until the 1970s.

Among Chinese businessmen, Teochews stand out for their entrepreneurial spirit, like the Hokkiens, as early settlers. Their contributions to the economic development of Southeast Asia are significant, amassing substantial capital.

> *"The Teochews, a major Chinese dialect group in Southeast Asia, were the pioneer planters in Singapore, and their community politics was played with skill and sophistication. Their economic influence is widely felt in parts of East and Southeast Asia such as Hong Kong, Thailand, Singapore, and Malaysia."*
>
> (Yen, 2002)

In Singapore, Seah Street is named after the Teochew merchant Seah Eu Chin, known as the "King of Gambier" due to his extensive gambier and pepper plantations (Song, 1984). Arriving in Singapore in 1823, Eu Chin founded the Ngee Ann Kongsi in 1830 to oversee the welfare and religious affairs of local Teochews. Within 20 years, he became one of Singapore's wealthiest Chinese person (Trocki, 2006). Appointed a Justice of Peace in 1867, he resolved disputes within the Chinese community. His legacy continued through his sons, Seah Cheoh Seah, Seah Liang Seah, Seah Song Seah, and Seah Peck Seah, with streets like Eu Chin Street and Liang Seah Street honoring the family (Savage & Yeoh, 2013). The Seah family maintained leadership of the Ngee Ann Kongsi after Eu Chin's death (Yen, 1986). Seah Liang Seah, his second son, managed the family business, Eu Chin & Co., while also serving as an entrepreneur and charitable leader.

Currently, a notable Teochew family is the William Cheng family. William Cheng founded the Lion Group Malaysia, which introduced the Parkson department store chain in 1987. Through Lion Corporation Bhd., he controlled six other listed companies, including Amsteel Corporation Bhd. and Angkasa Marketing Bhd. (Zin, 1999). The origins of Lion Corporation trace back to Cheng's father's company, Teck Chiang Foundry Co. (Chin, 2008). Diversifying in the 1950s, the family established Tuck Heng Manufactory Ltd. and Teck Chiang Manufactory Ltd. in Singapore. In 1968, Lion Metal Manufacturing Sdn. Bhd. was founded to produce steel components. These companies combined in 1973 to form Lion (Teck Chiang) Sdn. Bhd., renamed Lion Corp in 1981 and listed on the KLSE in 1982

(Gomez, 2012). The Lion Group has grown dramatically, owning over a hundred subsidiaries and demonstrating the Cheng family's successful business expansion.

2.3.5 Hainanese Chinese

The Hainanese, originating from Hainan province, are often associated with the saying, "Wherever there is the embrace of the sea, you'll find the souls of Hainan" (Lockard, 2013). Due to the island's remote maritime location and infertile soil, Hainanese inhabitants were compelled to seek livelihoods beyond their shores. Most of them hailed from the Wencheng or Qiongzhou districts and were originally farmers and fishers (Guang, 2012; Tan, 1990; Tim, 1972).

Starting in the 19th century, the Hainanese began settling in the Straits Settlements of Malacca, Penang, and Singapore, as well as in North Borneo. Although concentrated in Selangor and Malacca, they also represent the largest language group in Kemaman, Terengganu, while maintaining a notable presence in Penang and Johor Bahru. However, Hainanese is not a dominant dialect in any specific city or state (Lee et al., 2014).

Among the last southern Chinese sub-dialect groups to migrate to Malaya, the Hainanese faced challenges due to the late opening of Hainan Island to foreign trade and a conservative emigration attitude. By the time they arrived, more lucrative trades had already been occupied by earlier immigrants. Consequently, many Hainanese found work in the service sector, particularly as chefs, waiters, and servants in hospitality industry and affluent households (Han, 2012). Their cooking skills contributed to their reputation in Western cuisine (Wang, 2009).

In Singapore, many Hainanese men were employed as sailors on trading vessels, though this occupation was less documented in British census records from 1921 to 1947. Following the WWII, as the fall of British and Peranakan families unfolded, more Hainanese entered the hotel industry, establishing their own restaurants and kopitiams (Lai, 2010). Hainanese cuisine, including dishes like Hainan chicken rice and chicken chop, gained regional popularity and attracted tourists. The Hainanese are also recognized for their excellent coffee, particularly in kopitiams across Southeast Asia (Lai, 2006).

Prominent Hainanese businessmen include Choot Ching Khoon, founder of the renowned 'Salute Kopi O' brand (Chin & Jusoh, 2021; Yeoh, 2008). Fleeing war-torn Hainan at just 11 years old, Choot settled in Penang, where he started a coffee factory and built Kun Kee Food Industries Sdn. Bhd. His son, Choot Ewe Seng, now a prominent figure in the coffee industry and executive adviser to the Penang Chinese Chamber of Commerce, expanded the family business internationally, reaching markets in Singapore, China, and New York City. The Choot family also diversified into property development, IT, and oil palm plantations (Trisha, 2021).

In the early 20th century, a saying among the Nanyang Chinese community noted: "Fujian has Tan Kah Kee, and Hainan has Wee Cheow Keng" (Fu & Han, 2001). This reflects the esteem in which Wee Cheow Keng held. Cheow Keng Road in Singapore commemorates his contributions. Unlike many contemporaries, he received advanced education, enabling him to become a director of Sze Hai Tong

Bank, now part of OCBC Bank. He founded the Singapore Qiongzhou Association and served as its first chairman, emerging as a key leader for Hainanese in the region (Guo, 2012). His involvement spanned various industries, including rubber plantations, real estate, banking, insurance, and foreign exchange. His son, Wee Tin See, continued his legacy, managing diverse business ventures and contributing greatly to the local economy, particularly in banking.

2.3.6 Foochow Chinese

The Foochows, originating from the Foochow prefecture in Fujian Province, China, have a notable history of migration to Nanyang. The prefecture comprises 10 counties, and despite differences in sub-dialects, the people from these areas are collectively identified as "Foochow" due to their shared dialect (Kiu, 1997). Although they represent a smaller proportion of the Chinese population in Malaysia, Foochows have significant contribution to the country's economic development (Zhao, 2016).

The initial wave of Foochow migration occurred during the early Ming Dynasty, gaining momentum with Zheng He's trade missions that established a settlement in Malacca. A major migration wave followed the Opium Wars, particularly in 1844, when Foochow was designated as one of five ports for foreign trade. This designation spurred significant trade growth between Foochow and Nanyang (Hsü, 1995; Kuhn, 2008). Many Foochows also migrated as contract laborers, settling in regions such as Yong Peng, Sitiawan, Sungai Pelek, Miri, and Sibu (Hock & Suryadinata, 2012).

In Sarawak, the Foochows are the largest Chinese dialect group. The migration began in earnest in 1900 when Wong Nai Siong, the "Kang Choo" or "Port Master" of the Foochow, led a group of Foochows to the Rejang River. He negotiated to bring in a thousand settlers primarily for agricultural activities in Sibu (Ling & Thock, 2015). This migration faced numerous challenges, including disease and difficult living conditions. By 1905, many settlers had either died from malaria or left for other regions. Despite these hardships, the Foochow community displayed remarkable strength, eventually becoming dominant in various occupations in Sarawak, especially in Sibu (Lockard, 2003).

A prominent figure among the Foochows is Robert Kuok, recognized as Malaysia's richest entrepreneur. In 1959, he formed a partnership with a government agency and Japan's Nissan Sugar Manufacturing to establish Malayan Sugar, Malaysia's largest sugar refinery, which supplied 80% of the country's needs (Lin, 1989). Kuok varied his range of operation into several sectors, founding Federal Flour Mills (FFM) in Penang, Johor Flour Mills, and Perlis Plantations, and expanding his operations across Malaysia, Singapore, Indonesia, and beyond. His family continues to lead in business, with his daughter, Kuok Hui Kwong, chairing Shangri-La Asia, while his son, Kuok Khoon Ean, holds significant positions within the Kuok group.

Another influential Foochow entrepreneur is Tiong Hiew King, founder of the Rimbunan Hijau (RH) Group, initially focused on timber processing and trading.

The company has diversified into various sectors, including newspaper publishing, finance, and agriculture. Tiong also owns Oregon Group in New Zealand, which is involved in construction and farming. His family plays active roles in the business, with his son Chiong Ie becoming Chairman of Rimbunan Sawit Bhd. and other family members serving on the board of RH Group.

2.3.7 Kwongsai Chinese

The Kwongsai Chinese are often mistakenly conflated with the Cantonese, but they are a distinct group originating from Guangxi, China, with their own dialect, culture, and characteristics (Tan, 1997). Seeking better futures, Kwongsais migrated to Nanyang, arriving in smaller numbers compared to other sub-dialect groups such as the Hokkiens and Cantonese (Niew, 1969). Initially settling in Selangor, they later moved to Bentong, Pahang, in search of improved opportunities (Chen, 1987).

According to Zhuang Guotu's classification of Chinese immigration to Southeast Asia, Kwongsai immigrants were primarily part of the third wave, the autonomous migration period, spanning from the early 20th century to the 1950s (Zhuang, 2008). Significant migration began after the Opium Wars, driven by labor demands in the Nanyang region. As early settlers in Bentong encouraged their relatives to join them, the Kwongsai population grew. However, unlike the earlier-arriving Hokkiens and Cantonese, the Kwongsais lacked business insight, primarily working in labor-intensive sectors such as mining and rubber plantations (Leo & Peter, 1996).

The Kwongsais are predominantly found in Pahang and Perak, with a notable presence in Johor. In Bentong, they formed the majority of the Chinese population. The establishment of *"huiguan"* (Chinese associations) provided mutual support and unity against ethnic oppression, enabling the Kwongsai community to thrive in Bentong, Mentakab, and Raub (Yen, 1991). Unlike other Chinese sub-groups that adopted a "self-preservation" mindset, the Kwongsais were proactive, joining the Malayan People's Anti-Japanese Army to resist Japanese occupation. This courage may stem from Guangxi's historical struggles with poverty and oppression, which shaped their robust nature (Zhao, 1996).

During the colonial period, Pang Dun Wu, originally from Bobai County in Guangxi, faced adversity after losing his parents. At 19, he traveled to Singapore, starting as a hired laborer while saving diligently. He eventually founded "Yuan He Ke Zhan" (源和客栈), a shelter for migrants from his hometown, providing accommodation and job opportunities that stabilized the lives of Kwongsais (Wang, 1988). He co-founded the Sanhe Association in Singapore (Chen, 1989) and established Yuanhe Company (源和记) in 1903, marking a significant milestone in his entrepreneurial journey. Dun Wu's recruitment efforts for laborers were crucial to the development of Singapore and Malaysia during this period.

In Malaysia, Looi Hei Tyng stands out as a prominent Kwongsai figure. Currently the chairman of North Elegance Property Sdn. Bhd., he is also the vice president of The Associated Chinese Chambers of Commerce and Industry of Malaysia (ACCCIM) and a former president of the Guangxi Association of Malaysia. Hei

Tyng's family has roots in Nanyang dating back to 1930 when his grandfather emigrated, establishing a livelihood in rubber tapping, vegetable cultivation, and pig farming. Inheriting a strong work ethic, Hei Tyng entered the real estate sector in 2000, capitalizing on Malaysia's emerging market and the opportunities presented by the "Belt and Road Initiative." By 2015, his ventures had thrived, showcasing the hardy and entrepreneurial spirit characteristic of the Kwongsai community.

2.3.8 Henghua Chinese

One the Henghua Chinese, also known as Xinghua or Heng Hwa, are a distinct sub-dialect group among Chinese Malaysians, originating from a prefecture-level city in eastern Fujian province, specifically Putien and Hsienyu (T'ien, 1983). Extreme poverty in Putien prompted many Henghuas to migrate to Nanyang, where they established cohesive communities across Southeast Asia, including Sarawak, Negeri Sembilan, Selangor, Perak, Malacca, and Singapore. They maintain unique clan associations, temples, and ceremonial customs to preserve their residential pattern of "widespread dispersal and small-scale clustered living" (Zheng, 2009).

Despite being the smallest Chinese dialect group in terms of population, the Henghuas have distinct occupational characteristics. Faced with competition from other dialect groups, they shifted their focus to the transportation sector. They dominated the rickshaw industry, working as pullers and laborers earning the saying: "For travel, seek out the Henghuas" (Au, 1991). Over time, their involvement expanded to trishaws, bicycles, and eventually included roles as bus and taxi drivers. The Henghuas also engaged in the motorcycle and automobile spare parts industry, with many pursuing careers as mechanics (Nanyang University, Department of History, 1971).

In Sarawak, the Henghuas contributed to agriculture, particularly rice production (Ngu, 2011). The Brooke administration viewed their settlement development as satisfactory due to their successful provision of rice to Sibu with modest investment (Lockard, 2009; Niew, 1976). Their contributions to the transportation industry are well-recognized, as many transitioned to taxi and bus driving and bicycle shop ownership as demand for rishaw services declined due to the rise of bicycles, motorcycles, and automobiles. Beyond transportation, the Henghuas expanded into sectors such as oil palm plantations, real estate development, and electrical appliances.

Ng Teng Fong, a notable Henghua entrepreneur, was born in Putien and relocated to Singapore at six. With little formal education, he started working in his parents' soy sauce factory and worked as a bicycle repairman. His first venture was a provision shop, which led him to find his niche in property development. In 1960, he established the Far East Organization (FEO), becoming a prominent real estate tycoon (Suryadinata, 2012). His legacy continues with his eldest son, Robert Ng Chee Siong, managing the Sino Group in Hong Kong, while his younger son, Philip Ng Chee Tat, has served as CEO of FEO since 1991 and as Singapore's Non-Resident Ambassador to Chile and Argentina (MFA Press Statement).

Another prominent Henghua entrepreneur is Ng Chee Peng, who founded Ban Lee Heng as a bicycle shop in Seremban, Negeri Sembilan, in 1946. A well-known local entrepreneur, Chee Peng's business transformed in 1960 when he met Loh Boon Siew, becoming the exclusive distributor of Honda Motorcycles in Negeri Sembilan. After nearly two decades, he expanded into car distribution, officially becoming a Honda car distributor in 1976. In the early 1980s, his son Johnnie joined the dealership, significantly contributing to its growth and later serving as managing director in the 1990s. Today, Billy Wong leads this three-generation dealership, embodying the values of the brand they represent (Zheng, 2014).

2.3.9 Peranakan Chinese (Baba and Nyonya)

The Peranakan Chinese community is a unique ethnic group in Nanyang, distinct from the broader Chinese community despite identifying as Chinese (Pue, 2017; Tan, 1988). This group, often referred to as Baba and Nyonya, consists of individuals of mixed Chinese and Malay heritage resulting from marriages between Chinese men and Malay women (Lee & Tan, 2000; Koh & Ho, 2009). Originating in Malacca, many Peranakan Chinese migrated to Penang and Singapore as these regions developed (Poh-Seng, 1969).

From the late 19th to the mid-20th century, they were commonly known as the Straits Chinese, born in the British-controlled Straits Settlements of Singapore, Penang, and Malacca (Khoo, 1996; Rudolph, 1998). While maintaining a Chinese identity, the Peranakan Chinese distanced themselves from the kinship ties and political allegiances that characterized other Chinese groups, with many not speaking any Chinese dialects. Instead, their mother tongue was Baba Malay, a creole language blending Malay with elements from various languages including Chinese, Portuguese, Dutch, Tamil, and English (Lee, 2008).

Early Peranakan Chinese were known as shopkeepers and entrepreneurial traders, with substantial involvement in real estate, shipping, and banking (Khoo, 1996). Their English education and fluency facilitated their appointments as community leaders by British authorities. In the 20th century, they adeptly engaged with the government, leveraging political support to enhance their business interests. Among the Chinese community, the Peranakan were pioneers in both business and governance, often acting as middlemen in colonial society.

Tan Cheng Lock is a prominent figure representing the Peranakan Chinese in Malaysia, known for his roles as a businessman, community leader, and politician (Lim, 1960). Coming from a wealthy Straits Chinese family with shipping and plantation interests (Tregonning, 1979), he founded United Malacca Berhad (UMB) in 1910. UMB adeptly navigated challenges like the 1921 rubber crisis and the Great Depression, diversifying into oil palm cultivation in response to market changes and government policies. The Tan family managed UMB with a focus on professional management rather than nepotism, reflecting a mindset distinct from traditional Chinese values (Gatfield, 1997; Redding, 1990).

Another notable figure is Tan Tock Seng, born in Malacca in 1798, who became one of Singapore's most prominent philanthropists and community leaders. After moving to Singapore in 1819 and starting as a vegetable seller, he partnered with J. H. Whitehead, significantly increasing his wealth (Mulliner, 1991). Appointed as the first Asian Justice of the Peace by Governor William J. Butterworth, he earned the title "Captain of the Chinese" for helping early Chinese immigrants resolve disputes (Dhoraisingham & Samuel, 1992). Tan Tock Seng founded the Thian Hock Keng Temple, Singapore's oldest temple, which known as the Hokkien community's main place of worship. His philanthropic legacy was continued by his son, Tan Kim Ching, who supported the development of Tan Tock Seng Hospital, and his grandson, Tan Chay Yan, who made significant contributions to banking and insurance, and served on Malacca's municipal council.

2.4 Public Policies and Chinese Businesses in Malaysia

The literature on economic and enterprise development in East Asia frequently adopts a political economy perspective, emphasizing the "developmental state" to serve as the reason for the dramatic rise of companies in the region during the latter half of the 20th century. Nevertheless, the limitations of this framework became evident after the East Asian currency crisis of 1997 (Jomo, 2001). This book diverges from conventional family business research by moving beyond the developmental state perspective, employing concepts of organizational synthesis and historiography in business, inspired by the well-known work of Chandler (Gomez, 2007), to examine the rise of family firms in this area. This approach is particularly relevant in Malaysia, where the government's focus on educational investment distinguishes it from other East Asian developmental state economies, thus enabling it to stay up-to-date with global knowledge employment (Woo-Cumings, 2019).

As stated by Gomez (2009), there is poor interest is seen among scholars to pursue the topic of Chandler's work. This reinforces Gomez's (2007) argument that understanding the evolution and enterprise development in East Asia—especially in Malaysia—is essential. Scholars have identified weaknesses in the "market-leading strategy" (Wade, 1990), which can lead firms to "get the prices wrong" (Amsden, 1989). This study emphasizes the historical context of family businesses, examining family trees, roles, and new product development milestones within the food, plastics, and rubber industries, tracing back to their incorporation. Addressing the analytical gap by assessing successful family SMEs that effectively codify and commercialize their tacit knowledge, the study employs Chandler's concept of "organizational capabilities" to illustrate how cumulative learning within an enterprise is critical for profit-oriented entrepreneurs. This learning drives them to explore niche markets, specific economic sectors, or branded production essential for industrialization (Chandler, 1990; Gomez, 2009).

The New Economic Policy (NEP), announced by Prime Minister Tun Abdul Razak in 1970, aimed to bridge the gap in inter-ethnic economic disparities, particularly between Malays and Chinese (Gomez & Jomo, 1999). However, the implementation of this affirmative action diverged from its original intent to support

Malay SMEs. The government's focus shifted toward wealth restructuring through involvement in public enterprises across several categories, including departmental enterprises, statutory bodies, and government-linked companies (GLCs) such as the Heavy Industries Corporation of Malaysia (HICOM) and Petroliam Nasional Berhad (Petronas).

To bolster Bumiputera corporate equity, the government established trust agencies, including Perbadanan Nasional Berhad (Pernas) and Permodalan Nasional Berhad (PNB), which aimed to accumulate wealth on behalf of the ethnic group (Gomez & Jomo, 1999; Woon, 1989). Originally set to run from 1970 to 1990, the NEP aimed for Bumiputeras to own 30%percent of corporate equity by 1990. By that time, Bumiputera ownership had increased to approximately 19%, a significant rise from 1.5% in 1969 (Gomez, 2013).

The NEP's implementation led to widespread discontent among non-Bumiputera communities, largely due to inadequate responses to the challenges faced by poor Chinese in new villages and predominantly Indian plantation workers (Gomez & Jomo, 1999). In reaction, Chinese politicians and businessmen sought to redirect the focus of public enterprises toward sectors dominated by foreign interests, albeit unsuccessfully (Jesudason, 1989). Notably, significant Chinese-controlled entities, such as Malayan Banking Berhad, fell under state or Malay private control after bank runs, prompting Chinese businessmen to favor short-term investments with quick returns (Jesudason, 1989; Tan, 2001; Yoshihara, 1988). Figures like Loy Hean Heong and Khoo Kay Peng began cultivating relationships with Malay politicians with influence to secure state access (Gomez & Jomo, 1999).

Many Chinese family businesses in Malaysia have engaged in Original Equipment Manufacturing (OEM) and private labeling with multinational corporations (MNCs), linking family business literature with tacit knowledge conversion in partnerships with foreign firms. Recent scholarly works highlight the interplay between personal experience and business strategy, emphasizing the importance of both "private" and "business" critical incidents. Additionally, there is a contemporary interest in venture creation aimed at understanding enterprise development in rapidly industrializing and industrialized countries, including family businesses (Aldrich, 1999; Gartner et al., 2004; Thornton, 1999). Consequently, entrepreneurial historiography has become crucial for understanding long-term shifts in economic structures related to business growth and economic development (Jones, 2005). Such research is increasingly prevalent in the Malaysian context.

In Malaysia, existing studies have predominantly focused on large-scale Chinese businesses, with limited attention given to Chinese family-owned SMEs, including informal enterprises. This literature gap may arise from the government's implementation of developmental state policies between 1981 and 2003, particularly during Mahathir Mohamad's premiership. These state-led strategies, modeled after Japan's post-war economic growth, played a vital role in Malaysia's rapid economic development. Mahathir aimed to support domestic enterprises and foster large Chinese business groups, inspired by East Asian corporate models such as South Korean *chaebols* and Japanese *zaibatsu*.

Mahathir particularly favored the family-controlled *zaibatsu* system over the *keiretsu* model, which emphasized broader corporate equity dispersion. The *zaibatsu* system, which evolved into the keiretsu model post-World War II, highlighted strong connections between financial and industrial sectors as a means of driving industrialization (Morck & Nakamura, 2003). He used these corporate models as blueprints to promote the emergence of large, internationally recognized Malaysian Chinese conglomerates, aiming for rapid industrialization. Significant studies on large Malaysian firms prior to Mahathir's tenure—such as those by Lim (1981), Sieh (1982), and Tan (1982)—highlighted directorship patterns and interlocking ownership among large firms, focusing particularly on Chinese-owned businesses and foreign companies.

By the early 2000s, leading firms in Malaysia were predominantly GLCs, although several Chinese family-owned firms, including those belonging to the Lim, Yeoh, Quek, Kuok, Tan, and Lee families, emerged as significant publicly-listed companies. Gomez's influential work, *Chinese Business in Malaysia: Accumulation, Ascendance, Accommodation*, provides an in-depth analysis of eight large publicly listed Chinese firms, all family-owned[8]. Furthermore, he carried out a comparative study of small- and medium-sized Chinese family businesses in the UK and Malaysia, utilizing data from the UK Companies House (Gomez, 2007). His findings indicate that many Chinese family business owners in Malaysia preferred their heirs to pursue professional careers, which hindered the development of these family firms (Gomez, 2004). This reluctance to develop their enterprises stemmed from discriminatory public policies, including affirmative action, and a lack of governmental support for SMEs owned by ethnic Chinese (Gomez, 2009).

Moreover, many Malaysian Chinese businesses, especially in the manufacturing sector, are controlled by foreign interests. Research into the relationships between Malaysian Chinese family businesses and foreign firms is still in its nascent stages (Abdul Rahman, 2006). After Indonesia and Thailand, Malaysia ranks third in the extent to which large firms, primarily Chinese family-owned, dominate the market (Claessens et al., 2000). In 2009, several Chinese family business owners were listed among the 40 richest individuals in Malaysia (Singh, 2008).

Since gaining independence in 1957, Malaysia's natural resources have significantly boosted export trading and economic diversification. The share of rubber in agro-based industries declined from nearly 70% of total output value to about 65% between 1963 and 1967 (Lim, 1977). Malaysia's industrial diversification includes two primary types: agro-based industries transitioning from rubber to palm oil production, and manufacturing-related production evolving from primary to secondary industries. By 1990, the economy had become more industrialized, focusing on knowledge-intensive sectors like electronics and ICT services, which attracted foreign direct investment (FDI) and contributed to national GDP growth.

To attract FDI, many domestic cottage businesses transitioned into export-oriented manufacturing industries during the early 1970s, supported by policies such as the Investment Incentives Act of 1968 and the establishment of the Malaysian Industrial Development Authority (MIDA) in the mid-1960s, which provided funding for SMEs. During the colonial and immediate post-colonial periods, foreign enterprises, particularly British-owned, dominated the economy. However, Puthucheary (1960) observed a strong Chinese presence in manufacturing, with many family-owned businesses involved in traditional food production and rubber. Most small-scale businesses were concentrated in these sectors (Tan, 1982).

A comparison of the top 100 companies in Malaysia from 1970 to 2001 shows that only Rothmans, a foreign-owned enterprise, retained its leading position (Gomez, 2007; Lim, 1981). This indicates that many Malaysian companies, including Chinese family-owned manufacturing firms, did not adequately invest in research and development and lacked the pioneering tacit knowledge essential for growth in the manufacturing sector.

2.5 Malaysian Chinese Businesses in the Rooting Innovation in Nanyang

To thrive in competitive industries, particularly the food sector, some Malaysian CFBs have effectively codified tacit knowledge through strategic planning and partnerships with larger food agencies. These collaborations enhance product efficiency, quality, and variety, enabling these businesses to sustain themselves across generations. In contrast, many Malaysian CFBs still rely on traditional knowledge passed down from their ancestors in China, especially in food production, as demonstrated by companies like TPC Plus, Baker's Cottage, and Amoy Canning. Family ownership and control are central to these enterprises, with the next generation being groomed from an early age in family traditions, particularly in traditional food production. This transfer of tacit knowledge is crucial for long-term sustainability, helping these businesses maintain their competitive edge and strong market position both in Asia and globally.

In Malaysia, the new generation of CFBs leverages the Chinese diaspora market to drive business development, particularly in the food industry, instead of relying solely on inter-ethnic collaborations. Many CFBs prioritize assigning specific roles to family members to safeguard trade secrets and prevent the leakage of traditional production methods. Neubauer and Lank (1998) highlight that a significant strength of family businesses is their alignment with the family's values, which positively influences business practices, family dynamics, and societal contributions. In Malaysian Chinese family culture, the founder's values are paramount, shaping how CFBs conduct their operations, though this may not always be obvious to non-family employees.

The interplay of tacit knowledge and innovation in CFBs involves the creation, application, evolution, and transfer of knowledge. This learning process is vital for "self-transcending" growth. For CFBs, innovating practices involves actively studying theoretical concepts to guide practical applications, subtly enhancing their analytical and problem-solving skills. These foster added value and competitive advantages in the marketplace.

The promotion of vertically integrated firms is crucial for CFBs to produce a variety of products derived from founders' tacit knowledge. Initially, these businesses face significant challenges in achieving market acceptance. Thus, CFBs focus on preserving traditional Chinese production practices across generations, allowing them to adapt more slowly to changes than other industries. To maintain a prominent presence, they must continuously upgrade skills and innovate. Ongoing research is recommended to explore how new start-ups within CFBs can enhance competitiveness by creating niche markets, particularly in Malaysia's uniquely diverse economic landscape.

Notes

1 The Peranakan Chinese, also known as Straits Chinese or Baba-Nyonya, are descendants of Chinese immigrants who came to the Malay Archipelago between the 15th and 17th centuries. They adopted many local Malay customs while retaining Chinese traditions, creating a unique hybrid culture that includes a distinct language, cuisine, and social practices.

2 See Mak & Him (1992).

3 The term *Fangyanqun* (方言群) refers to a group or cluster of regional dialects within a language. In the context of the Chinese diaspora, it typically describes the linguistic communities formed around different Chinese dialects.

4 The Chinese concept of *Jia* (家), meaning 'family' or 'home,' extends beyond the immediate nuclear family to include the extended family, ancestors, and even future generations. It encompasses a collective sense of identity, responsibility, and continuity. In traditional Chinese culture, *Jia* serves as the fundamental social unit, where values such as filial piety, loyalty, and mutual support are deeply embedded, influencing both personal and business relationships.

5 In the context of Nanyang (which refers to Southeast Asia, especially in the historical sense of Chinese migration), "sinkheh" (新客) is a Hokkien term that means "new guest" or "newcomer." It was commonly used to describe the early Chinese immigrants arriving in Southeast Asia, particularly during the late 19th and early 20th centuries. These sinkheh were typically individuals or families from southern China. The term "sinkheh" highlights their status as newcomers, distinct from the more established Chinese migrant communities that had been in the region for longer. It also reflects the challenges they faced in integrating into the local society, building new lives, and forming networks within the existing Chinese communities and with other ethnic groups in Southeast Asia.

6 Rén Shēng (仁生), is deeply rooted in Confucian values. It derives from Rén (仁), one of Confucius' core virtues, which emphasizes compassion, benevolence, and humaneness in interpersonal relationships. In Confucian thought, Rén is the moral foundation for creating a harmonious society, where individuals are expected to act with kindness and empathy toward others, thereby contributing to the welfare of mankind.

7 Hakka mountain songs (*Shange*, 山歌) are a form of traditional folk music originating from the Hakka people. Typically performed in the Hakka dialect and have played an important role in preserving Hakka cultural identity across generations.

8 See Gomez (1999).

3 Reviewing Chinese Businesses in Southeast Asia and Key Concepts of Family-Owned Chinese Businesses in Malaysia

It is argued that family-owned Chinese businesses succeed due to Chinese values linked to successful business practices. Founders are typically diligent, committed, have business acumen, rely heavily on trust, practical, they are customer-centered, frugal, concerned with image, and profit-oriented. These traits are not only found in founders but are also expected from successors and staff, as expressed by founder Tsao: "The prospective heir should have the wisdom to learn from the invaluable experiences of the founder." However, the outlook dims when considering Chinese businesses' response to evolving global commerce trends. Chinese businesses differ significantly in structure, capabilities, and activities from international best practices. They tend to be smaller, more diversified, vertically integrated, localized, and less focused on proprietary processes and products compared to global counterparts. While this does not hinder Chinese businesses from engaging with the international business environment, it often limits them to low-value, low-margin activities where cost competition is the main option available.

3.1 Review of Chinese Businesses in Southeast Asia

Understanding the dynamics of Chinese family businesses in Southeast Asia is crucial for accurately examining the growth and succession of Chinese family businesses in Malaysia. These nations share a history of migration, leading to their diaspora dispersing across various countries through similar but diverse migration paths. Moreover, geopolitical factors also wield significant influence, given that these Southeast Asian nations were once colonial territories and gained independence around the same period, thereby nurturing strong political and commercial ties. By grasping the regional outlook, valuable perspectives can be made on the positioning and development of Chinese family businesses in Malaysia, enabling a deeper comprehension of their distinct trajectories within this shared heritage and diverse geopolitical pressures.

DOI: 10.4324/9781032705842-3

3.1.1 Chinese Businesses in Singapore

In 1963, Singapore joined the Federation of Malaysia, but political and economic differences led to its expulsion in 1965, becoming an independent nation. Despite achieving independence around the same time, Singapore rapidly surpassed Malaysia in economic progress, earning its place as one of the Four Asian Tigers alongside Hong Kong, South Korea, and Taiwan (Barro, 1998). Often considered an economic "miracle," Singapore transitioned from a developing to a high-income economy under the leadership of the former Prime Minister Lee Kuan Yew (Huff, 1995). With one of the world's most open economies, Singapore consistently ranks among the least corrupt nations (Peng et al., 2018), while also maintaining a highly pro-business environment with low tax rates and the highest per-capita GDP based on equality in purchasing power (Vietor & White, 2016). The country's primary exports include electronics, chemicals, and services, thus positioning it as a major hub for wealth management (Long & Tan, 2011). Additionally, Singapore's strategic geographic location makes it a key center for international trade, with its port being one of the busiest in the world (Lee, 1984; Wong et al., 2023).

Singapore's history as a commercial hub began in 1819 when Sir Stamford Raffles established it as a free port, leading to a significant influx of Chinese immigrants, who became the majority by 1840 (Freedman, 1960). Today, Singapore's population stands at 5.92 million, with ethnic Chinese making up about 51.2% (Population in Brief 2023: Key Trends, 2023). Among the Chinese sub-dialect groups, Hokkiens and Teochews, known for their business insight, are particularly prominent. (Wee, 2014).

Small- and medium-sized enterprises play a significant role in Singapore's economy. In 2022 SMEs contributed 48% (S$284 bil) of Singapore's total enterprise nominal value-added and employed 71% of Singapore's total workforce of 3.63 million (*Singapore Economy*, 2023). Many of these SMEs are Chinese-owned (Tan & Fock, 2001; Lee & Tan, 2001). Of Singapore's top 100 corporations, 69 are family-owned, with Chinese families playing a dominant role in industries such as construction, hospitality, real estate, and trade (Tan, 2011). These Chinese family businesses have a preference for public listing, maintaining a maximum 90% shareholding as allowed by law (Tan & Fock, 2001). As these businesses transition between generations, they face challenges balancing family values with business growth. Some firms, like Hong Leong Group, Far East Organization, and UOB Group, rely on professional management while maintaining family control (Ong, 2019). However, family legacies can sometimes restrict external managers if family visions conflict with broader business goals.

The evolution of Chinese education in Singapore has also influenced the business landscape, with more Chinese students from English-speaking families changing the sociolinguistic profile. The government has promoted Chinese education through curriculum reforms, emphasizing the language's cultural and economic importance (Curdt-Christiansen, 2014). While Singaporean Chinese initially obscured their ethnic heritage, their growing national progress led them to re-embrace their roots. This is a consideration for Malaysian Chinese businesses, which have remained deeply attached to their ethnic identity.

Despite their shared cultural heritage, the Chinese communities in Singapore and Malaysia have developed distinct business environments. Singapore's Chinese community has flourished by capitalizing on the country's favorable economic conditions and global connections, participating in international trade and making strategic financial investments. In contrast, Malaysian Chinese face a business environment shaped by inconsistent government regulations. Nonetheless, both communities contribute uniquely to the economic systems of their respective nations while pursuing different paths in their entrepreneurial endeavors.

3.1.2 Chinese Businesses in Indonesia

Indonesia, with a population of around 277 million, is the fourth most densely populated nation globally and home to the world's largest Muslim population (Indonesia Population, 2023). Despite representing just 7% of the total population, Chinese Indonesians wield significant economic and financial influence, controlling a large share of the nation's wealth and business (Backman, 2001; Chua, 2004; Globe Asia, 2016). Chinese Indonesians form the fourth largest overseas Chinese community, following Thailand, Malaysia, and the United States. Their immigration to Indonesia predates the arrival of Westerners, with many arriving initially as sojourners with plans to return home (Wang, 1996). Over time, Chinese migrants, primarily traders, settled across Indonesia, particularly in Java, Sumatra, and Kalimantan (Thung, 2012).

Historically, the Chinese in Indonesia have been supported by Chinese-language schools, ethnic media, and clan associations (Suryadinata et al., 2003; Suryadinata, 1997). However, compared to other Southeast Asian nations, Chinese Indonesians have faced significant prejudice and ethnic conflicts, shaping a complex relationship with their heritage. Despite this, Chinese immigrants have long been integral to Indonesia's business sector. Their involvement in trade, dating back to the colonial period, helped them establish strong business networks through cultural integration and *guanxi* (Fee & We, 2004). By the time of independence, Chinese entrepreneurs had set up small businesses catering to their ethnic communities, with employees often recruited based on shared dialects.

Currently, Chinese Indonesians control 26 of the 30 major business conglomerates in the country, spanning industries such as cement, paper, textiles, and food (Jomo & Folk, 2013. These businesses have grown by leveraging family ties and trusted networks. During the New Order regime (1966–1998), assimilation policies pushed Chinese Indonesians to blend with the local Pribumi population, leading to inter-ethnic business collaborations. Despite challenges, such as enforced assimilation and anti-Chinese sentiment during political instability in the 1990s (Chua, 2004; Suryadinata, 1978), Chinese businesses continued to thrive.

Today, Chinese conglomerates like Texmaco, Sinar Mas, and Salim Group maintain control through holding companies and trusted networks, appointing Indonesian Pribumi and relatives to key positions. These entrepreneurs also form partnerships with the rising Pribumi middle class, blending business acumen and public-sector expertise to expand their market reach. Successive generations of Chinese Indonesian entrepreneurs continue to adapt, capitalizing on evolving political and economic conditions (Coppel, 2013; Hoon, 2008; Wijaya, 2019).

In contrast to the Malaysian Chinese, who represent the second-largest ethnic group, Indonesian Chinese are a minority and have faced more severe assimilation policies. Despite this, their notable achievements in business underscore their resilience and entrepreneurial spirit, making their success even more remarkable.

3.1.3 Chinese Businesses in Thailand

Chinese migration to Thailand has a rich history, starting when many Chinese moved to Southeast Asia seeking better economic opportunities back in the 18th century. The dominant Chinese sub-dialect group in Thailand is the Teochew, followed by the Hakka, Hainanese, Hokkien, and Cantonese (Luangthongkum, 2007). This migration fostered networks of immigration, trade, and remittance. Thailand has historically been open to Chinese migrants, unlike some countries with stricter immigration policies. Although Thai nationalism surged in the 1930s, creating tensions between the Sino-Thai and Thai communities (Laothamatas, 1988; Sidel, 2012; Sugihara, 2004; Vu, 2013), the Chinese population's position in the national economy remained strong, supporting the growth of Chinese businesses across various sectors (Suehiro, 1992).

Today, Sino-Thais constitute around 14% of Thailand's population, making them the largest overseas Chinese community globally. Thailand has the second-largest concentration of Chinese after Malaysia, creating a dynamic, diverse economic and cultural environment. Education has been crucial for Chinese migrants and their descendants, particularly in Mandarin and Thai, which has facilitated integration into Thai society and business circles. Bilingual proficiency has enabled smoother business interactions and fostered stronger ties within the Thai business community (Kuhn & Liu, 2006). Skinner (1957) argued that Thailand successfully integrated Chinese immigrants better than neighboring countries like the Philippines, Indonesia, and Malaysia. However, other scholars have suggested that rather than fully assimilating, many Sino-Thai descendants maintain their Chinese identity while embracing their cultural heritage (Vatikiotis, 2003).

The Sino-Thai community has long been entrepreneurial, dominating industries such as trade, commerce, finance, and manufacturing (Auansakul, 1995). Overseas Chinese family businesses are often characterized by their small scale and simple structure (Redding, 1993; Weidenbaum, 1996). Research has shown that Chinese immigrants actively seek out business opportunities, frequently relying on close-knit communities and family networks to build and sustain their enterprises (Ling et al., 2021; Sahakijpicharn, 2007). Over time, younger generations of Sino-Thais have combined traditional values with modern business practices, resulting in innovative approaches that balance cultural heritage with Thai societal norms. This blending of traditions and modernization significantly shapes their business values, customer relations, and market strategies.

One prominent example is the Charoen Pokphand Group (CP Group), known as the Chia Tai Group in China. Founded in 1921 by Chia Ek Chor, an immigrant from Shantou, Guangdong, CP Group has been under the control of the Chearavanont family for generations (Burch, 1996; Hewison, 2003). The family's second generation expanded the business abroad and diversified into sectors like animal feed, telecommunications, and manufacturing. Their guiding philosophy of benefiting the country, people, and business has cemented the CP Group as Thailand's most respected company and largest private enterprise (Pananond, 2001).

In conclusion, the evolution of Chinese family businesses in Thailand reflects a balance between tradition and modernity, driven by communal support systems, education, and shifting cultural identities. As successive generations of Sino-Thais navigate this complex landscape, they continue to integrate traditional values with modern entrepreneurial approaches, shaping Thailand's economic and cultural landscape.

3.1.4 Chinese Businesses in Philippines

The ethnic Chinese population in the Philippines comprises about 20% of the total population (Soriano, 2016). FilipinoChinese enterprises have significantly driven entrepreneurship in the nation over the past 50 years, similar to other Southeast Asian countries with ethnic minority groups (Khan et al., 2017; Susilo & Sugihartati, 2020; Gonzales, 2021). The presence of Chinese in the Philippines can be traced back to pre-colonial times, when Chinese traders engaged in coastal commerce (Yeo & Gloria, 2022). In the late 16th century, the Spanish's presence further attracted Chinese immigrants, and by the early 17th century, Manila had over 20,000 Chinese residents, mainly Hokkiens (Carstairs, 1899; Wickberg, 1964).

During the Spanish colonial period, the Chinese played a key role in trade and business operations, serving as merchants, craftsmen, and food suppliers (Wickberg, 1964). The period from 1850 to 1898 was significant for the Filipino Chinese community, as immigration regulations eased, facilitating economic growth (Camba & Lung, 2021; Tan, 2021). The Philippines was one of the first Southeast Asian nations to develop an export-oriented economy, benefiting the Chinese community, which established connections with the local elite (Koning, 2011; McVey, 1992).

However, the Filipino Chinese experienced a decline in economic status during American colonization. During the Japanese occupation (1941–1945), unity between Filipino Chinese and native Filipinos fostered a sense of belonging, with many Chinese viewing the Philippines as their homeland (McCoy, 1994). Post-independence, the Retail Trade Nationalization Act of 1954 forced many Filipino-Chinese to shift from retail to manufacturing due to citizenship issues (Palanca, 1995).

The Filipino economy faced recessions in 1997, 2008 (Tan, 2001; Yap et al., 2009), and during the COVID-19 pandemic. However, the broader challenge for the Philippines was its failure to keep pace with economic developments in other Southeast Asian nations. While the country focused on light industry, heavy industry and agricultural reforms were neglected, causing it to lose ground in sectors like aviation and port commerce (Bravo, 2017; David, 2003).

Despite anti-Chinese sentiments post-World War II, the situation improved in 1974 when the Philippines established diplomatic relations with China, granting legal recognition and political rights to the Chinese community. This integration bolstered the economic standing of Filipino Chinese businesses, similar to the experience in Thailand. Many Filipino Chinese businesses remain family-owned, and prominent magnates include the Sy, Tan Caktiong, Lucio Tan, and Ty families. Henry Sy, the founder of SM Group, was the wealthiest man in the Philippines for 11 years, succeeded by his children (Berou Jr, 2012).

Filipino Chinese businesses have adapted to economic and policy changes, with the younger generation increasingly focusing on globalization (Rivera & Tullao, 2023). As part of the Chinese supply chain, these businesses are well-positioned to benefit from China's rise as the world's second-largest economy (Camba & Lung, 2021).

3.1.5 Chinese Businesses in Vietnam

The experiences of the Chinese in Vietnam (Hoa) and Malaysia have diverged in politics, culture, and commerce, thus shaping unique paths for each community. The Chinese Vietnamese hold citizenship and nationality, though their ancestral ties to the Han Chinese vary. Chinese migration to Vietnam began over a thousand years ago, with the Han dynasty's feudal rulers initiating an assimilation policy between the Han-Tang and Viet communities (Nguyen, 1993). Migration intensified in the late 17th century, following the Opium Wars, and continued into the 20th century as Chinese merchants sought better markets (King, 1987; Trung Vu Nguyen, 2009). Further migration occurred after 1954, particularly among Hakka Catholics fleeing communist persecution in the north (Spence, 1996).

Cantonese speakers make up the largest group among the Chinese Vietnamese, while other dialects found include Teochew, Hokkien, Hainan, and Hakka (Van Trang, 2015).

Although a minority, the Chinese Vietnamese have long played a vital role in commerce, they organized into "*bangs*," unifying bodies based on language and origin that supported cultural, social, and business activities (King, 1987). However, after 1975, the Communist government seized many Chinese businesses, forcing a large number to flee as "boat people." This persecution led to the Sino-Vietnamese War, but later economic reforms and an open-door policy restored their influence in Vietnam's economy (Khanh & Phuong, 1997).

Today, Chinese Vietnamese account for just 1.4% of the population, yet they make up a huge portion of the economy, particularly in banking, industry, and trade (Share, 1994). They lead at all levels of commerce, largely working within family businesses rather than seeking government or state-owned employment (Van Trang, 2015). Most Chinese Vietnamese family businesses are relatively young, with many still under founder control, such as Vuu Khai Thanh's family, which rose to prominence in the 1980s with cooperatives like Binh Tien and Van Thanh, producing rubber slippers for export (Pham et al., 2019).

Despite their growth, these businesses face challenges in restructuring governance and transferring knowledge to the next generation. Internal governance, rooted in family ties, can hinder modernization, making education and strategy development key priorities (Pham et al., 2019). Compared to Chinese businesses in other Southeast Asian countries, Vietnamese Chinese family firms are still developing, a reflection of Vietnam's political system and policies. Culturally, the Chinese Vietnamese are highly assimilated, like to the Thai Chinese, while maintaining distinct business strategies typical of Chinese communities elsewhere. Unlike capitalist or constitutional monarchies, Vietnam's communist state influences the trajectory of Chinese businesses, which remain focused on adapting to local and global economic shifts.

3.1.6 Chinese Businesses in Brunei

Brunei's Chinese community has a long history, predating the arrival of Islam in Southeast Asia. The Chinese played a key role in trade with the Brunei Sultanate before this activity went south in the 18th and 19th centuries. The discovery of oil in 1929 attracted more Chinese immigrants, and by 1960, they made up 26% of the population (De Vienne, 2011). However, the Chinese population has since decreased to 9.5% of Brunei's population of 445,400 (Laporan Banci Penduduk dan Perumahan [BPP], 2021). The Hokkien are the largest Chinese group, followed by the Foochow, with smaller communities of Hakka, Cantonese, Teochew, and Henghua. The Hokkien, although they are small in number, the Hokkien have a strong presence in Brunei's business sector, often partnering with Malaysian Chinese businesses (Richter, 1999).

Since Brunei's independence in 1984, the national policy of Melayu Islam Beraja (MIB) has emphasized the role of Malay Muslim Monarchy, with the Chinese community actively participating in localizing economic and cultural practices (Ho, 2021). Many Chinese Bruneians have assimilated culturally and educationally, while maintaining intra-ethnic networks and playing significant roles in both government and private sectors. Some Chinese have converted to Islam and follow Syariah regulations (Pang, 2015). Brunei also respects Chinese culture, with Chinese New Year recognized as a national holiday, and Chinese names preserved, contrasting with assimilation policies in the Philippines, Indonesia, and Thailand (Ho & Ho, 2021).

Chinese Bruneians are engaged in the national economy, supported by institutions such as the Chinese Chamber of Commerce, which fosters cooperation with the Malay Chamber of Commerce. Many Chinese entrepreneurs maintain strong ties with the monarchy, a practice mirrored in Malaysia and Thailand. Although the private sector is small and reliant on government contracts, Chinese businesses, particularly family-owned ones like Hua Ho, Soon Lee, Sim Kim Huat, and First Emporium Group, continue to thrive (Hayat, 2017; Pang, 2019). Historically, Chinese Bruneians were involved in retail and commodity trading, but now many are opting for white-collar jobs over traditional retail (Pang, 2015).

Despite their population decline, the Chinese community continues to play a vital role in Brunei's economy. Family businesses remain prominent, resisting external partnerships or licensing, and the community retains strong ties to regional networks across Southeast Asia. While the "Ali Baba" phenomenon, where local businesses partner with foreign entities, exists in Brunei, Chinese businesses have largely preserved their independence (Thien, 2012). Overall, the Chinese Bruneians benefit from Brunei's stability, political cohesion, and cross-border networks, positioning them well for continued success in the nation (Pang, 2019).

3.1.7 Chinese Businesses in Laos

Chinese migrants have had a significant presence in Laos since the late 1600s, initially integrating well into local life in Ban Lan. However, newcomers arriving in the early 1900s faced challenges assimilating into Laotian society (Laungaramsri, 2019). Their migration was driven by economic and political factors, with many settling in northern Laos or Vientiane. The treatment of Chinese migrants has fluctuated over time, with periods of both acceptance and suppression (Chen Jun, 2022). Today, Chinese account for about 1 to 2% of Laos' population. These migrants included various Han subgroups such as Cantonese, Yunnanese, Hainanese, Teochew, and Hakka, as well as minority groups like the Miao and Yao, some of whom came to Laos after facing challenges in Thailand or Vietnam (Halpern, 1961). While the distribution of Chinese dialect groups in Laos is similar to that in Thailand, the Yunnanese community holds more significance in Laos (Skinner, 1957).

During French colonial rule, the Chinese migrant population in Laos was smaller compared to other Southeast Asian regions, and education played a vital part in preserving Chinese cultural identity. Chinese migrants established their own schools, often without French instruction, leading many graduates to pursue further education in Taiwan or China (Halpern, 1961; Peng, 2013). In the 1950s, the Chinese in Laos became an influential urban ethnic minority in cities like Pakse and Luang Prabang, but after the rise of the communist government in 1975, their communities declined significantly (Hlaing, 2006; Rossetti, 1997; Stuart-Fox, 1979).

The Lao communist government has alternately disrupted and facilitated economic activities. From 1975 to 1986, reforms targeted the agricultural sector, reducing landowner privileges and promoting collective ownership (Michaud, 2013). The Greater Mekong Subregion (GMS) program, initiated in 1992, significantly increased the number of Chinese migrants in Laos by improving road networks between Kunming and Bangkok (Southiseng et al., 2008). This boosted trade and reinforced ties between Yunnan and Southeast Asia, contributing to economic development in Laos (Walsh, 2011).

Danielle Tan (2012) challenges the notion that Laos is a passive victim of globalization, arguing that Chinese involvement has strengthened the Lao government rather than undermining it. The GMS program has facilitated trade between Southeast Asia and China, and Chinese family businesses have become active in various sectors, particularly infrastructure projects like roads and dams (Andriesse,

2011). Many small and medium-sized Chinese enterprises in Laos focus on trading and services, though they face challenges such as an unclear legal framework, limited access to credit, and insufficient government support (Walsh, 2011).

In conclusion, Chinese migration to Laos reflects the evolution of traditional trade routes into modern economic corridors. However, Chinese businesses often rely on personal relationships, family ties, and social networks to navigate challenges due to limited government and financial support. More extensive research is necessary to gain better understanding the Chinese community's ongoing role in Laos, as current studies remain limited.

3.1.8 Chinese Businesses in Myanmar

The Sino-Burmese, or Burmese Chinese, comprise around 3% of Myanmar's population (Than & Kyi, 1997), with their migration occurring in multiple waves. These migrants were driven by political, economic, and social factors, including security concerns, famine, and business opportunities (Liu et al., 2019). Early Yunnanese traders settled in Mandalay in the mid-18th century, engaging in trade, mining, agriculture, and craftsmanship , a term used when referring to handcrafts, emphasizes the skill, artistry, and dedication involved in creating objects by hand. This can include pottery, weaving, woodworking, and other artisanal practices (Yang, 2003). During British rule in the 19th century, a larger wave of Chinese immigrants arrived, forming two primary groups: the Hokkien and Cantonese, who traveled by sea, and the Yunnanese, who entered overland (Yi Li, 2015). Today, the Yunnanese have become the largest Chinese group in Myanmar, especially in Yangon, historically dominated by Hokkien and Cantonese communities.

Myanmar's prolonged civil conflicts and autocratic rule have left much of the country underdeveloped, with about a quarter of the population residing in conflict zones governed by armed factions (Burke et al., 2017; Egreteau & Jagan, 2013). These factors, along with Myanmar's global isolation, have hampered the private sector's growth (Rieffel, 2010). The lack of regulatory oversight has forced many businesses to operate informally, often relying on personal networks and connections to navigate the challenging business environment (Bissinger, 2014; Gravers, 2015).

The Chinese community in Myanmar consists of several subgroups, including the Hakkas, Hokkiens, Cantonese, Kokang, Panthay, and Tayoke Kabya (Stamp, 1930; Smith & Allsebrook, 1994). These groups have established a prosperous middle class and hold significant influence over the country's economy. Chinese entrepreneurs own four of Myanmar's five largest banks: Myanmar Universal Bank, Yoma Bank, Myanmar Mayflower Bank, and Asia Wealth Bank (Turnell, 2009). Additionally, many retail, wholesale, and shipping businesses are Chinese-owned, with close ties to military elites enabling these entrepreneurs to gain economic advantages (Mangan, 2018).

Chinese business influence is particularly strong in Yangon and Mandalay. In Yangon, the Hokkien community leads family-owned businesses in teak logging, and the trade of rice, beans, and legumes, while the Cantonese are known for handicraft manufacturing and artisanal retail. In Mandalay, Chinese enterprises have transformed the city into a vibrant economic hub, with a focus on trade and foreign investments (Myint-U, 2011; Roberts, 2016). Overseas Chinese investors use bamboo networks to funnel capital into Myanmar, with the Sino-Burmese community playing a crucial role in these ventures.

Research on Myanmar's private sector has been historically limited due to restrictions imposed by previous military regimes. This has contributed to Myanmar's poor ranking of 182nd out of 189 countries in the World Bank's 2014 Doing Business Index, reflecting its difficult business environment. However, since the transition to a civilian government in 2016, there have been efforts to improve the economy, with expectations of continued growth in the coming years.

3.1.9 Summary

The comparative study of Chinese businesses across Southeast Asia reveals a rich tapestry of historical migration, cultural integration, and economic evolution, offering valuable insights into how Chinese communities have shaped and been shaped by their environments. This analysis underscores both the unique trajectories and common threads linking Chinese business practices across the region.

Thailand demonstrates a high degree of assimilation where Thai Chinese have deeply integrated into local networks. Their adaptability is evident in their large-scale investments and international expansion, allowing them to maintain a significant presence across various sectors.

In **Singapore**, the Chinese community is characterized by high professionalism and innovation. The city-state's role as a global financial hub and its supportive business environment have fostered the growth of CFBs. Singaporean CFBs, with their emphasis on modern corporate governance, contrast sharply with the more traditional CFBs in Malaysia, reflecting the advantages of operating in a dynamic, globally connected economy.

Indonesia highlights the resilience of the Chinese community amid historical challenges. Despite periods of discrimination and economic restrictions, Chinese Indonesians have established a significant economic presence. Recent regulatory relaxations have allowed for business expansion, showcasing the community's perseverance and adaptability.

In the **Philippines**, government support and an open economic environment have facilitated the professionalization and diversification of Chinese businesses, though regulatory inconsistencies and political instability continue to pose challenges. **Vietnam** illustrates how historical experiences of acceptance and persecution have shaped the Hoa community's economic activities. Despite a complex regulatory environment, Vietnamese Chinese entrepreneurs have adapted to local and international markets, thriving amid ongoing political and economic challenges.

In **Brunei**, the Chinese community, though declining in population, remains influential. The integration of Chinese businesses into Brunei's economy is marked by strong familial ties and a focus on cultural preservation, with the nation's stability providing a conducive environment for business.

Laos and **Myanmar** reflect the difficulties faced by Chinese businesses in less developed and politically unstable settings. In Laos, Chinese SMEs contribute significantly to infrastructure and local services despite regulatory and credit challenges. In Myanmar, political instability and a weak regulatory framework affect Chinese economic activities, but strong political connections and extensive networks help navigate these challenges.

Overall, the study highlights the diverse experiences of Chinese businesses in Southeast Asia, shaped by historical, cultural, political, and economic factors. Malaysia serves as a notable example of how Chinese businesses can thrive in a supportive yet challenging environment. Despite regulatory and economic hurdles, Malaysian Chinese businesses effectively balance cultural preservation with adaptation to local norms. Malaysian Chinese entrepreneurs leverage ethnic-based networks and familial ties, maintaining their cultural identity while engaging in diverse economic activities. Malaysia's relatively stable political and economic environment supports business growth, although regulatory challenges and economic shifts pose ongoing hurdles. Compared to some neighbors, Malaysia's infrastructure and business environment are more developed, aiding business stability. In contrast, Thai and Singaporean Chinese show higher degrees of assimilation and professionalism. Thai Chinese have integrated deeply into society, while Singaporean Chinese businesses benefit from a highly professional environment. In Indonesia, Vietnam, Philippines, Laos, and Myanmar, Chinese businesses face more challenging conditions, characterized by political instability, regulatory inefficiencies, and varying economic environments. The common thread across the region is the adaptability and perseverance of Chinese entrepreneurs. Regardless of the country, Chinese entrepreneurs have demonstrated a capacity to balance cultural preservation with local integration, leveraging ethnic networks and familial ties to navigate complex economic and political landscapes. This comparative analysis enriches our understanding of Chinese business practices and the broader implications of ethnic entrepreneurship in shaping regional economies. As Southeast Asia evolves, the experiences of Chinese businesses offer valuable lessons in navigating economic landscapes and contributing to regional development.

3.2 Reviewing Key Concepts of Chinese Businesses

The global economy is dominated by family businesses, accounting for 80 to 98% of enterprises and contributing 37% of Fortune 500 companies, while generating over 75% of the GDP in various nations (Poza, 2010). Despite their prominence, over 50% of family business startups fail within the first five years (Goldberg, 1996; Ryan et al., 2001), and only about one-third survive to the second generation, with one-third of those advancing to the third generation[1]. Although research on family businesses is extensive in Western contexts (Zahra & Sharma, 2004), there is a notable gap in studies focusing on Malaysia. A Malaysian business publication reports that nearly 80% of businesses in Malaysia are small- and medium-sized enterprises owned by Chinese families (Draim, 2001). The historical and cultural ties within East and Southeast Asia support the integration of Malaysian Chinese family businesses into the broader category of overseas CFBs (Redding, 1993; Yeung, 2004), with the Chinese community playing a significant role in Malaysia's economy.

CFBs in Malaysia are often seen as primarily focused on dynasty modes, emphasizing the establishment, preservation, and enhancement of knowledge and innovation practices within the family lineage. Nevertheless, they face challenges in evolving into a modernized form of CFB that blends traditional and contemporary practices (Loy, 2012). Founders expect successors to emulate and apply tacit knowledge inherited from them, as exemplified by founder Tsao's assertion that heirs should learn from their invaluable experiences (Tsao, 1993).

Koiranen (2002) identifies two essential components of a family enterprise: ownership management and family participation across at least two generations. He emphasizes that ownership authority should remain within the family, excluding external parties. Chua et al. (1999) describe family businesses as those governed by family members who pursue business objectives through a dominant coalition across generations, focusing on sustainability. Chua's research highlights integrity and dedication as vital traits for family enterprises in Western contexts, while interpersonal skills, historical performance, and expertise are crucial for advancement. Astrachan et al. (2003) categorize three key themes in family business growth: past experience, controlled power, and organizational culture. Understanding the influence of generational transitions on organizational outcomes is essential, given that leaders in family businesses prefer to maintain family oversight (Zahra & Sharma, 2004). Therefore, investigating the roots of ethnic entrepreneurship in Chinese enterprises is vital for comprehending their successes.

In discussing ethnic entrepreneurship from the supply perspective, scholars often put the emphases on the characteristics and resources that migrants use to establish their businesses (Bonacich, 1973; Weber & Kalberg, 2013). Bonacich (1973) emphasizes the role of cultural factors in initiating and developing ethnic businesses, while Portes (1995) focuses on the significance of social networks, including family and intra-ethnic ties. Critics have pointed out that these approaches can be too narrow in focusing solely on social capital (Engelen, 2001). As a result, researchers started taking demand factors into consideration, such as economic conditions and state policies impacting ethnic enterprises (Jones et al., 2000; Ram et al., 2003; Waldinger et al., 1990), though demand-oriented studies often fail to notice the importance of networking and ethnic resources.

To address this gap, Waldinger et al. (1990) introduced an interactive model that combines both supply and demand aspects of ethnic entrepreneurship, focusing on group characteristics and opportunity structures. Another significant model, the mixed embeddedness model, examines how business opportunities are shaped by the host country's economic conditions. Kloosterman (1999) identifies two opportunity types: ethnic-based products and opportunities arising when native shop owners leave areas with higher migrant populations. Migrants are thus seen as integrating into the social, economic, and political frameworks of their host countries. Both the mixed embeddedness model and the interactive model highlight the critical role of market conditions in shaping opportunities and demand for ethnic entrepreneurs.

To comprehend Chinese businesses in Malaysia, this study categorizes the business strategies into two parts. The first part is the resources element which as adapted from Kloosterman and Rath (2001) and Waldinger et al. (1990), and the second part is the opportunity structure adapted from Waldinger et al. (1990). The viability of these concepts in an assessment of Chinese-owned enterprises in Malaysia will be explained in the next chapter.[2]

3.3 Resources

Mulholland (1997) stated that businesses require class and ethnic resources, for instance skills, education and property. When these entrepreneurs first arrived as migrants, they brought with them their own resources: ethnicity, knowledge, financial capabilities, and identity. Additionally, they possessed social resources in the form of friends and family ties. To break free out of their niche ethnic circle, gain better resources, and serve a bigger market, firms may resort to developing their connections with non-ethnic resource owners and markets. If utilized effectively, these resources can be a vital driving force that catalyzes the growth of the enterprises. In the present study, resources are viewed from the supply perspective of ethnic entrepreneurship.

3.3.1 Class Resources

Class resources are generally referring to material goods, for instance wealth, "bourgeois values, attitudes, and knowledge" (Light & Bonacich, 1988). Social class provides a socialization context with economic, symbolic, and cultural resources that influence psychological functioning and behavior, affecting focus, self-orientation, and individual self-definition (Goudeau et al., 2017). The concept of class operates through the imbalanced distribution of both symbolic and material resources, possessing an implied and hidden quality (Hilmar, 2022; Jarness, 2013).

Education is important for entering the business world, with higher levels of education linked to increased success in new venture creation and growth (Mohammed et al., 2014). Education helps entrepreneurs overcome internal barriers and better navigate external market challenges. This is supported by Basu (2011) who claims that market strategies are influenced by educational attainment, skill levels, and prior business experience. Moreover, a recent study indicates poor training and education as a primary cause of frequent failures among SMEs (Saah, 2022). Although increased educational qualifications enable individuals to advance socially through professional careers, the relationship between education and success varies by industry. In the banking sector, higher education levels positively influence profitability (Dinçer et al., 2019), whereas in the hospitality industry, educational level has a negligible impact. Plus, while education opens up professional opportunities, it has been reported that people with better qualifications have lower tendency for self-employment (Clark & Drinkwater, 2010).

In addition to education and knowledge, financial resources are a crucial component of class resources. Bourdieu (2018) identifies three forms of capital: economic capital (convertible into money and institutionalized as property rights), cultural capital (convertible into economic capital under certain conditions and institutionalized as educational qualifications), and social capital (social obligations or 'connections' convertible into economic capital and institutionalized as titles of nobility). These factors play a vital role in business development and advancement. Credit from financial institutions is seldom used during the start-up phase (Raijman & Tienda, 2000; Townsend, 2005; Tienda, 2001). Instead, loans from informal sources and personal savings provide majority of the start-up capital (Bates & Robb, 2013). An entrepreneur's initial social class position significantly influences the availability of financial resources from family and ethnic lending sources. Social networks often determine the availability of investment capital or start-up funding, with ties to close networks being mainly influenced by the entrepreneur's social background (Basu, 1998; Dunstan et al., 2004; Portes & Zhou, 1992).

Since ethnic minority entrepreneurs are more prone to experience bigger financial barriers (Ram et al., 2003), this limits their ability to compete in a competitive environment (McPherson, 2019). In Malaysia, the New Economic Policy had varying effects on different social classes within the Chinese community. While Chinese entrepreneurs collectively progressed, larger companies outperformed smaller ones. Upper-class Chinese entrepreneurs emerged as the most successful beneficiaries, whereas smaller enterprises faced increased competitive pressures (Koon, 1997).

3.3.2 Ethnic Resources

The establishment of ethnic enterprises is influenced by various factors, including geographic location, job opportunities, education, cultural and religious differences, generation, local demographics, economic conditions, and origins (Volery, 2007). Ethnic entrepreneurs, as defined by Zhou (2004), are individuals who manage their own businesses, share a recognized cultural heritage, and are embedded within specific social structures that shape their actions, connections, and economic exchanges. This embedding influences the dynamics of ethnic economies, which differ from both ethnic and non-ethnic counterparts. Chaganti and Greene (2002) suggest that the definition of "ethnic entrepreneur" should focus on the individual's involvement in their ethnic community rather than simply their ethnic background.

Migrants sharing a common nationality and ethnic heritage often maintain similar cultures, values, and societal norms, fostering trust and understanding that facilitate connections within their ethnic communities (Berry, 2005; Sam & Berry, 2010). This support system among migrants is critical, as it enhances trust, communication, access to credit, and cultural compatibility, leading to the formation of economic clusters that reinforce cultural value systems[3]. Ethnic resources can significantly aid business startups. By utilizing social networks and community resources, migrants can navigate cultural adjustments in diverse host countries without fully assimilating into the dominant culture[4]. However, an overreliance on these ethnic networks may hinder long-term growth, resulting in greater failure rates and lower profitability (Bates, 1994). This dependence can restrict market growth and product diversification, limiting appeal to a broader customer base.

Hofstede's research (1980, 2001) on cultural dimensions across 64 countries highlights the stability of culture and values over time and across different environments. First-generation migrants often face challenges in assimilating into the their new environment, which can negatively affect the initiation, development, and growth of ethnic enterprises (Hofstede, 2001; Zhou & Bankston, 2016). However, cultural values and norms may lose significance among the descendants of these migrants. Koning and Verver (2012) observe that second- and third-generation ethnic entrepreneurs in Southeast Asia increasingly disregard traditional cultural values and norms.

The definition of identity is both an individual and collective process, with entrepreneurship playing a role in shaping identity through interactions within similar groups. Individuals recognize their collective identity based on shared characteristics, forming cultural networks. New perspectives view identity as dynamic, adapting to social changes and learning over time. Factors such as history, traditions, and future aspirations shape identity, with location and time influencing cultural and national identities. Economic success can further facilitate identity development. As ethnic entrepreneurship transitions across generations, there is often a shift in identity from migrants to their descendants[5]. Migrants tend to adopt a new national identity while preserving their cultural roots, gradually integrating into the host society. Over time, their descendants may shift from a cultural to a national identity, diminishing the influence of cultural norms on business practices.

In Malaysia, studies revolving the relationship between identity, business, and the evolution of tacit knowledge innovation within Chinese family-owned firms across generations are limited. As generational shifts occur, evolution in cultural identity could affect how ethnic resources are utilized. The link between the utilization of these resources and the growth of ethnic entrepreneurship warrants further investigation, as alterations in ethnic resources significantly influence the market conditions faced by ethnic businesses.

3.3.3 Knowledge Factors

Enterprises can achieve a competitive edge by blending their traditional strengths with technological innovations (Porter, 2001). For family businesses, particularly, the ability to convert tacit knowledge into codified forms relies on the next generation's capacity to drive innovation through new technologies. Innovation, defined as the creation of new services, processes, or products, and the use of existing knowledge in creative ways, is crucial for economic success. Scholars emphasize that this innovative capacity is essential for rapidly introducing new products and adapting to processes, thereby maintaining a firm's competitive advantage (Barney, 1991; Dosi et al., 1992; Lall, 1995).

The effective transfer of tacit knowledge into economically viable products through enhanced knowledge sharing is vital for family businesses (Nonaka, 1994). This process ensures that the organization's capabilities are communicated and structured. Technological learning has a crucial role in the competitive success of family firms, directly influencing their developmental potential and entrepreneurial dynamics (Zahra & Covin, 1995). Family businesses that operate in widely-varied national markets can access information that enhances their technological capabilities, but the challenge lies in maintaining the business beyond the second generation (Kets de Vries, 1994; Lansberg, 1988).

Majority of the available literature on family businesses primarily focuses on European and American contexts, which have different operational frameworks. In the U.S., family businesses typically prioritize performance-based systems, whereas families (in this context, referring to business families in the U.S., discussing the characteristics of family businesses in general, not necessarily limited to Chinese businesses) emphasize relationship-based systems (Handler & Kram, 1988). This divergence often leads to internal conflicts stemming from strategic decisions regarding innovation and the utilization of tacit knowledge (Ward, 1987).

The evolution of family businesses in the U.S. is significantly influenced by industrial restructuring. Research has highlighted the economic contributions of small family enterprises, which continue to play crucial roles throughout U.S. business history, despite certain inefficiencies (Jones & Rose, 2013). Scranton notes that while government support has its limitations, the resilience of these small businesses is commendable, as many entrepreneurs are driven by both risk and hope for success (Scranton, 1997).

The goal of the present work is to investigate how tacit knowledge is transformed and maintained in codified forms, examining the interplay between entrepreneurship, tacit knowledge, and organizational change. Understanding how the antecedents of innovative capacity affect business development across generations is critical, especially since the transformation of tacit knowledge is often challenging due to its inherent ambiguity. Previous studies suggest that knowledge management in family enterprises is typically implied rather than explicitly articulated (Glisby & Holden, 2003). A significant barrier to innovation is the reluctance to share information, with family members often distrusting outsiders regarding professional management. The conversion of this tacit knowledge into codified forms generally requires time.

Cooperation and mergers can enhance organizational capabilities, particularly as family enterprises expand internationally. Successful transformation is aided by strong interpersonal skills that promote collaboration (Hutchings & Michailova, 2003). Japanese researchers have created a knowledge matrix to help family businesses sustain operations by fostering logical thinking and problem-solving (Nonaka, 1995). Traditionally, founders have led successors in a paternalistic structure to maintain family harmony (Redding & Witt, 2011). As successors adopt more egalitarian leadership styles, fostering a culture of innovation and creativity becomes essential (Ling & Fang, 2003).

3.3.4 Chinese Network

Social capital, particularly social networks, plays a crucial role in the establishment of entrepreneurial ventures (Afandi et al., 2017; Strobl et al., 2014). Portes (1995) argues that ethnic entrepreneurs significantly benefit from participation in social networks, which are integral to migrants' cultural frameworks. These networks facilitate employment acquisition and business establishment while providing access to information, influence, control, and resources such as financial support and labor (Adler & Kwon, 2002; Klyver et al., 2011). They also foster community unity and help maintain order within ethnic groups.

Family ties are a key component of social capital (Herrero, 2018). From the outset of migration, social ties can extend outward from close family and co-ethnic friends. Family connections are particularly vital for ethnic entrepreneurs, serving as a primary resource in initiating ventures (Weidenbaum & Hughes, 1996). These ties encompass guidance, financial support, and labor, with high trust levels fostering strong connections that yield both sacrifices and benefits. For many immigrants, family is the first source of employment and start-up capital. Chinese entrepreneurs often seek initial funding from family and kinship networks before getting external support for business partners or employees. Family members involved in the business generally show greater productivity, especially when wages are low, due to their vested interest in its success (Sanders & Nee, 1996). However, excessive dependence on familial connections can stifle innovation and the influx of new ideas, limiting the business's market prospects (Laursen et al., 2012).

In the face of restrictions imposed by some host countries on Chinese businesses, migrants often relied on their own resources and unified within their communities to navigate challenges and alleviate insecurities (Mackie, 1992; 2003). Early Chinese settlers in Southeast Asia formed interconnected networks based on sub-ethnic ties[6]. Co-ethnic networks provide access to resources such as business guidance and relationships with suppliers and customers. The "bamboo network" represents the economic connections among the Chinese diaspora in Southeast Asia, including Malaysia (Ciorîia, 2018). Intra-ethnic networks offer diverse information and resources compared to family networks. In the Chinese community, competition is intertwined with *guanxi*, or relationships, which are essential for business success (Yeung, 1999). The depth of an ethnic enterprise's integration into its intra-ethnic networks correlate with its exposure to new products and business practices, enabling entrepreneurs to gather valuable insights and innovate in response to competition.

While ethnic relationships are vital, they can also limit growth and resource access for minority enterprises. To expand, these businesses must break into mainstream markets, making inter-ethnic ties essential for diversification (Gomez, 2003; Jakobsen, 2014; Yew & Tan, 2022). Many ethnic businesses cater to niche markets with limited purchasing power, resulting in intense competition and saturation. In order to overcome these challenges, businesses must broaden their target audience. To achieve this, Chinese entrepreneurs need connections beyond family and intra-ethnic networks to understand the broader market's needs and behaviors, a trend evident in Malaysia.

Chinese entrepreneurs benefit from their extensive networks—family, intra-ethnic, and inter-ethnic—which provide insights into market demands and consumer behavior. While networks are often seen as resources, they also represent opportunity structures, particularly in the Malaysian context. Although Chinese businesses can thrive through inter-ethnic networks, this area remains underexplored. Existing research has primarily focused on family connections and intra-ethnic ownership, neglecting the significant role of inter-ethnic relationships in business growth and diversification.

This research will investigate how *guanxi* fosters the growth of Malaysian Chinese family businesses (CFBs) across generations. Historically, CFBs in Malaysia have adapted to various economic and political shifts, evolving from sectors like rubber cultivation and tin mining to banking, property development, and technology (Whah, 2007). Given that local Malays comprise the majority ethnic group and have economic policies that favor them, this study will explore *guanxi*'s role in promoting business growth and the importance of inter-ethnic relationships in securing opportunities within the Malaysian landscape. This research is particularly relevant as generational changes within businesses have spurred tacit knowledge innovations (Xavier et al., 2021).

3.4 Opportunity Structure

The present study employs the opportunity structure elements that are adapted from the interactive model (Waldinger et al., 1990). The opportunity structure consists of two main elements: the local market and the role of the state. For a business to thrive, an initial demand for specific products or services is required. Ethnic enterprises initially cater to the needs of co-ethnic members by offering products and services from their home country, typically including basic necessities like food and clothing. However, over time or with the emergence of new generations, the demand from consumers for these products or services may change. The government's role is also vital in determining the success of ethnic-based entrepreneurship. Beyond providing moral support, the government can offer financial assistance and implement policies to support migrants in their entrepreneurial endeavors.

3.4.1 Local Markets

The prosperity or lack of success of ethnic-based businesses relies on whether they can effectively fulfill the local markets with their products or services. Significant factors also include the resources accessible to migrant entrepreneurs, both collectively and individually. Furthermore, education helps entrepreneurs overcome internal barriers and navigate external market barriers. A lack of proficiency in the host country's language among ethnic groups can serve as a challenge in overcoming market barriers. Additionally, a lack of knowledge about the host nation's market conditions and governmental regulations is a typical issue. This disadvantage hinders their opportunities because of the communication barrier and lack of career-related skills.

The business landscape in Malaysia is unique due to the presence of various ethnic groups, each operating and conducting business in distinct ways they consider most effective (Minai & Lucky, 2011). Specific ethnicities excel in particular industries and engage in specific endeavors. The Chinese have long been at the forefront of the business sector. For example, it was reported in 1991 by the Malaysian Business that the Chinese owned the majority of wholesale trade at 82%, over half of retail trade at 58%, half of equity in the construction sector, and approximately 40% of the manufacturing sector (Gomez et al., 2004).

Chinese businesses in Malaysia developed under two main market opportunities. First, during the migrant period, immigrants had specific needs and preferences unmet by the non-ethnic sector, leading to businesses specializing in ethnic consumer products (Zhou & Bankston III, 2016), such as *"Eu Yan Sang,"* a traditional Chinese medicine store. Second, they targeted markets under-served or ignored by the majority business groups, thus creating an opportunity for ethnic businesses to dominate (Freedman, 1998). Examples include the Hainanese in culinary and catering services, the Henghuas in transportation, and the Hokkiens in the manufacturing sector. Chinese entrepreneurs leveraged their strengths while avoiding weaknesses in language and sector-specific knowledge.

The market witnessed internal competition among co-ethnics as they ventured into similar businesses targeting a specific ethnic niche. Consequently, Chinese businesses often find themselves in intense competition due to closely emulating each other's commercial footsteps, leading to market saturation. Traditionally, they employ strategies such as extending operating hours, providing personalized year-round service, and offering lower prices to maintain their economic standing. However, as identities evolved, particularly with the emergence of a new generation, there has been a gradual decline in the emphasis on traditional strategies, products, and services based on ethnicity. Investigating why and how the new generation of entrepreneurs innovate and change their business strategies is fascinating. Is it because they choose to enter different or larger markets for the sake of ensuring greater profits? It is also necessary to determine if these businesses still cater to specific market needs. The success of Chinese businesses often highlights market conditions as a crucial factor. Nevertheless, market conditions and structures are highly depending on the government policies and local economic environment.

3.4.2 Role of the State

Modern societies are increasingly shifting from fixed social and established frameworks toward a state of fluidity, with mobility becoming a prominent feature. Spatial mobility is expanding from local or regional scopes to encompass national and global dimensions (Barbosa et al., 2018). Homogeneity in society is gradually being replaced by diversity (Calhoun, 2020), leading to future societies characterized by a 'multi-color' composition of cultures, social structures, ethnicities, and religions.

Ethnic entrepreneurship is mostly comprised of people who self-employ (Waldinger et al., 1990). When hiring employees, this type of entrepreneurship creates job opportunities by employing immigrant workers (Van Delft et al., 2000). The job creation function for immigrants can be expanded further when highly entrepreneurial groups start hiring workers from different ethnic backgrounds (den Butter et al., 2004; Knight, 2015; Light et al., 1999).

Policymakers recognize the tremendous potential of ethnic entrepreneurship as a feasible and promising approach to addressing employment challenges faced by cultural minorities. Recent policy trends view diverse environments as fertile grounds for new SMEs, benefiting from rich cultural and ethnic diversity. Policies to reduce ethnic unemployment usually involve welfare assistance and focus on improving the position of minorities. By addressing their needs such as improving education, language skills, and overall knowledge, unemployment among minorities can decrease.

In Malaysia, from 1957 to 1969, the government adopted a laissez-faire approach. During this period, Chinese capital experienced significant growth, while Malays only saw slight improvements, remaining on the outskirts of mainstream economic progress. This unequal development led to discontent and the race riots of May 13, 1969.

In response, the Malaysian government implemented the New Economic Policy (NEP) in 1971, aiming to develop a Malay entrepreneurial community within a single generation. During the NEP's implementation, Chinese businesses employed diverse strategies to navigate the evolving economic landscape. Some diversified their operations and entered new markets to ensure adaptability. Emphasis on improving efficiency and fostering innovation was paramount for Chinese businesses. Partnerships facilitated project development and market expansion, exemplified by the Ali-Baba system, where a politically-linked Malay individual obtains a contract and delegates tasks to a non-Malay, typically Chinese, individuals (Koon, 1997; Siddique & Suryadinata, 1982). Strategic investment in talent development underscored their commitment to adaptation and resilience in the face of changing economic policies.

However, a financial downturn in the mid-1980s and changes in the domestic social hierarchy prompted the government to implement various economic adjustments (Gomez & Jomo 1999; Siddiqui, 2012). These included relaxing economic policies to attract more foreign investments. In 1986, the government- initiated deregulation and liberalization of the NEP to promote private sector growth, followed by the privatization of the public sector. The National Development Policy (NDP, 1991-2000), the Sixth Malaysia Plan, and Vision 2020 marked a shift toward fostering inter-ethnic business partnerships (Jomo, 2005; Lee, 2023; Osman, 1992).

Malaysian Chinese entrepreneurs are navigating a new form of capitalism shaped by digital technology and globalization, where knowledge, technology, capital, and innovation are essential for success. Policymakers should embrace Malaysia's ethnic diversity and create inclusive policies that recognize the Chinese community's educational advancements, fostering equal rights and opportunities to boost economic growth and international competitiveness.

3.5 Small- and Medium-Sized Enterprises: The Malaysian Dimension

As indicated in the government's Economic Transformation Program, SMEs are vital in fostering knowledge-intensive economic conditions in the Malaysian economy. In Malaysia, the SME Corporation Malaysia standardized that an SME is characterized based on "its annual sales turnover, assets and number of full-time employees." Although SMEs have different criteria and definitions in different countries based on government policy, generally SMEs can be categorized as shown in Tables 3.1 and 3.2.

Figure 3.1 indicates SME contribution to GDP in 2022 as documented by Department of Statistic Malaysia, Economic Planning Unit. In 2022, Malaysian SMEs mainly comprised of the service sector at 89.2&, meanwhile the manufacturing and agriculture sectors only made up of 5.3% and 1.1%, respectively. The massive differences between these sectors are owing to the changes in global trends, thus pushing both the manufacturing and agricultural sectors to the services sector. Indeed, Figure 3.2 further illustrates its GDP contribution, 37.8% in 2017 to 38.4% in 2022. Nevertheless, when compared to Japan, South Korea, Hong Kong, and New Zealand, Malaysian SMEs contribution to the country's GDP is seen to

Table 3.1 Micro, Small, and Medium Enterprise Definitions

Size/Sector	*Agro-based Industries*	*Manufacturing-related production*	*Professional services*
Micro	Less than RM300,000	Less than RM300,000	Less than RM300,000
Small	Between RM300,000&less than RM3 million	Between RM300,000 & less than RM15 million	Between RM300,000 & less than RM3 million
Medium	Between RM3 million & RM20 million	Between RM15 million & RM50 million	Between RM3 million & RM20 million

Source: SME Corporation Malaysia (2022a).

Table 3.2 SME Definition Based on Number of Full-time Employees

Size/Sector	*Agro-based Industries*	*Manufacturing-related Production*	*Professional Services*
Micro	Less than 5 employees	Less than 5 employees	Less than 5 employees
Small	Between 5 & 30 employees	Between 5 & 75 employees	Between 5 & 30 employees
Medium	Between 30 & 75 employees	Between 75 & 200 employees	Between 30 & 75 employees

Source: SME Corporation Malaysia (2022a).

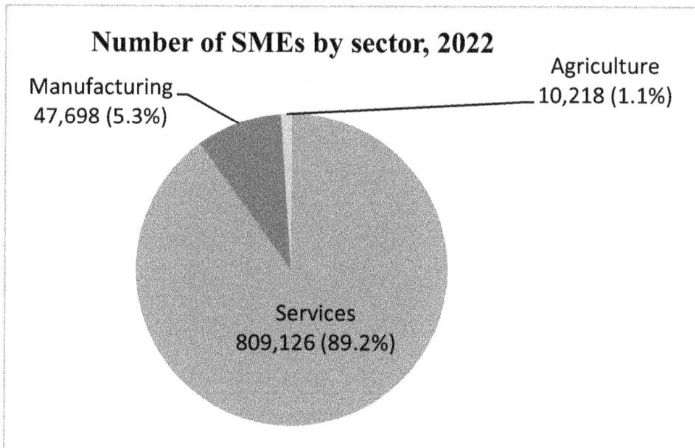

Figure 3.1 SME Contribution to GDP in 2022.

Source: SME Corporation Malaysia (2022b).

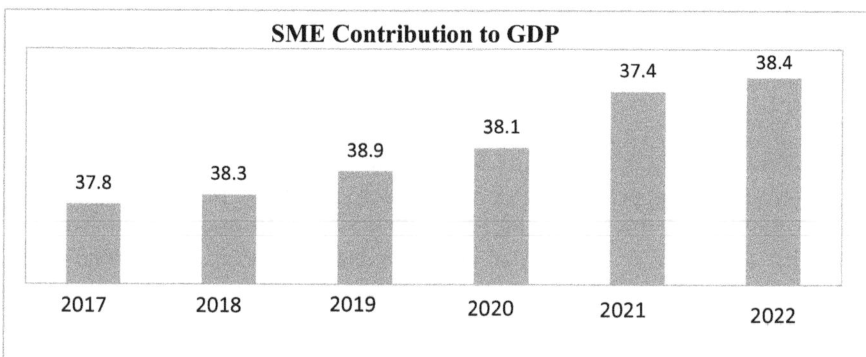

Figure 3.2 SME Contribution to GDP, 2017–2022.

Source: Department of Statistic Malaysia, Economic Planning Unit.

be at the lowest as depicted in Figure 3.3, demonstrating that there are rooms for improvement on productivity levels and structural issues.

Malaysia‘s contribution of SMEs to GDP remains low compared to other countries, particularly regarding product commercialization and R&D collaboration with the government. The Malaysian government has made limited efforts to foster new business establishment and promote entrepreneurial intentions compared to Japan and Hong Kong. For instance, Kyoto University has developed strategies linking regional innovation to business incubators, recently collaborating with China's Tsinghua University on the MEXT-funded Katsura Innovation Park, a hub for creative ventures and R&D.

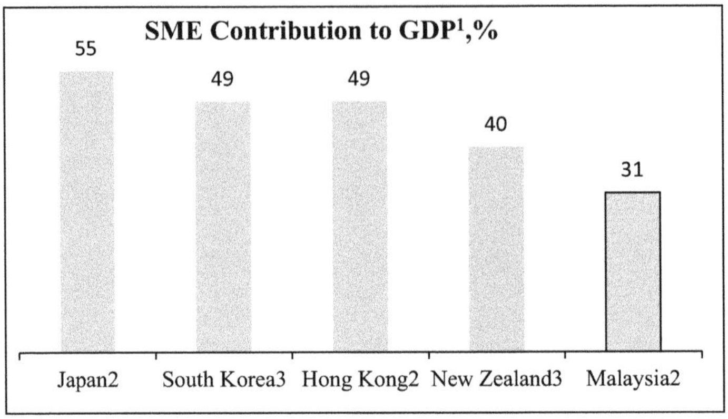

Figure 3.3 SME Contribution to GDP between Japan, South Korea, Hong Kong, New Zealand, and Malaysia.

Notes:
1. Calculated as value added to economy, when contribution to GDP not available.
2. 2008
3. 2006

Sources: 'Strategy Package for Higher Growth and Structural Change, 2009'; Economic Planning Unit; MOF Policy Research Institute, Japan.

In contrast, Hong Kong boasts strong innovation policies and institutional mechanisms that support SMEs through industry-university partnerships, ranking third in the Global Innovation Index in 2009 and 2010 and 27th in industry-university partnerships. These collaborations enhance product commercialization and nurture a culture of innovation.

Despite Malaysia's rich natural resources offering export and economic diversification opportunities since independence in 1957, its agro-based industries, primarily rubber, saw a decline in share by the late 1960s. The economy shifted toward knowledge-intensive industries, such as electronics and ICT, by 1990, attracting direct foreign investment and bolstering GDP growth.

3.6 Small- and Medium Enterprises Growth Model

Kazanjian (1988) developed a model outlining four stages of growth for new firms based on a study of 105 companies. These stages—conception and development, commercialization, growth, and stability—reflect how a firm's organizational design responds to sequential challenges. Hanks et al. (1993) expanded this model to include a fifth stage, decline, resulting in a five-stage growth model that remains consistent with Kazanjian's initial stages. As firms progress, they must adapt their organizational structures to address common growth challenges (Chandler, 1962). Failure to do so can lead to growth crises (Adizes, 1989; Greiner, 1972) or "growing pains" (Flamholtz, 1986). For this study, we will adopt the five-stage model by Hanks et al. (1993) to focus on SMEs.

Greiner (1998) identified five driving forces for growth among SMEs: creativity, direction, delegation, coordination, and collaboration. His model emphasizes that business growth requires the development of new products, managerial systems, structural changes, and market expansion.

Collaboration, as noted by Greiner, can also emerge through networks like *guanxi*. Research by Peng and Luo (2000) and Luo (2003) indicates a positive link between entrepreneurial *guanxi* and business performance. Li and Liu (2010) differentiate between embedded *guanxi* (social ties formed through kinship or friendship) and market *guanxi* (networks built via market transactions). Small businesses often rely on embedded *guanxi* for operational flexibility, while larger firms leverage market *guanxi* for expansion. This study will emphasize market *guanxi* due to its relevance for Malaysian Chinese family businesses.

The model's first stage is the start-up, where the firm focuses on product or service development, often facing initial rejection from stakeholders (Hanks et al., 1993; Kazanjian, 1988). The expansion stage follows, characterized by team assembly and product launch, resulting in public availability. In the maturity stage, high sales revenue indicates market acceptance, but challenges arise in production and distribution. Managers may hire professionals to facilitate growth (Kazanjian, 1988). The diversification stage involves generating new products and penetrating non-co-ethnic markets to boost revenue (Hanks et al., 1993). Finally, the decline stage shows a slowdown, potentially due to excessive bureaucracy (Hanks et al., 1993). While revitalization may be necessary, this stage will not be relevant for this study, as most of chosen firms are currently operational and not in decline, with the exception of one case.

Despite existing research on ethnic minority firms in Malaysia, none have utilized this SME growth model as a primary perspective. This research aims to apply this model to evaluate the evolution of Chinese family-owned SMEs in Malaysia, with a discussion of the conceptual model and methodology in the next chapter.

Notes

1 See Ward (1987).
2 See conceptual framework in Chapter 4.
3 See Portes & Zhou (1992).
4 See Pires & Stanton (2000, 2005).
5 See Xavier & Gomez (2018).
6 See Skinner (1957) and Redding (1990).

4 Constructing a Phenomenological Framework in Family-Owned Chinese Businesses

This chapter outlines the research methodology and procedures used to address the research problem identified in the previous chapter. Researchers have increasingly advocated for more in-depth qualitative case study research to enhance enterprise development theory. Given that enterprise development is a time-dependent process, employing a longitudinal case study approach, such as biographic history, is essential. This approach captures a firm's complete development from its founding to the present, highlighting that enterprise development strategies are interconnected with overall business operations. Thus, examining the enterprise development process of Chinese family businesses in Malaysia within the context of their life cycle and critical events is crucial. Case study evidence is necessary to assess the ability of these businesses to sell goods and services internationally. When researching family businesses, it is vital to use case-intensive methodologies to ensure data collection goes beyond superficial insights. This is particularly important for sensitive topics like tacit knowledge, innovation, and generational change, as highlighted by previous researchers.

> *"... exploratory investigations into the complex relationships between proprietarily ownership and managerial control favor an emphasis on qualitative research methods rather than more quantitative survey techniques. Detailed case studies using both participant and non-participant observation are more likely to yield insight into the control strategies pursued by owner-proprietors and the coping responses developed by managers and other employees."*

The case study approach emphasizes an understanding of the dynamics present within a single setting. As highlighted, the case is "a phenomenon of some sort occurring in a bounded context...your unit of analysis".

4.1 Conceptual Framework

This study employs a qualitative approach to examine the evolution of Chinese family businesses (CFBs) in response to changes in the Malaysian business landscape, involving 12 family-owned businesses across three industries. The case

DOI: 10.4324/9781032705842-4

studies provide interdisciplinary insights into family business dynamics through the lenses of tacit knowledge innovation, anthropology, and history, facilitating an examination of key concepts influencing the growth of CFBs in Malaysia. A conceptual framework was outlined based on current literature and theories.

This framework evaluates the effect of generational change on CFBs from three perspectives: resources (including class resources, ethnic resources, knowledge factors, and Chinese networks), opportunity structures (local market dynamics and state roles), and tacit knowledge innovation (transforming tacit knowledge into codified forms, R&D, product development, and adaptation). These factors inform strategy implementation among Malaysian CFBs and shape their developmental trajectories. Despite growing research on family enterprises, there remains a gap in understanding how to enhance organizational capabilities, particularly in codifying and developing tacit knowledge into major branded products (Leonidou et al., 1998). The framework (refer to Figure 4.1) aims to identify triggers for significant changes in family businesses as new generations take the helm, facilitating enterprise development.

To analyze CFBs effectively, the conceptual framework integrates conceptual tools from various disciplines and theories (Leonidou et al., 1998). Prior research highlights that organizational characteristics, such as family histories, age, education, and goal-setting (Davis & Harveston, 2000), alongside resources (Busenitz & Lau, 1996; Portes & Zhou, 1992), local market adaptation, and state roles (Aldrich et al., 1984; Ng & Ng, 2003), significantly influence strategic direction during generational transitions (Fernández & Nieto, 2005; Gallo, 1995; Gomez-Mejia et al., 2011). These factors contribute to either positive or negative outcomes for CFBs, impacting strategies for enhancing organizational capabilities, improving R&D, forming partnerships, and securing financing for niche markets and branded products (Kelly et al., 2000; Morck & Yeung, 2003). The conceptual framework thus connects CFB profiles and organizational changes to strategic management and enterprise development in Malaysia's multicultural context.

4.1.1 Delineation of Conceptual Framework

A careful review of existing literature on family businesses, particularly case studies, highlights the substantial impact of organizational change over time (Chandler, 1997; Chandler et al., 1999) and the emphasis on nurturing tacit knowledge innovation in shaping business evolution (Damanpour, 1991; Hurley & Hult, 1998; Siguaw et al., 2006). However, there are relatively few studies focusing on trans-generational strategy implementation within family businesses (Prajogo & Ahmed, 2006).

The first stream of research explores human perspectives regarding generational change. The success of tacit knowledge innovation is largely dependent on an organization's capabilities, quality management, and resource utilization, which influence organizational outcomes (Habbershon & Williams, 1999; Sirmon & Hitt, 2003; Shane, 2003; Corbetta, 1999; Ward, 1987, 1999, 2008).

In Western contexts, studies reveal that technological innovations drive manufacturing processes in capital-intensive industries, influencing organizational change and development (Chandler et al., 1999). As roles within enterprises become

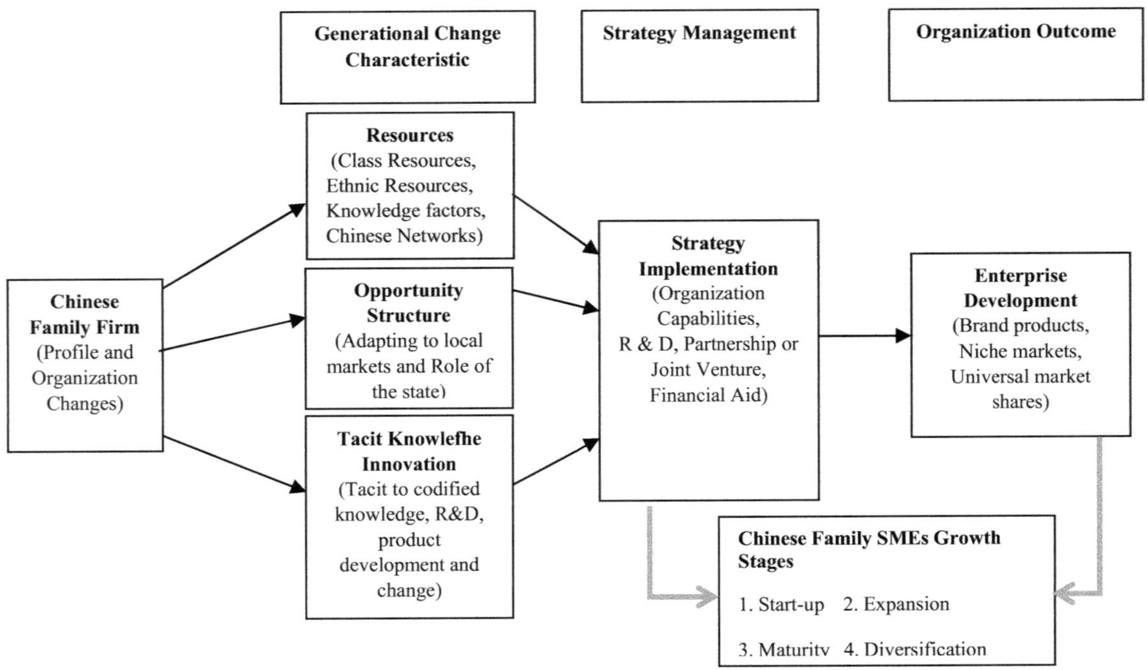

Figure 4.1 Conceptual Framework. Created by the author.

more specialized, management structures evolve, leading to hierarchies where low, middle, and top managers operate increasingly independently of founding families (Chandler, 1997). The transition to financial capitalism from family capitalism necessitates greater investments and financial strength, with external financiers participating in top management decisions (Chandler, 1997). This shift transforms family businesses into modern enterprises capable of competing in national and international markets (Chandler, 1990; Elbaum & Lazonick, 1987.

Innovation is seen as a systemic approach to enhance organizational capabilities (Daft, 1982; Damanpour, 1991). Innovation capacity is used in reference to the ability of an organization to implement new processes and managerial skills (Damanpour, 1991; Hult et al., 2004; Siguaw et al., 2006). To ensure the success of innovation, this endeavor depends on organizational capabilities that recognize the importance of strategic change, even in family businesses (Burns & Stalker, 1994). Key antecedents of innovation capacity include handling cross-functional teams, fostering top-down relationships, enhancing customer relationship management, and improving skills and talent. However, many family businesses struggle to nurture and catalyze innovation due to their inherent cultures, which may inhibit innovative dynamics despite having existing knowledge and expertise (Zahra et al., 2006).

The family businesses' ability to survive largely hinges on how the subsequent generation drives enterprise development. Literature suggests that family members generally prefer to pass on the ownership and leadership responsibilities to their heirs rather than spending their wealth (Chang et al., 2010; Kim et al., 2008; Zahra, 2005). Effective capital management is essential for ensuring business sustainability across generations (Habbershon & Williams, 1999; Lim et al., 2010). This entails making the appropriate investment in strategic partnerships, R&D, and organizational capabilities (Chen & Hsu, 2009; Kim et al., 2008; Munari et al., 2010; Sirmon & Hitt, 2003). Open communication regarding family involvement and constructive ideas are critical to fostering organizational flexibility and innovation (Craig & Dibrell, 2006). Ultimately, family businesses need to develop various strategic implementations to achieve organizational outcomes that support long-term enterprise growth and competitive advantage (Salvato & Moores, 2010).

In Malaysian CFBs, transitions in control and ownership profoundly influence company development (Penrose, 1980). The process of enterprise development generally unfolds in three stages: establishing business partnerships, transitioning to self-ownership or family business structure, and shifting to managerial control. The lengthy transition from partnerships to family enterprises typically culminates during generational shifts, particularly between the second and third generations (Chandler, 1977; Penrose, 1980). Case studies, such as that of Li & Fung, illustrate effective strategies for resolving family conflicts and ensuring business continuity. This Hong Kong-based family-controlled multinational successfully employs mechanisms like "pruning the family tree" and "listing and de-listing" to navigate pivotal development and succession phases. The resilience of Li & Fung defies the prevailing notion that family businesses struggle to survive beyond three generations (Victor & Wong Siu Long, 2016). This paper explores how Li & Fung exemplifies successful generational transitions and sustainable enterprise development.

4.2 Methodology

It is imperative to select the right research techniques that allow the scholar to answer the research questions in mind (Morse & Richards, 2002). In the current study, an overall qualitative research method is employed, using a phenomenological approach. The case study method is mainly applied to track the implications of generational changes on CFBs in Malaysia.

4.2.1 Phenomenological Research

Phenomenological research involves a comprehensive description of lived experiences, requiring the researcher to adopt an open perspective, setting aside preconceived opinions and judgments about observable facts (Finlay, 2009). This approach focuses on studying the "essence" of human experiences related to specific phenomena as described by the study's participants. In this study, the phenomenological method is chosen because it centers on understanding the experiential significance of the reviewed company owners.

Phenomenological researchers aim to uncover new, intricate, and vivid descriptions of a phenomenon as it is experienced. Wertz (2005) describes phenomenology as a "low-hovering, in-dwelling, meditative philosophy" that emphasizes the concreteness of person-world relations and prioritizes lived experience, with all its indeterminacy and vagueness, over established knowledge. Since this study seeks to examine the real-life settings, experiences, and generational shifts within CFBs in Malaysia, the phenomenological research method is the most appropriate approach.

4.2.2 Qualitative Research

One of the reasons why qualitative research is typically less undertaken is because it can be challenging to describe family businesses in an accurate manner, including case studies (Handler, 1989). Considering the nature of most family businesses that values privacy, it is understandable that precise information about them is not readily available. Plus, the standard definition of family business has not been established. Table 4.1 demonstrates the overview of selected family business studies using an interpretive approach.

In Table 4.1, an interpretive approach to family business research seeks to offer new insights using the concepts used by the existing theory through innovative interpretations (Ainsworth & Wolfram Cox, 2003). This value-added interpretation allows theoretical frameworks to be modified and ultimately, enhancing our understanding of the research topic.

4.2.3 Case Study Method

A case study is defined as "an in-depth, empirical investigation of a single instance or setting to explain the processes of a phenomenon in context" (Tharenou et al.,

Table 4.1 Selected Family Business Studies Using an Interpretive Approach

Author (year), publication	*Topic*	*Theory/concepts*	*Empirical material (data collection)*	*Main findings and contribution*
McCollom (1992) *Family Business Review*	Family and non-family employees' experiences of membership in a family business system	Family business system theory	565 stories from family-owned retail firms	The anecdotes describe relations between family and business systems in daily processes.
Cole (1997) *Family Business Review*	Role of women and impact of gender issues on women's working lives	Gender, role and rules	Study of women in context of their business family in nine firms (interviews)	Women are treated as invisible by other women. Also, they do not accept traditional roles, take longer to make decisions, advance as fast as men, and believe that having children hinders their professional advancement.
Johannisson and Huse (2000) *Entrepreneurship & Regional Development*	Recruiting non-family board members	Governance, contrasting ideologies (paternalism, managerialism, entrepreneurialism)	Pilot survey of 12 family businesses, case research into two family businesses (interviews)	Activating the board by adding non-family members enforces managerialism and challenges dominant ideologies of paternalism.
Hall et al. (2001) *Family Business Review*	Corporate entrepreneurship as strategic renewal and a change process	Culture and learning	Case research into two family businesses (interviews and observations)	Some cultural patterns preserve traditional ways of doing business, others facilitate change. To support entrepreneurship, a process of high-order learning in which old cultural patterns are questioned and changed is needed.
Ram (2001) *Human Relations*	Impact of family dynamics on management of professional service firm	Small business management, family system, kinship ties, household	Case research in one family business (interviews, company visits, observations and documents)	Household relations (rather than entrepreneurial individual) are important for understanding operations; tendency to underplay female partner; employees both value 'family' aspects of organizational culture.

Table 4.1 (Continued)

Author (year), publication	*Topic*	*Theory/concepts*	*Empirical material (data collection)*	*Main findings and contribution*
Fletcher (2000) *Journal of Small Business and Enterprise Development*	Professionalization of the family business	Networks, culture, organizing	Ethnography of one family firm (observation, interviews, documents)	Employees form cultural organizing by invoking emotional categories to trade away variance, divergent views and new practices.
Ainsworth and Wolfram Cox (2003) *Organization Studies*	Dynamics of compliance, resistance and control	Culture, shared understanding of divisions, interpretive divisions	Case research into two small family firms (interviews, site visits, observations, documents)	Employee perspectives offer insights on critical aspects of family business cultures, as well as on the symbolic, material and ideological meaning of family.
Hall et al. (2006) *Handbook of Research on Family Businesses*	Family and ownership influence on micro strategic processes of change	Arena, legitimacy, role and value, social interaction	One case illustration of a medium-sized family business	Challenging strategic implementations can lead to role confusion, questioned legitimacy, and decreased organizational efficiency.
Hamilton (2006) *International Small Business Journal*	Role of women in founding and establishing family businesses	Patriarchy, identity, gender, entrepreneurship	Study of two generations in three business families (interviews)	Women resisting and challenging patriarchy owing to their previously marginalized role on family businesses.

Steier (2007) *Journal of Business Research*	Family's role for entrepreneurial start-up	Entrepreneurship, narrations, family ties	Case research into one start-up (interviews, company visits, documents)	Family is an important "sub-narrative" to understand start-up processes.
Nordqvist and Melin (2008) *Long Range Planning*	The role of actors in strategic planning processes	Strategy-as-practice, champions	Case research into two family business strategic planning processes (interviews, observations and documents)	Strategic planning champions as key strategic practitioners.
Hall and Nordqvist (2001) *Family Business Review*	Professional Management	Culture and symbolic interactionism	Case research into five family firms (interviews, observations)	Professional management consists of formal and cultural competence. Family members can also be professional managers.

Source: Compile by author.

2007). The case study method emphasizes context, aiming to provide a theoretically grounded understanding of complex phenomena rather than just a description (Tharenou et al., 2007). In researching ethnic businesses, adopting case-intensive methodologies is recommended to capture the key characteristics relevant to themes like generational change (Litz, 1997).

Yin (2003) distinguishes between single and multiple case study methods. While single case studies are useful for unique cases or longitudinal studies, they have limited external validity. In contrast, multiple case studies allow for careful selection to explore commonalities or differences, providing greater external validity (Eisenhardt, 1989; Yin, 2003). Therefore, to investigate the evolution of CFBs in Malaysia, a qualitative multiple case study approach—utilizing in-depth interviews and business report analysis—would be most appropriate.

4.2.4 Unit of Analysis

The unit of analysis in this study is the family business, focusing on the evolution of CFBs in Malaysia, particularly within the context of ethnic businesses (Crabtree & Miller, 1992; Yin, 2009). To gather information, various mechanisms were employed to study 12 family businesses in food production, plastics manufacturing, and rubber manufacturing. Interviews were conducted primarily with members of the new generation managing these firms.

As registered companies, these businesses are required to submit annual reports to the Companies Commission, detailing equity distribution, annual turnover, major acquisitions, and new subsidiaries. This research adopts a longitudinal case study approach, examining firms that have successfully undergone generational transitions.

The case studies analyze "family history, milestones, and knowledge transfer across the second, third, and fourth generations," focusing on themes such as "generational change, innovation capacity, and enterprise development." A comparative analysis was performed regarding objective setting, organizational changes involving man, machine, and materials, and innovation across generations, which are critical for understanding strategy implementation and organizational outcomes.

The study achieved an 80% response rate from Chinese family CEOs, predominantly from the second generation, resulting in 38 completed questionnaires from family members and staff of the 12 CFBs. Five cases were excluded due to refusals for in-depth interviews. The selection included only those businesses with at least one family member on the Board, allowing for a diverse range of generational perspectives.

The focus on food, plastics, and rubber production highlights how these firms have effectively retained and developed tacit knowledge, a core factor in their market uniqueness. The productive development of tacit knowledge has led to the adoption of new skills and technologies from China to Nanyang Malaysia, enabling the creation of innovative products for local markets. Well-educated family members are committed to disseminating and developing new knowledge, shaping production processes, upgrading machinery, and recruiting professional managers to enhance brand products and explore niche market opportunities.

4.3 Sampling Method

Qualitative data typically focuses on small samples as it allows the researcher to extract data more effectively when the appropriate cases are selected through snowball and criterion sampling (Patton, 1990). Thus, qualitative methods employ purposeful sampling to "select information-rich cases whose study will clarify the questions under study" (Patton, 1990).

4.3.1 Criterion Sampling

Criterion sampling is the selection of cases that fulfill a certain "criterion of importance" (Patton, 1990). The ethno-cultural aspects of family firms is relevant in first generation Chinese family business because the initial tacit knowledge in the production is intimately linked to cultural tradition and institutions. The empirical investigation is a multiple case design comprising of 12 case studies. The case studies were selected according to the following criteria (see also Table 4.1 and Table 4.2):

1. The family business has survived at least two generations.
2. The sampling lists of family businesses comprising two industries will later be categorized as large-, medium-, and small-scale Chinese family SMEs. They are mostly located in West Malaysia, typically in highly industrialization states such as the Klang Valley, Penang, Selangor, Perak, Malacca, and Johor.
3. Established a solid track record up to 2023, with a strong reputation or recognition in the domestic market with observable changes in terms of organizational structure, resources, opportunity structure, and tacit knowledge innovation milestones across generations.
4. Strong financial capabilities from annual sales, net profits, potential for growth, and not likely to fail in the future.
5. Nature of business with manufactured products clearly established and the roles of the founder and the next generation are clearly recognized.
6. Availability and willingness to consent to a focused in-depth interview.

4.3.2 Snowball Sampling

Snowball sampling is used to identify information-rich informants and cases by asking the "right people" who are most suitable to talk to. According to Patton (1990), by inquiring for the relevant individuals to talk to, this will result in snowballing effect as the number of interview candidates grows, especially if the names are repeatedly suggested by different people.

Table 4.2 Sampling Research Area and Reason for Choosing Food Productions

Chinese Family enterprise	*Nature of Business*	*Location/ Area*	*Recognitions*	*Reason to Choose*
1. London Biscuit Est: 1994 2nd Generation Large Scale SME	Ready to Eat Products (snack food, cake rolls and candies manufacturer)	Desa Cemerlang Industrial Estate Ulu Tiram, Johor State	- MMITI Product Industry Excellence Award 2004.	- 2nd Generation family business. - Husband, wife and their children's leadership roles clearly seen. - Able to see the evolution from a family business to snack food and the London Biscuit group.
2. King's Confectionery Est: 1977 - 2nd generation - Medium scale SME	Ready to Eat Products (bakeries and confectioneries manufacturer)	Taman Kepong Industrial Estate, Kuala Lumpur State	- Malaysia's largest retail confectionery chain with nearly 90 outlets	- 2nd generation family business. - Sister and brother leadership roles are clearly seen. - Able to see the evolution from a hawker center to outlet retailing and café franchising.
3. Leong Hup International Berhad and Baker Cottage Est: 1994 - 3rd generation - Large scale SME	Ready to Buy Products (bakeries and confectioneries manufacturer)	Wisma Westcourt, Jalan Kelang Lama, Kuala Lumpur	- Best Mooncake Award in Malaysia	- 3rd Generation family business. - Grandson's leadership role clearly seen. - Able to see the evolution from a subsidiary of Leong Hup poultry farm to diversification into a retail confectionery chain.
4. Besfomec Est: 1948 - 3rd generation - Medium Scale SME	Ready to Buy Products (traditional essence drinks and herbs)	Alor Gajah Industrial Estate, Malacca State	- Good Manufacturing Practice (GMP) - HHACCP Certification	- 3rd generation family business. - Father and son leadership roles clearly seen. - Able to see the evolution from herbal products to Besfomec essence and nutrition supplement medicine.

5. Hei Hwang Est: 1975 - 2nd generation - Small Scale SME	Ready to Buy Products (Coffee Powder and Health Supplement Powder Manufacturer)	Ipoh Silibin Light Industrial Estate, Perak State	- Golden Brand Award of Ipoh Coffee in China. - Singapore's Most Promising Health Supplements	- 2nd generation family business. - Father and sons leadership roles clearly seen. - Able to see the evolution from Chinese traditional herb drinks to coffee powder manufacturer and health supplements from herbal remedies.
6. Kam Lun Tai (Loy Kee) Est: 1972 - 2nd Ggneration - Small Scale SME	Ready to Eat Products (Restaurant Business and Mooncakes Manufacturer)	Cheras Jaya Industrial Estate, Selangor State	- Mooncake Superbrand Award in 2001 - Golden Chef Award-Paris 2000	- 2nd generation family business. - Father and son leadership roles clearly seen. - Able to see the evolution from a hawker center to restaurant business, food catering and mooncakes and food related manufacturer.

Source: Compiled by the author.

Table 4.3 Sampling Research Area and Reasons for Choosing Plastics Productions

Chinese family enterprise	*Nature of business*	*Location/area*	*Recognitions*	*Reason to choose*
1. SKP Resources Berhad Est: 1974 2nd generation Large Scale SME	High Precision Plastic Injection (Plastic Audio Parts and Accessories)	Jalan Kuang, Johor state	- Enterprise 50 award - Excellent quality management systems Pioneer products	- 2nd generation family business. - Father and son leadership roles clearly seen. - Able to see the evolution from design to finished products, servicing MNCs.
2. LH Plus Sdn Bhd Est: 1947 3rd generation Medium Scale SME	Plastic Houseware (Plastic Houseware Manufacturer)	Shah Alam, MahSing Industrial Park, Selangor State	- CEO Callum Chen named one of 25 Notable Processors 2007 by Modern Plastic	- 3rd generation family business - Father and son leadership roles clearly seen. - Able to see the evolution from a local manufacturer to OEM for MNCs, developing a personal design culture.
3. Syarikat Perniagaan Kemajuan Est: 1973 2nd generation Medium Scale SME	High Precision Plastic Injection (Plastic Injection for Semiconductors)	Kepong Baru Industrial Estate, Kuala Lumpur State	- National semiconductor award for supplying packaging rail 1991 - Fairchild award of excellence 2000	- 2nd generation family business. - Father, son and daughter leadership roles in two family partnerships are clearly seen. - Able to see the evolution from fabrication to plastic manufacturing and MNCs in semiconductors.

Source: Compiled by the author.

Table 4.4 Sampling Research Area and Reasons for Choosing Rubber Productions

Chinese Family Enterprise	*Nature of Business*	*Location/ Area*	*Recognitions*	*Reason to Choose*
1. Top Glove Corporation Berhad Est: 1991 - 2nd generation - Large Scale SME	Rubber Latex gloves and protective products (Rubber gloves manufacturer)	Setia Alam, Selangor state	- Export excellence awards 2023 - Reader's Digest Trusted brand awards 2023 - Sustainability and CSR Malaysia Awards	- 2nd generation family business. - Father and son leadership roles clearly seen. - Able to see the evolution from design to finished products, servicing export trading in the US and European market.
2. Fun Keong Rubber Manufactory (M) Sdn Bhd. - Est: 1934 4th generation - Medium Scale SME	Rubber based motorbike tires and tubes (rubber tires and tubes manufacturer)	Klang, Selangor State	- Top Achiever Convention 2020 - Export excellence awards 2020	- 4th generation family business. - Father and son leadership roles clearly seen. - Able to see the evolution from a canvas shoe manufacturer from Hong Kong to motorbike tires manufacturer with the branding of FKR.
3. Aerofoam Manufacturing (1969) Sdn Bhd Est: 1969 - 2nd generation - Medium Scale SME	Natural rubber latex-based bedding products (mylatex bedding products)	Port Klang, Selangor State	- MEP awards 2022 - Crystal Cabin awards 2018 - Sirim awards for product quality (MS679:1999)	- 2nd generation family business. - Father, and daughter leadership roles are clearly seen. - Able to see the evolution from the metal fabrication industry to natural latex bedding manufacturer with the brand of Aerofoam, mylatex under USTherapedic technology.

Source: compiled by the author.

Notes on abbreviations:
EST - Establishment
HACCP - Hazard analysis and critical control points
=MITI - Ministry of International Trade and Industry
MNC - Multinational Corporations
OEM - Original Equipment Manufacturing
R&D - Research and Development
SMEs - Small and Medium Enterprises
TCM – Traditional Chinese Medicine
UAE - United Arab Emirates
UK - United Kingdom
WTO – World Trade Organization

4.4 Selected Cases

Out of 12 Malaysian Chinese businesses that were incorporated in this study, six of them were from the food industry, three from the plastic industry, and the other three from the rubber industry. Of these, 11 of them were established in Malaysia, while one of them was established in Hong Kong at first. All 12 also deal with ethnically and culturally based local Chinese brand products and services and have been operated for at least two generations. Tables 4.2, 4.3, and 4.4 list the selected firms with their sampling criteria.

4.5 Data Sources and Triangulation

Good qualitative research usually involves collecting data from diverse sources, including interviews, observational data, records from archive, and theoretical notes (Morse & Richards, 2002). The case study approach may encompass documentation, archival records, interviews, observations, and physical artifacts (Yin, 2003). This study will utilize in-depth interviews with first, second, and third generation owners of CFBs and analyze business documents, archived newspaper articles, journals, and media reports. Data triangulation, as described by Decrop (1999), will be employed by incorporating various types of materials to enrich the study's findings.

4.5.1 Primary Data

The present study carried out the primary data collection method through in-depth interviews with founders, second- or third-generation owners of Chinese Family Businesses (CFBs) in Malaysia. Interviews are have been determined to be the most suitable approach of "exploring and highlighting processes" (Barbour, 2008; Ghauri, 2004). Additionally, some interviewees requested that their conversations not be directly quoted. To fulfill the obligation as interviewer, this study will honor their requests by presenting the content in a comprehensive and synthesized manner rather than through direct quotes, ensuring the confidentiality and respect for the interviewees' preferences.

The annual reports of these CFBs were also used as a primary source of data. These annual reports provide information as follows:

i) a list of shareholders and how shareholding patterns have changed with each generational shift;
ii) list of directors and how they changed over time, especially after a generational shift or in response to public policies;
iii) the companies they acquired, established, sold or closed down;
iv) when they began to diversify, if they did; and
v) joint ventures they established, including with foreign firms.

The data extracted from these reports offer valuable information that allows the researcher to gain better understanding of the evolution of these Chinese family enterprises.

4.5.2 Secondary Data

Industry articles and reports from Companies Commission of Malaysia (SSM)[1]and Federation of Malaysian Manufacturers (FMM)[2], archived data from the local newspapers, local and international business magazines and journals were gathered as the secondary data source. In addition, videos from Astro[3] were also included as data source. These data was used to triangulate primary data information which is necessary to strengthen the study design (Patton, 1990). By combining data sources, the findings can be validated and cross-checked.

4.6 Design of Interview Guide

Annual reports and annual returns of each chosen firm were viewed from the time of incorporation. After in-depth historical information from company records filed with the Companies Commission of Malaysia was compiled, the interviews were conducted as planned. The interview data collection was regarded as "conversations with a purpose" (Marshall & Rossman, 2014).

The researcher contacted potential Chinese family businesses (CFBs) by telephone to discuss their participation, explaining the study's purpose and assuring confidentiality. Initial reluctance to participate was common due to business management demands, but the researcher emphasized the study's potential to enhance understanding of CFB evolution in Malaysia. Despite these efforts, some declined to participate.

Confirmed appointments with willing participants were made via telephone, with some requesting interview questions in advance, which were sent via email. The semi-structured interviews lasted approximately 60 minutes and allowed flexibility for new topics while focusing on core study concepts. Participants included shareholders or directors, who offered insights into generational change, resource evolution, opportunity structures, and tacit knowledge innovation.

The interview questions were designed to explore the participant's role in the firm, their historical perspective, and how resources, opportunity structures, and tacit knowledge innovation were managed across generations. A total of 12 questions were formulated, tailored to capture significant aspects of the company's history and pivotal changes. Information from annual company reports was utilized to refine these questions based on the interviewee's position.

Before conducting the final interviews, a pilot study was conducted with three participants—two potential participants and one researcher—to ensure the clarity and relevance of the questions. Feedback from the pilot study indicated that the questions were easily understood and pertinent to the study, leading to minor revisions for better comprehension. Annual and financial reports from the Companies Commission of Malaysia were analyzed prior to the interviews, enhancing the preparation and focus of the interview process.

4.7 Data Analysis

Applying an explanatory approach to data analysis allows for a greater understanding of the field data through the process of creating order, structure, and meaning out of the collected data (Freeman et al., 2006).

4.7.1 Content Analysis

Content analysis is an analytical technique "that extracts thematic information from qualitative materials" (Tharenou et al., 2007: 253) and allows written or spoken material to be analyzed systematically. At this stage, the interviews and secondary data sources were identified and categorized. Tharenou et al. (2007) recommended an interpretative style[4] of analysis which aids in creating new insights regarding subjects with limited knowledge.

4.7.2 Explanation Building

As recommended by Yin (2009), explanation building was used as another analytic technique in which the data are analyzed through a series of iterations, followed by gradually presenting an extensive explanation (Yin, 2009). The formation of a relevant and convincing explanation was achieved by analyzing the transcripts and revisiting the literature which helped in refining the study modus operandi. Plus, the case documents were constantly visited in identifying converging and diverging themes.

4.7.3 Cross-case Analysis

Cross-case analysis increases the cross-case generalization where interconnecting issues across cases and themes are identified (Simons, 2009; Yin, 2009). For the purpose of this study which explores the evolution of CFBs in Malaysia, cross-case generalization between the firms in the different industries can be made.

4.8 Limitations

Qualitative methods offer in-depth exploration of social and economic processes within specific contexts but are often time-consuming and costly (Griffin, 1985). Despite their usefulness, interviews have notable limitations. The research outcomes from qualitative data may not be generalizable to larger populations, as they are typically not subjected to statistical testing for significance or chance (Atieno, 2009).

Firstly, interviewees may disclose only what they are willing to share about their perceptions, which can be subjective and vary with time and circumstances (Alshenqeeti, 2014). Walford (2007) asserts that "interviews alone are an insufficient form of data to study social life."

Nevertheless, qualitative methods and interviews remain the most suitable approach for addressing the research questions and objectives of this study.

Notes

1 The Companies Commission of Malaysia (Malay: Suruhanjaya Syarikat Malaysia, abbreviated SSM) is a statutory body formed under an Act of Parliament that regulates corporate and business affairs in Malaysia. The SSM was formed in 2002 under the Companies Commission of Malaysia Act 2001, assuming the functions of the Registrar of Companies and Registry of Business.
2 Malaysia representing over 3,000 manufacturing and industrial service companies of varying sizes, the FMM is the officially recognized and acknowledged voice of the industry. Making Malaysian Industries Globally Competitive.
3 Astro is the brand name of the Malaysian direct broadcast satellite pay-television service.
4 Interpretative analysis explores in detail how participants make sense of their personal and social world. In this study, interpretative analysis is critical as the researcher tries to understand from the view of the participants.

5 Ethnic Chinese Businesses in the Food Industry

This chapter presents a historical review and analysis of the development of Chinese family businesses in the food production industry. Initial interviews were conducted by the researcher to identify companies that fulfill the criteria of this study and address the research questions. The study begins by profiling the organizational changes and enterprise development in six Chinese family SMEs. The focus is on how these enterprises have evolved, particularly through the transfer and application of tacit knowledge, explores how tacit knowledge is cultivated through innovation, emphasizing skill enhancement, top-down management improvements, and R&D initiatives. These strategies include partnerships with foreign firms to develop new pharmaceutical products (e.g., Besfomec Industries Sdn. Bhd.), advancing R&D in food technology for export-oriented products in the biscuit industry (e.g., London Biscuits Berhad), and upgrading production capabilities to introduce Ipoh coffee and a range of organic health beverages (e.g., Hei Hwang Food Industries). The findings in this chapter offer a chronological analysis of Chinese family SMEs in food production, tracing their journey from initial establishment to subsequent changes in ownership and product development, with emphasis on tacit knowledge innovation across generations.

5.1 Industry Background

Malaysian cuisine is a captivating blend of flavors, intricately woven through history and shaped by a diverse array of cultural influences (Lee, 2017). This culinary landscape reflects the country's appreciation for both global and local food traditions. The increasing popularity of international fast foods, including halal options, illustrates Malaysia's seamless integration of modern tastes with cultural acceptance. To truly appreciate the distinctive character and global appeal of Malaysian cuisine, it is essential to explore the historical layers that have shaped it.

The origins of Malaysian cuisine date back to ancient times, rooted in indigenous ingredients and cooking methods. For millennia, trade along the maritime Silk Road linked the Malay Archipelago and North Borneo with distant lands, facilitating the exchange of spices, ingredients, and culinary techniques (Hall,

DOI: 10.4324/9781032705842-5

2010; Heng, 2022). Influences from traders arriving from China, India, and the Middle East significantly enriched Malaysian cuisine with diverse flavors and cooking styles.

Colonialism marked a crucial chapter in the evolution of Malaysian food culture. The arrival of the Portuguese (Desai, 1969), Dutch (Arasaratnam, 1969; Purcell, 1947), and later the British (Mills et al., 1960) introduced new ingredients, culinary methods, and cultural influences to the Malay Archipelago and North Borneo. Additionally, the influx of Chinese immigrants, primarily of Hokkien, Hakka, Cantonese, Hainan, Teochew, and other southern Chinese descendants, was spurred on by British colonial policies. These immigrants established Chinese settlements in urban areas, and their culinary styles, influenced by southern China, became a key component of Malaysian-Chinese cuisine (David & Chee-Beng, 2001; Tan & Tan, 2024). These colonial powers not only left their imprint on local cuisine but also transformed the agricultural landscape, introducing cash crops like rubber and palm oil that would shape Malaysia's economy for generations. The country's rich natural resources, coupled with its diverse population, have provided fertile ground for food research, cultivation, production, and processing, building a vibrant culinary industry rooted in deep cultural traditions.

Food plays a vital role in Malaysian society, serving as a medium for cultural expression, social cohesion, and identity formation. The fusion of Malay, Chinese, Indian, and indigenous culinary traditions embodies Malaysia's multicultural ethos and reflects the harmonious coexistence of diverse communities. Street food stalls and hawker centers serve as vibrant social spaces where people from all walks of life gather to enjoy the varied flavors of Malaysian cuisine.

The food industry is a cornerstone of Malaysia's economy, contributing significantly to employment, agricultural production, and export revenues (Saleh & Ndubisi, 2006; Webster, 2014). Malaysia's reputation as a gastronomic destination fuels culinary tourism, attracting millions of visitors annually and generating income across the hospitality and service sectors (Hashemi et al., 2023). The food production and processing industry accounts for around 10% of the manufacturing sector's output, growing at approximately 3% annually (MIDA, 2021). The 12th Malaysia Plan (12MP) prioritizes productivity growth through enhanced food production, urging SMEs to leverage advanced technologies such as digitalization and niche capabilities.

The Malaysian food industry is predominantly driven by SME firms, with key growth areas including halal food, convenience food, functional food, food ingredients, and health food. However, the industry faces challenges from rapid urbanization, environmental degradation, and climate change, which threaten agricultural productivity and food security, highlighting the need for sustainable practices and innovation in food production (Bala et al., 2014). Additionally, the globalization of food supply chains and shifting consumer preferences pose challenges for traditional food artisans and small-scale producers.

In this chapter, we examine six Chinese family-owned businesses in Malaysia's food industry: London Biscuit Berhad, King's Confectionery Sdn. Bhd., Leong Hup International Berhad and Baker Cottage, Besfomec Industries Sdn. Bhd.,

Hei Hwang Food Industries (M) Sdn. Bhd., and Kam Lun Tai (Loy Kee) Sdn. Bhd. The selection of these case studies is based on specific criteria aligned with the Chinese Family SMEs Growth Stages and the characteristics of generational change discussed in Chapter 4.

5.2 Case Study One: London Biscuits Berhad

5.2.1 Introduction

London Biscuits Berhad (LBB) traces its roots back to 1981 when it was established as a confectionery manufacturer in Malaysia. However, it wasn't until 1994 that a pivotal moment occurred in its history with the acquisition by the Liew family, led by Dato' Sri Liew Kuik Hin. This acquisition injected fresh vigor into London Biscuits Berhad, setting the stage for significant growth and expansion in the years to come.

From its inception, London Biscuit has been committed to crafting delectable treats that resonate with consumers' palates, ranging from classic biscuits to innovative snack offerings. London Biscuit's primary strategy revolves around acquiring other food companies to gain access to their tacit knowledge within the food industry. This includes technologies, expertise, and market insights. Leveraging this acquired knowledge, London Biscuit then further develops and introduces new products and marketing strategies. For instance, they acquired Khee San Berhad, with expertise in candy manufacturing, and Kinos Food Industries Sdn. Bhd., which boasts a mature and well-established distribution network. With a product range spanning various confectionery delights, including biscuits, cakes, and snacks, London Biscuit has captured the hearts and taste buds of consumers across Southeast Asia. The company's dedication to quality and innovation has earned it a prominent position in the market, with distribution channels extending to over 35 countries in the region.

London Biscuit's journey in the business world has seen it transition from a family-owned enterprise to a publicly listed company. In 2002, the company achieved a milestone by successfully listing on the Second Board of Bursa Malaysia, followed by a transfer to the Main Board in 2003, signaling its growth and prominence in the market. Its listing on the stock exchange has provided the company with access to capital and enhanced visibility in the market, facilitating its growth and expansion initiatives.

However, like many businesses, London Biscuit Berhad has encountered challenges along the way. Despite its initial successes, the company faced financial difficulties in recent years, marked by declining revenues and financial constraints, leading to a restructuring process and changes in leadership. In 2019, the company defaulted on a significant debt repayment to the Bank of Nova Scotia, leading to its placement under PN17 status by Bursa Malaysia. Subsequent actions included the sale of its stake in Khee San, and the resignation of family members from the board and executive management. In 2020, London Biscuits divested its assets to Mamee-Double Decker, the leading Malaysian brand for instant noodles and noodle snacks in Malaysia. Thus, London Biscuits is currently facing a winding-up petition and has pledged cooperation in the interim liquidation process.

5.2.2 Stage One: Start-up

Its beginnings as a small family enterprise, the family business established by the late Dato Low Nam Hui, originating from Hakka-Hopo family in Guangdong, China, who migrated to Malaysia in pursuit of opportunities. Born in 1918 under a different name, he chose the name "Nam Hui"(南辉) with the hope that he, as an individual seeking a livelihood from China to Nanyang, could shine brightly in the south (南) and create brilliance (辉). In 1929, at the age of 11, he arrived in Kuala Lumpur from China and attended primary school for 4 years. He followed his parents to cultivate vegetables in Ampang area, and at 17, he moved to Johor. Initially, he made a living by planting pineapples, and soon after that he opened a grocery store. During the Japanese occupation of Malaya, he participated in the Malayan Anti-Japanese Guerrilla War. After World War II, he ventured into the transportation business and later switched to the timber trade, establishing Low Nam Hui Co. Sdn. Bhd. in Johor Bahru.

After many years of operation and development, he created a diversified business empire, venturing into various fields, including palm oil, tourism, hospitality, transportation, and property development, among others. London Biscuit is one of the branches of the family business. Nam Hui was also one of the founders of the Southern University College, often selflessly dedicating himself to Chinese education. In 1974, he led the fundraising campaign for the initial development fund of Foon Yew High School and personally donated RM 100,000. He held positions such as Chairman of the Johor Bahru Chinese Chamber of Commerce, President of the Johor Chinese Chamber of Commerce and Industry, Honored President of the Federation of Chinese Chambers of Commerce and Industry of Malaysia, President of the Malaysian Hopo Association, and founding President of the World Low Family Reunion Association. These positions further expanded Nam Hui's networks and established his extraordinary personal influence. The Johor Tower (刘南辉大厦) owned by the Low's family in Johor Bahru is an important symbol. Nam Hui's biography also mentions his deep friendship with the Johor royal family. His success in his career is inseparable from his close relationship with members of the royal family, including those of the Johor and Pahang royal families.

Dato Liew Kuik Hin, the eldest son of Nam Hui, graduated from Nanyang University, Singapore in 1965 with a Bachelor of Commerce and Accounting. After finishing his studies, he followed his father's footsteps by joining the family-owned business. From a Chinese cultural perspective, conducting business involves looking to the long term, preparing for the future, and considering potential risks (未雨绸缪)[1]. It emphasizes foresight, prudence, and proactive planning for what lies ahead. Recognizing the imminent decline of the timber sector and the increasing challenges in obtaining government licenses due environmental issues and anti-monopoly regulations, Kuik Hin displayed remarkable foresight. This foresight prompted him to pivot toward the food industry, foreseeing greater opportunities for growth and sustainability in the long term. This transformation began in 1981 with the acquisition of London Biscuits (Johor) Sdn. Bhd., a corn snacks factory, marking the family business's entry into the food sector.

In the dynamic landscape of the food industry, staying ahead requires not only astute market awareness but also the ability to innovate products that resonate with consumers. London Biscuit, with its roots tracing back to a family timber business, demonstrates this through its strategic product innovations driven by deep-seated tacit knowledge. Kuik Hin aimed to transform the traditional Chinese snack, typically made with corn flour, into a Nanyang snack food brand. By enhancing its shelf life for consumption and preservation, the goal was to create a commercially viable food product that could be rapidly mass-produced and exported to other countries.

5.2.3 Stage Two: Expansion

Under the leadership of the Liew family, London Biscuits embarked on a path of innovation. In 1998, the company made a strategic move into cake manufacturing, introducing London Pie Cakes, a range of individually packaged cakes with center-filled cream in various flavors. Following the success of this venture, the roll cake segment was expanded in 2000 and Swiss roll cakes were introduced. These initiatives propelled London Biscuits to become the largest domestic cake manufacturer, offering a diverse portfolio that includes round, layer, and roll cakes.

The second generation of the Liew family, comprising sons and daughters, infused innovation into the business by implementing advanced technologies like robotic arms and customizing warehouses. These innovations not only optimized production processes but also positioned the company for export success, earning accolades and recognition. Expansion through acquisitions played a crucial role in London Biscuit's growth strategy, to be the largest roll cakes producer in Southeast Asia.

In 2005, the company acquired its first subsidiary, Kinos Food Industries Sdn. Bhd., a move that synergized product ranges and distribution channels, strengthening London Biscuit's market position. Subsequently, in 2007, London Biscuit acquired a majority stake in Khee San Berhad, a prominent player in sweets, candy confectionery, and wafer manufacturing, further diversifying its product portfolio and market reach.

Moreover, acquisition of the Malaysia largest egg poultry farm underscored its commitment to product excellence and market leadership. By acquiring companies with complementary offerings and expertise, London Biscuit expanded its capabilities and enhanced its market positioning. Focused initiatives in branding campaigns across both Malaysia and Singapore were undertaken to boost the London Biscuit brand's value and market position, thereby augmenting its presence and attractiveness to consumers.

5.2.4 Stage Three: Maturity

Over the years, London Biscuit demonstrated a keen understanding of market trends and consumer preferences. By acquiring factories specializing in various products such as teacup biscuits, pie cakes, and Swiss rolls, the company strategically diversified its product portfolio to cater to evolving consumer demands. In Chinese culture, achieving goals more easily needs wisdom. This includes understanding human nature, catering to preferences (投其所好)[2]. Applying this wisdom to business is a natural inclination among the Chinese.

In response to shifting consumer preferences, London Biscuit continued to innovate its product line. Implementing a Customized MRP System and the introduction of twist wrap packaging machines reflected the company's agility in adapting to technological advancements and streamlining operations.

Recognizing the global fame of Disney cartoons, London Biscuit made a strategic maneuver. Leveraging Nam Hui's networks in Hong Kong, London Biscuits obtained a Disney license in Malaysia for its Yummies brand. This license allowed for the incorporation of classic Disney characters onto cake and corn confectionery products marketing, appealing to a wider audience beyond cultural boundaries, and thereby bolstering its market visibility. Additionally, it facilitated entry into the China market from Hong Kong.

5.2.5 Stage Four: Diversification

Under the leadership of the second generation, London Biscuit embarked on a path of innovation and expansion, aiming to reach beyond the Chinese market, and into the global Muslim market. London Biscuit demonstrated its adaptability and responsiveness to global market demands by obtaining a Halal certificate for its Mizu brand biscuits series. This strategic decision opened doors to the UAE market, catering to the preferences and dietary requirements of Muslim consumers, thereby further diversifying the company's consumer base. Leveraging their astute market insights, London Biscuit introduced a range of corn-based snacks and biscuit cup products, each boasting a variety of flavors tailored to cater to diverse consumer preferences.

Malaysia's prominence as a global hub of Halal products stems from its substantial Muslim population, with Halal standards deeply ingrained in the country's cultural and religious fabric. Renowned for its rigorous adherence to Halal guidelines, Malaysia has emerged as a global leader in certifying Halal products and services. This authenticity extends beyond domestic borders, with Malaysian Halal certification widely recognized and respected worldwide, further solidifying the country's influence in Halal standards. Using this certification, London Biscuit was showcasing innovative tacit knowledge in strategically venturing into new markets.

Moreover, in line with its commitment to innovation, London Biscuit invested in cutting-edge technology to produce Khee San candies and sweets infused with tropical fruits. Using the latest advancements, not only enhanced product quality, but also solidified its position as the largest candy manufacturer in Malaysia, capturing the hearts of consumers with delightful tropical flavors.

Furthermore, recognizing the growing demand for snack products London Biscuit focused on new product development in the snacks category, introducing competitively priced potato chips in 2010. This strategic move allowed the company to tap into new market segments and broaden its product offerings, appealing to a diverse range of consumers beyond traditional Chinese markets.

In addition to product innovation, London Biscuit also employed other marketing strategies, including TV sponsorships and exhibitions. Using these TV sponsorships allowed the company to reach a wider audience and increase brand visibility through television advertising. Furthermore, leveraging the exhibition method for product promotion provided an unconventional yet effective approach to showcase London Biscuit's offerings to potential customers. While relatively uncommon in the food industry, exhibitions served as a platform for direct engagement with consumers and facilitated brand awareness in a tangible and interactive manner. These diverse marketing strategies contributed to London Biscuit's ability to effectively promote its products and expand its market presence in innovative ways.

5.2.6 Stage Five: Decline

Despite its achievements, London Biscuit encountered challenges in recent years. Even in the face of immense challenges and operational difficulties, family businesses often find solace and resilience in the unity of their kin. Drawing upon the collective strength and support of family ties, they navigate through turbulent waters and emerge unscathed. This resilience is a testament to the wisdom ingrained within Chinese culture, where the bonds of family serve as a pillar of strength in times of adversity.

In 2020, London Biscuits embarked on a significant transformation by divesting its assets to Mamee-Double Decker, a renowned Malaysian brand recognized for its instant noodles and noodle snacks. This strategic decision likely arose from several factors. Firstly, Mamee-Double Decker's strong foothold in the Malaysian market provided London Biscuits with an opportunity to leverage its distribution network and brand reputation to expand the reach of its products. Moreover, aligning with a well-established player like Double Decker enabled London Biscuits to streamline operations, cut costs, and refocus on its core business activities. Additionally, this sale may have been driven by financial considerations, allowing London Biscuits to access capital for investment in other ventures or to address financial challenges. Despite the change in ownership, this move signifies a commitment to unlocking synergies, enhancing competitiveness, and ensuring long-term sustainability in the ever-evolving food industry landscape. It also indicates that the ambition to continue the legacy of Nanyang snack foods persists, driven by passionate market players.

The choices made by the Liew family epitomize the wisdom outlined in Sun Tzu's "The Art of War," where it is said that "to know when to fight and when not

Figure 5.1 The former London Biscuit Berhad Building with its New Mamee Bakery Sdn Bhd. Signboard After the 2020 Acquisition by Mamee-Double Decker. Photograph by the author.

to fight is the height of wisdom" (知可以战与不可以战者，胜)[3]. Recognizing the importance of strategic retreat as much as bold advancement, the Liew family's decisions exemplify their astute understanding of when to push forward and when to withdraw. This tactical acumen underscores the significance of knowing when to seize opportunities and when to exercise prudence, echoing the timeless wisdom of Chinese philosophy and strategy.

5.2.7 Ownership Pattern and Financial Performance

London Biscuit is a public limited company operated in the manufacturing and trading of confectionery and related foodstuffs. However, the company is currently in the process of winding up. As of the last available information, the company had a total issued share capital of 258,305,981 ordinary shares and 51,296,652 shares of other types. This indicates the extent of ownership and investment in the company by shareholders.

The year 2019 marked a significant turning point in the history of London Biscuits, led by the Liew family. Unfortunately, due to health reasons, Nam Hui resigned from his position within the company. Subsequently, in July 2019, London

Table 5.1 London Biscuits Berhad Balance Sheet, 2018–2022

(RM)	*2022*	*2021*	*2020*	*2019*	*2018*
Non-Current Assets	479,766,000	440,732,560	581,869,204	588,400,917	587,356,209
Current Assets	335,659,000	304,458,144	293,571,110	237,920,815	151,266,367
Non-Current Liabilities	0	131,177,128	103,785,577	50,112,555	67,070,649
Current Liabilities	314,401,000	210,959,900	251,802,743	289,737,325	249,875,504
Share Capital	206,484,000	186,533,789	186,533,789	186,533,789	163,556,789
Reserve	162,423,000	216,519,887	211,282,479	0	181,394,097
Retain Earning	0	0	0	193,067,993	0

Source: Companies Commission of Malaysia (SSM).

Table 5.2 London Biscuits Berhad Income Statement, 2018–2022

(RM)	*2022*	*2021*	*2020*	*2019*	*2018*
Revenue	308,703,000	426,021,317	436,507,512	402,539,026	359,995,183
Profit/(Loss) Before Tax	18,341,000	21,283,039	24,994,900	22,740,567	21,513,819
Profit/(loss) After Tax	13,658,000	17,238,848	22,418,889	18,198,429	17,311,670
Net Dividend	0	-5,367,448	0	0	-1,422,235

Source: Companies Commission of Malaysia (SSM).

Biscuits was placed under PN17 status by Bursa Malaysia. In response to these challenges, strategic decisions were made, including the sale of a 20% stake in Khee San and the gradual reduction of family members' stakes in the company. As a result, several family members also resigned from their positions on the board of directors and executive management. To manage the company's affairs during this transition, a liquidator has been appointed.

Following the withdrawal of the Liew family from London Biscuits Berhad, the company embarked on a winding-down process, as evidenced by its financial performance over the years. From 2018 to 2022, there was a noticeable decline in both revenue and profitability. Revenue decreased steadily from RM 359,995,183 in 2018 to RM 308,703,000 in 2022. Similarly, profit before tax and profit after tax experienced a downward trend, indicating operational challenges and decreasing profitability.

Additionally, the absence of net dividends in 2022, coupled with a significant negative net dividend in 2021, suggests financial difficulties and a lack of returns for shareholders. These financial indicators align with the decision of the Liew family to withdraw from the business, likely driven by the company's deteriorating financial health and prospects.

Furthermore, the balance sheet reflects a reduction in both non-current and current assets over the years, while liabilities remained relatively stable. This could signify divestment activities or asset liquidation as part of the winding-down process. With the Liew family's departure, the company may have struggled to maintain its competitive position and sustain operations, leading to the need for a controlled exit strategy.

Overall, the financial data points to a winding-down process for London Biscuits Berhad following the withdrawal of the Liew family. The declining financial performance, absence of dividends, and potential asset reductions indicate a challenging transition period for the company as it navigates the aftermath of the family's departure and seeks to manage its affairs during the winding-down phase.

5.3 Case Study Two: King's Confectionery Sdn. Bhd.

5.3.1 Introduction

King's Confectionery Sdn. Bhd., a renowned confectionery enterprise deeply rooted in the vibrant tapestry of Malaysia's culinary heritage. Originating from the rich traditions of the Hainanese Chinese, King's Confectionery has carved a niche for itself as a purveyor of delectable baked goods and pastries that delight palates across the nation.

With a diverse product range spanning from mouthwatering cakes and pastries to savory buns and breads, King's Confectionery caters to a wide spectrum of tastes

Figure 5.2 Exterior View of a King's Confectionery Shop. Photograph by the author.

and preferences, all while upholding the highest standards of quality and authenticity. Operating across various regions in Malaysia, from urban centers to serene rural locales, King's Confectionery has established itself as a household name, beloved by millions of customers. King's Confectionery has successfully expanded its reach into the Bangladesh market, further solidifying its global position in the confectionery industry.

As a family-owned enterprise, King's Confectionery is guided by a legacy of passion and dedication passed down through generations. With the involvement of the second and subsequent generations of the Wong family, the company continues to thrive, adapting to evolving consumer demands and market trends while staying true to its founding principles of excellence and innovation. In today's dynamic market landscape, King's Confectionery remains committed to providing unparalleled culinary experiences, blending tradition with innovation to create moments of joy and indulgence for its valued customers.

5.3.2 Stage One: Start-up

Rooted in the Chinese Hainanese culture, King's Confectionery's story is one of passion, dedication, and the mastery of tacit knowledge passed down through generations. The Hainanese Chinese established themselves as culinary experts in the history of Malaya due to their role in serving both British colonial households and Peranakan Chinese families. Their culinary skills and adaptability contributed to their reputation for creating dishes that satisfied the diverse tastes of these communities.

Elder Wong was born in 1912 in the province of Hainan, China. By the age of 16, he managed to master the skills of making the perfect cup of coffee and tea. Elder Wong migrating from *Hainan* to Malaya in 1929. It all began in 1960, amid the bustling streets of Batu Arang, Rawang, where a small *Kopitiam* business served as the humble birthplace of King's Confectionery. Wong extended an invitation to his wife and daughters to join him in crafting mouthwatering dumplings and brewing aromatic coffee, setting the stage for what would become a legacy of culinary excellence.

Elder Wong's tacit, intimate knowledge about coffee made his business famous among locals and thus had motivated his eldest daughter, Wong Yoke Khing, to take over the business. As the years unfolded, Yoke Khing emerged as a visionary in her own right. Trained in the art of cakes and breads at the esteemed Coliseum Cafe and Taiwan, known for its highly systematic and professional culinary and baking knowledge, she set out to carve her own path in the world of pastry-making. She wanted to transform Chinese pastries and street food into dishes that every ethnic group in Malaysia, including Malays, Chinese, and Indians, could enjoy and would love to eat. With her father's guidance, the family transitioned from a stall in Rawang to a bustling coffee house on Jalan Sultan, where Wong Yoke Khing's pastry house began to take shape.

She later married Eng Man Hin who worked as a bank manager at the time. They started their first bakery by selling an array of pastries and cakes in Kepong's wet market. Eventually, they opened their first outlet in Jinjang and later, they opened another one in Kepong. In 1977, the establishment of the King's Confectionery factory warehouse marked a pivotal moment in the company's history, enabling the distribution of pastries to outlets across Malaysia.

Under the leadership of Elder Wong and Yoke Khing during the first generation, King's Confectionery distinguished itself by focusing on distributing Hainanese traditional food recipes and brewed coffee, appealing to housing residents with a penchant for authentic flavors. With Yoke Khing at the helm, the family business flourished, expanding its operations to manufacture and design a diverse range of pastries and baked goods. During Yoke Khing's leadership, King's Confectionery not only focused on retailing but also ventured into wholesaling, marking a pivotal expansion in its distribution network. This strategic move allowed the company to reach a wider audience and establish its presence beyond individual outlets. This era marked the birth of King's pastries, centralizing business operations and setting the stage for further growth.

5.3.3 Stage Two: Expansion

After holding the position of CEO from 1973 to 1990, Yoke Khing passed on the leadership role to her younger brother, Wong Lei Hoy, who majored in business administration in a university in Australia. In the second generation, led by Lei Hoy, King's Confectionery underwent a transformation into a franchising powerhouse, expanding its reach from retail shops to *Kopitiam* lifestyle cafes. Lei Hoy also understands that if the goal is to extend the customer base beyond the neighborhood, obtaining a Halal certificate is necessary.

Incorporated in 1993, King's Confectionery's commitment to quality and diversity has been steady. Certified Halal by Jabatan Kemajuan Islam Malaysia in 1996, the company's vision of delivering excellence in bakery products to Malaysia's multicultural society became a reality. Embracing franchising as a strategy, the company penetrated rural and urban markets alike, establishing outlets in every Tesco store in Malaysia. The Wong family's strategic decision-making, coupled with the recruitment of experienced COOs, propelled King's Confectionery to new heights, solidifying its position as a market leader. From its beginnings in a small *Kopitiam* to its status as a trailblazer in the confectionery industry, King's Confectionery stands as a demonstration to the enduring legacy of Chinese Hainanese culinary excellence and the power of tacit knowledge passed from one generation to the next. King's Confectionery has garnered a significant following among the Malay community. Notably, in many rural areas where the Malay community is concentrated such as Kedah, King's Confectionery has achieved excellent sales figures. This indicates that the company's strategic direction is correct.

Despite the common belief that obtaining Halal certification leads to increased revenue, King's Confectionery's journey suggests otherwise. Two main insights emerge from the company's experience: the importance of cultural adaptation and the need for comprehensive market strategies. King's Confectionery, rooted in Chinese Hainanese culture, initially focused on traditional recipes and flavors to attract customers. However, recognizing the multicultural nature of Malaysian society, the company embarked on a journey of cultural adaptation, aligning with the diverse dietary preferences of the population. This strategic move not only expanded the customer base but also demonstrated King's Confectionery's commitment to inclusivity and accessibility. Moreover, the company's experience highlights the significance of comprehensive market strategies beyond Halal certification. While Halal certification is essential for catering to specific consumer segments, it does not guarantee higher revenue on its own. King's Confectionery realized the importance of holistic marketing approaches, including product diversification, retail expansion, and franchising. By offering a wide range of baked goods and confectionery, expanding retail outlets, and embracing franchising, the company effectively tapped into diverse market segments, driving revenue growth and market penetration.

5.3.4 Stage Three: Maturity

Expanding from 25 to 90 outlets, King's Confectionery became the largest retail confectionery chain in Malaysia. Through dedication and innovation, production soared, giving rise to an impressive array of 50 to 120 new products by the 1990s. Drawing upon centuries of tradition and the innate understanding of flavor and technique passed down through generations, King's Confectionery continues to push the boundaries of creativity and innovation in the realm of baked goods.

During a visit to Hong Kong, the Wong family stumbled upon a pastry known as Portuguese egg tarts, which were not yet available in Malaysia. Recognizing the potential business opportunity, they discovered that these tarts originated from Macau. They subsequently traveled to Macau to learn the art of making Portuguese egg tarts before returning to Malaysia to produce them on a large scale. The enthusiastic response from customers validated their foresight, and Portuguese egg tarts soon became a beloved pastry among Malaysians. Discovering and introducing new products that are widely embraced by the public requires a deep understanding of customer tastes and consumption trends. This relies on the tacit knowledge passed down through family generations and the courage of the family business.

Another competitive advantage of King's is its cakes. The most prominent evidence of this advantage is their development of the pandan layer cake. The pandan layer cake is now a well-known cake in Malaysia, but many years ago, no one had thought of using pandan leaves, a unique plant with a refreshing aroma from the Nanyang region, as the main ingredient for making cakes, rather than just a flavoring. Using pandan to make layer cake not only results in a soft texture but also blends the fragrance of pandan leaves with that of the flour, highlighting both aromas. This makes pandan layer cake a unique Nanyang-flavored cake.

Throughout its evolution, King's Confectionery has remained true to its core values and objectives: ensuring continuity and stability across generations. The family's deep understanding of baking and marketing, combined with their relentless drive to innovate, has enabled the company to weather economic storms and emerge stronger than ever. King's Confectionery demonstrated its innovation and ability to meet the evolving needs of customers. King's Confectionery expanded its reach from retail shops to Kopitiam lifestyle cafes. Embracing franchising as a strategy, the company penetrated rural and urban markets alike, establishing outlets in every Tesco store in Malaysia and venturing into overseas markets such as Bangladesh.

5.3.5 Stage Four: Diversification

Seeing as most of King's Confectionery workers were from Bangladesh, Lei Hoy was convinced that expanding this company to Bangladesh was the right decision. His move came into fruition as King's Confectionery was very well received despite the fact that it is mostly a semi-rural country.

For many years, revenue in Bangladesh grew at a steady trend annually, and even surpassed the sales revenue in Malaysia. Therefore, Ley Hoi believed as the "market can take it, what with today's changing trends and demands," they were planning to expand their business into the concept of franchise stores. Furthermore, he was a firm believer that with the right technological advancement, especially automation, he will be able improve enterprise development, as well as creating new products to penetrate new market.

King's Confectionery (Bangladesh) Private Limited was established in Bangladesh in February 2003, with seven branches in and around Dhaka. It is a Bangladesh-Malaysia business venture and partnership. Just like their other franchises, these branches maintain a high level of hygiene and quality control throughout their entire manufacturing processes. To diversify the market, Yoke Khing leveraged her talent by establishing luxurious urban cafes, targeting middle and high-income consumers. This initiative showcases the transfer of tacit knowledge within the company, as it ventures into untapped market segments, further expanding its reach and customer base.

5.3.6 Ownership Pattern and Financial Performance

King's Confectionery Sdn Bhd. operates as a limited company with a total issued ordinary share capital of 2,100,000. The company is deeply rooted in familial ties, with key positions held by family members who contribute to its success and growth.

In terms of shareholding, Wong Lee Tong, the second brother, holds 672,000 shares, indicating a significant ownership stake in the company. As a director, his role likely involves strategic decision-making and overseeing operational aspects of the business. Wong Lei Hoy, the youngest brother, holds the largest portion of shares, with 798,000 shares. In addition to his role as a director, he also serves as the manager, indicating his active involvement in day-to-day management and leadership of the company. Wong Nyok Choo, the fourth sister, the R&D director, holds 630,000 shares, further solidifying the family's presence and influence within the company.

Table 5.3 King's Confectionery Sdn. Bhd. Balance Sheet, 2018–2022

(RM)	*2022*	*2021*	*2020*	*2019*	*2018*
Non-Current Assets	29,184,612.	31,110,033	13,354,464	14,676,441	15,876,339
Current Assets	20,423,107	21,550,045	24,196,847	26,182,295	27,187,353
Non-Current Liabilities	2,281,322	3,051,507	3,787,187	2,888,708	3,339,201
Current Liabilities	22,669,633	25,210,191	22,691,347	23,843,948	26,422,331
Share Capital	2,100,000	2,100,000	2,100,000	2,100,000	2,100,000
Reserve	19,318,677	19,318,677	0	0	0
Retain Earning	3,315,099	3,027,699	8,737,238	11,672,453	11,202,160

Source: Companies Commission of Malaysia (SSM).

Table 5.4 King's Confectionery Sdn. Bhd. Income Statement, 2018–2022

(RM)	*2022*	*2021*	*2020*	*2019*	*2018*
Revenue	34,102,160	33,047,726	36,108,723	44,926,049	53,971,634
Profit/(loss) Before Tax	281,595	-5,990,667	-2,938,306	619,372	982,644
Profit/(loss) After Tax	278,384	-5,993,074	-3,033,303	470,293	825,750
Net Dividend	0	0	0	0	0

Source: Companies Commission of Malaysia (SSM).

The shared ownership and active participation of family members ensure the familial nature of the business, with each member playing a crucial role in its operations and governance. From a family business perspective, King's Confectionery exemplifies the blending of familial bonds with entrepreneurial endeavors. This close-knit structure fosters a sense of unity, shared vision, and mutual trust, essential elements for the success and longevity of a family-owned enterprise.

Over the five-year period from 2018 to 2022, King's Confectionery maintained a stable financial position, with consistent levels of non-current assets and current assets. Despite fluctuations in liabilities, the company's share capital remained constant at RM 2,100,000, indicating a steady investment base. The introduction of reserves in 2020 signifies a strategic move to accumulate profits for future growth opportunities. Retained earnings reflect the company's profitability, although there was a slight decrease in 2021. Overall, King's Confectionery's balance sheet demonstrates prudent financial management, with a focus on maintaining liquidity, managing debt, and accumulating reserves to support long-term sustainability and growth.

Over the period from 2018 to 2022, King's Confectionery witnessed fluctuations in its financial performance as depicted in the Income Statement. Despite maintaining relatively stable revenue levels, the company experienced significant variations in profitability, with notable losses recorded in 2020 and 2021. These losses were attributed to factors such as operational challenges or economic downturns. However, King's Confectionery demonstrated resilience, with a return to profitability in 2022. Throughout this period, the company refrained from distributing dividends, indicating a focus on retaining earnings for potential reinvestment or financial stability. Overall, the income statement reflects King's Confectionery's commitment to navigating through financial challenges while striving for sustained growth and profitability in the confectionery industry.

5.4 Case Study Three: Leong Hup International Berhad and Baker's Cottage

5.4.1 Introduction

Leong Hup and Baker's Cottage stand as pillars of food industry, deeply rooted in the rich tapestry of Chinese heritage and entrepreneurial spirit. Founded by the Lau family, Teochew Chinese, the companies represent the culmination of generations of dedication to quality, innovation, and tradition. As prominent figures within the Malaysian Chinese community, Leong Hup and Baker's Cottage epitomize the values of unity and collaboration.

Leong Hup, initially established as a poultry farming enterprise in Muar, Johor, has evolved into a diversified conglomerate spanning various industry. Under the

Figure 5.3 Exterior View of Leong Hup International Berhad Factory. Photograph by the author.

stewardship of the second generation the third generation of Lau family, Leong Hup has expanded its reach beyond Malaysia to become a key player in the Southeast Asian market. In 2019, Leong Hup International made history with its successful listing on the Main Market of Bursa Securities, marking the largest poultry-related initial public offering in Southeast Asia. Adding to its diverse portfolio, Leong Hup expanded its reach by acquiring Baker's Cottage as a subsidiary, leveraging its "Farm-to-Plate" concept to offer the most affordable and highest quality roast chicken. With a focus on incorporating traditional Chinese recipes and techniques, Baker's Cottage has carved a niche for itself in the competitive bakery industry, captivating the hearts and tastes of consumers across Malaysia and beyond.

Today, both Leong Hup and Baker's Cottage continue to thrive under the visionary leadership of the third generation, embracing technological advancements, and leveraging their cultural heritage as a source of innovation and competitive advantage.

5.4.2 Stage One: Start-up

Founded in a rural town, Muar, Johor during the 1960s, Leong Hup traces its roots back to a modest vegetable wholesale business operated by the late Lau Leng Yeaw, father of the late Lau Bong Wong, who exemplified the diligent and resilient spirit characteristic of the Teochew people. Historically, the Teochew people originated from the eastern coastal region of Guangdong Province in China, where agriculture has long been a central part of the local economy. With fertile land and a favorable climate, agriculture flourished in this region, providing the Teochew people with a rich agricultural heritage. The geographical features have facilitated the cultivation of various crops such as rice, vegetables, fruits, and tea. Additionally, the proximity to the coastline has enabled the Teochew people to engage in aquaculture and fishing activities, further diversifying their agricultural practices. When the Teochew people's migration to other parts of Southeast Asia, including Nanyang and Thailand, brought their agricultural knowledge and skills to new territories. In these regions, they adapted to local climates and environments, continuing their agricultural traditions while also integrating with the local communities. As mentioned in Chapter 3, the Thailand leading agro-industry and food business, Charoen Pokphand Group were also founded by immigrants from the Teochew community.

Born in 1943 in Muar during the colonial era, the late Lau Bong Wong, lead his brothers in pioneering the livestock industry, he embodied the enduring ethos of hard work and perseverance. Throughout the entrepreneurial journey, he consistently showcased aspects of the Chaoshan culture, blending tradition with innovation to forge a path of success in the business landscape. The name "Leong Hup," symbolizing "龙合" in Chinese, embodies profound cultural connotations deeply rooted in Chinese values. "龙" represents the majestic dragon, a revered symbol of strength, success, and auspiciousness in Chinese culture. It epitomizes the extraordinary capabilities and accomplishments of the founders, Lau Bong Wong and Lau Chong Wang. Meanwhile, "合" signifies unity, collaboration, and harmonious partnership—a core principle in Chinese philosophy and family-centric business ethos. Together, "龙合" encapsulates the essence of Leong Hup, reflecting its founders' vision of collective endeavor, resilience, and prosperity. Thus, the name itself embodying the spirit of Chinese culture and values in its journey of excellence.

The business evolved into Leong Hup Poultry Farming, later renamed Leong Hup Contract Farming, implementing a vertical integration strategy to revolutionize poultry farming and embracing modern techniques to thrive in the competitive market in Malaysia. This strategic move allowed for economies of scale, enabling the distribution of day-old chicks and broiler chickens to larger markets such as Penang, Kuala Lumpur, Malacca, and even Singapore.

Leong Hup's decision to focus on chicken production is strategically aligned with the high demand and widespread consumption of chicken, which is consumed by all ethnic groups in Malaysia. As the most widely consumed meat in the country, this poultry gains its popularity due to its affordability, widespread availability, and alignment with cultural preferences. By prioritizing chicken production, Leong Hup ensures a consistent market demand, potentially higher profits, and relatively low maintenance costs. Additionally, the quick turnover of chicken production enables Leong Hup to generate revenue more rapidly compared to other livestock animals with longer production cycles.

5.4.3 Stage Two: Expansion

The transition into the second generation saw Leong Hup's listing on the Malaysian main board, marking a significant milestone in its expansion. The group ventured into broiler day-old chicks, contract farming, and retailing, establishing itself as Malaysia's main distributor of fresh chicken and processed meat. Inspired by the Lau family members, they expanded into the confectionery retail sector with acquired Baker's Cottage and later ventured into the TBC restaurant retail chain. This allowed them to tap into broader consumer markets, leveraging Chinese networks and family business principles to expand their reach. Under the stewardship of subsequent generations, including Lau Chia Nguang, Lau Eng Guang, and Lau Tuang Nguang, Leong Hup achieved vertical integration, encompassing breeder farms, butchery plants, and food processing facilities.

Subsequent expansions saw the establishment of operations across Southeast Asia, including Malaysia, Indonesia, Vietnam, Singapore, and the Philippines, tapping into vibrant consumer markets with significant growth potential. This expansion saw the formation of the Leong Hup Group, which strategically diversified its operations vertically, encompassing a spectrum of poultry-related endeavors across Southeast Asia. In Malaysia, Leong Hup ventured into feedmill production and trading through Emivest Berhad, while layer farming activities were spearheaded under Teo Seng Capital Berhad.

Beyond Malaysian borders, the Leong Hup's footprint extended into neighboring territories, including Singapore, where it engaged in food processing and trading activities under the Lee Say Group banner. In Indonesia, Leong Hup established a presence through PT Malindo Feedmill TBK, focusing on integrated poultry farming and feedmill production. Similarly, in Vietnam, the company ventured into integrated poultry and feedmill operations under the Emivest Vietnam Group. The strategic expansion into overseas markets demonstrates the Chinese concept of seeking rent and capturing larger market demand. By establishing poultry hatcheries and breeding farms abroad, Leong Hup positioned itself as a key player in the regional poultry industry, leveraging its expertise and network to target a wider market. In 2019, Leong Hup International made history with its successful listing on the Main Market of Bursa Securities, marking the largest poultry-related initial public offering in Southeast Asia.

5.4.4 Stage Three: Maturity

As Leong Hup evolved over the years, initially focusing on poultry farming, Leong Hup later diversified into the confectionery business, introducing a wide array of pastries, cakes, and other delicacies under the Baker's Cottage brand. Lau Chia Nguang, Lau Hai Nguan, and Lau Joo Heng, brothers and nephew of founder Lau Bong Wong, spearheaded Baker's Cottage's transition into a confectionery powerhouse. Leveraging their familial ties and expertise, they diversified the business from bakeries to a renowned mooncake brand. Drawing inspiration from traditional Chinese recipes and techniques, the company infused its products with a unique blend of flavors and textures that appealed to both local and international palates.

Baker's Cottage has not only preserved traditional recipes but also adapted them to meet the evolving tastes of a contemporary market. This delicate balance between honoring heritage and embracing change is a testament to the enduring relevance of tacit knowledge—a legacy passed down through generations, enriching both the business and the broader cultural landscape. One of the key products that defined the business was the mooncake—an iconic Chinese pastry enjoyed during the Mid-Autumn Festival. When targeting customer groups, Baker's Cottage develops different business strategies for traditional mooncake enthusiasts and customers who seek new flavors. On one hand, it strives to maintain the characteristics of traditional mooncakes, such as crafting exquisite five-nut mooncakes, where "five-nut" refers to almonds, walnuts, peanuts, sesame seeds, and melon seeds. Due to geographical and social factors, traditional Teochew mooncakes are not as elaborate as Cantonese mooncakes. Traditional Teochew mooncakes are typically sweet, whereas Cantonese mooncakes come in both sweet and savory varieties. On the other hand, it endeavors to introduce new and delicate flavors with a Nanyang twist. Leong Hup and Baker's Cottage introducing innovative flavors such as durian, pandan, and black charcoal, catering to changing consumer preferences while preserving the essence of this time-honored delicacy.

When we see roast chicken in a bakery, we may be surprised, and that's exactly Leong Hup's unexpected strategy. Leong Hup and Baker's Cottage established "Farm-to-Plate" concept to revolutionize the roast chicken market, offering the most affordable and highest quality roast chicken. By using company sourced ingredients and prioritizing sustainability, every roast chicken served is ensured

Figure 5.4 Exterior View of Baker's Cottage Shop. Photograph by the author.

to not only be delicious but also ethically produced. Through this strategic collaboration, Leong Hup and Baker's Cottage committed to providing their customers with a guilt-free dining experience that combines the convenience of fast food with the integrity of farm-fresh ingredients.

Additionally, the company's embraced technological advancements in food processing and production, commitment to R&D led to the development of other popular items such as ice-cream cakes, festive cookies, and savory snacks, further expanding its product portfolio and capturing new market segments. Through continuous innovation and a deep understanding of consumer trends, the company has remained at the forefront of the culinary industry, offering products that not only reflect Chinese cultural heritage but also resonate with modern consumers seeking authentic flavors.

5.4.5 Stage Four: Diversification

The third generation's entrepreneurial spirit led to the establishment of Baker's Cottage pastries and mooncakes, solidifying their presence in Malaysia's bakery industry. They embraced their heritage, incorporating tacit knowledge from poultry farming into bakery operations, ensuring a seamless transition. Their strategic vision involved tapping into the resources of the Leong Hup, transforming production processes and product offerings. By focusing on mooncakes, they focused on a niche market, capitalizing on traditional recipes while integrating modern technology. With a keen eye for innovation, they modernized manufacturing with automated technology, ensuring efficiency and quality. Concurrently, they centralized management, aligning with the Leong Hup's ethos and streamlining operations.

The strategic expansion into food processing and confectionery retail chains during the third generation exemplifies the Chinese concept of leveraging resources and knowledge transfer. By utilizing resources to streamline operations and minimize costs, Baker's Cottage successfully grew its retail outlets from 2 to 26 within a decade. Through research and development initiatives, they introduced a diverse range of products, including buns, pastries, counter cakes, ice-cream cakes, mooncakes, and festive cookies, catering to evolving consumer preferences. Moreover, the transfer of tacit knowledge from vertical integration strategies in chick farming to food processing and confectionery retail underscores the importance of generational learning and adaptation in Chinese family businesses. This seamless transition not only preserves traditional values but also fosters innovation and growth in new market segments.

As of June 2021, Baker's Cottage received certification from the Department of Islamic Development Malaysia (JAKIM) as halal. This signifies several advantages for the company. Being halal-certified opens access to a broader market segment, particularly among Muslim consumers who adhere to halal dietary requirements. This certification enhances Baker's Cottage's credibility and trustworthiness among Muslim customers. Moreover, halal certification can facilitate entry into international markets with large Muslim populations, enabling Baker's Cottage to expand its business globally. Obtaining halal certification presents significant advantages for Baker's Cottage, including increased market reach, consumer trust, and opportunities for growth both domestically and internationally.

Leong Hup consistently seeks to broaden its range of processed chicken food items by frequently unveiling new offerings for consumers. This includes the production of processed chicken meat products like frankfurters, nuggets, and chicken meatballs under the Halal-certified brand "Ayam A1" for the domestic market. Additionally, the company has outlined plans to establish additional Ayam A1 retail outlets, which will offer fresh and roasted chicken alongside existing outlets. As a component of the group's strategy for vertical integration, they established a rapidly expanding network of quick-service restaurants (QSR) including Baker's Cottage in Malaysia, LH Deli in the Philippines, and Sunny Chick in Indonesia. These restaurants specialize in providing high-quality, ready-to-eat poultry products at exceptional value, catering directly to consumers.

Their commitment to excellence extended to retail chains and cafes, where they introduced new mooncake varieties, cementing their status as a premier mooncake enterprise in Malaysia. In 2020 alone, Baker's Cottage opened more than 60 outlets, reaching different parts of Malaysia. Today, there are 178 outlets all over the country. Empowered with autonomy and access to group resources, they navigated the business landscape with creativity and foresight. Through their endeavors, the third generation Lau family members have not only upheld the legacy of Baker's Cottage but also propelled it to new heights, marking a chapter of continued success and innovation in the Malaysian culinary scene.

5.4.6 Ownership Pattern and Financial Performance

Leong Hup International Berhad operates as a public limited company under a limited by shares structure, boasting a total issued share capital of 1,505,131,992 ordinary shares. The board of directors features prominent individuals including Lau Eng Guang and Lau Chia Nguang, siblings of the company's founder, Lau Joo Hong, the founder's nephew, and Lau Joo Keat and Lau Joo Han, his sons. Additional directors include Chu Nyet Kim, Low Han Kee, Tay Tong Poh, and Goh Wen Ling, with Tan Sri Lau Tuang Nguang, another sibling of the founder, serving as both director and CEO.

Datin Paduka Rashidah binti Ramli brings invaluable experience to the board, having commenced her career in public service as an Administrative and Diplomatic Officer in 1984. She ascended to various senior roles within the Ministry of Foreign Affairs of Malaysia, including the Southeast Asia Division, Development Division, and Chief of Inspectorate. Her incorporation onto the board brings a unique advantage, with her extensive experience in public service adding a broader perspective to the company's decision-making processes.

The main Lau family shareholders comprise Lau Eng Guang, holding 20,045,400 shares (~ 1.33%); Lau Joo Heng and Lau Jui Peng, each holding 24,583,822 shares (~ 1.63% each); HN Lau & Sons Sdn. Bhd., representing Lau Hai Nguan, Lai Chong Koo, and their children, holding 28,633,207 shares (~ 1.90%); and CN Lau Holdings Sdn. Bhd., representing Lau Chia Nguang and his children, holding 58,935,607 shares (~ 3.91%).

Table 5.5 Leong Hup International Berhad Balance Sheet, 2018–2022

(RM'000)	*2022*	*2021*	*2020*	*2019*	*2018*
Non-Current Assets	3,431,812	3,411,240	3,228,404	2,904,308	2,576,103
Current Assets	3,160,389	2,918,574	2,466,399	2,504,830	2,257,892
Non-Current Liabilities	1,339,504	1,321,435	1,154,468	1,125,191	1,183,779
Current Liabilities	2,663,122	2,648,539	2,291,772	2,103,424	1,884,788
Share Capital	1,499,684	1,499,684	1,499,684	1,499,684	1,230,132
Reserve	505,360	307,376	213,757	141,525	7,709
Retain Earning	0	0	0	0	0

Source: Companies Commission of Malaysia (SSM).

Table 5.6 Leong Hup International Berhad Income Statement, 2018–2022

(RM'000)	*2022*	*2021*	*2020*	*2019*	*2018*
Revenue	9,042,702	7,153,520	6,040,664	6,054,756	5,746,572
Profit/(loss) Before Tax	326,555	140,315,	157,126	288,750	348,575
Profit/(loss) After Tax	243,874	95,890	117,523	212,987	246,753
Net dividend	0	-24,090	-20,075	-58,400	-58

Source: Companies Commission of Malaysia (SSM).

Over the five-year period from 2018 to 2022, the company demonstrated consistent growth in both non-current and current assets. Non-current assets rose from RM2.58 billion to RM3.43 billion, while current assets increased from RM2.26 billion to RM3.16 billion. This growth reflects the company's robust financial health, with strategic investments in long-term assets and maintained liquidity. Liabilities also grew, with non-current liabilities rising from RM1.18 billion to RM1.34 billion and current liabilities increasing from RM1.88 billion to RM2.66 billion. However, the strong asset base indicates a favorable debt-to-asset ratio, showcasing effective financial management.

Share capital remained stable at RM1.50 billion, while reserves saw a significant jump from RM7.71 million in 2018 to RM505.36 million in 2022, highlighting retained earnings and accumulated profits. This boost in reserves further enhances financial stability and risk resilience. Overall, the balance sheet reveals steady growth, prudent management, and resilience, setting the company up for sustained future success.

From 2018 to 2022, Leong Hup showed consistent revenue growth, rising from RM5.75 billion to RM9.04 billion, underlining its market expansion and increased sales. Despite fluctuations in profit before tax, ranging from RM140.32 million to RM348.57 million, Leong Hup remained profitable, reflecting its resilience in changing market conditions. Profits after tax stayed positive, between RM95.89 million and RM243.87 million, demonstrating effective expense management and sustainable earnings.

In 2022, Leong Hup opted not to distribute dividends, a shift from previous years, possibly to reinvest for growth or strengthen its financial base. Overall, LHI's income statement reveals strong financial performance, strategic management, and a solid foundation for future success.

5.5 Case Study Four: Besfomec Industries Sdn. Bhd.

5.5.1 Introduction

Besfomec Industries Sdn. Bhd. is a beacon of tradition and innovation in the realm of herbal healthcare. As a family-owned enterprise deeply entrenched in the rich tapestry of Chinese culture, Besfomec traces its roots back to the entrepreneurial spirit of Lau Tin Shun, a Hakka Chinese descent hailing from Guangdong Province, China. Specializing in traditional Chinese medicine, Besfomec has blossomed from its beginnings as *Xin Chun Woh* Chinese medical hall in Malacca in 1948 to a modern-day powerhouse, blending ancestral wisdom with cutting-edge research and development.

Spanning three generations, the family business's journey embodies the ethos of familial stewardship and intergenerational continuity. Led by Lau's son and subsequently by his grandchildren, Besfomec has evolved into a dynamic entity

Figure 5.5 Exterior View of Besfomec Industries Sdn. Bhd. Factory. Photograph by the author.

at the intersection of tradition and modernity. Their collective efforts have propelled Besfomec to the forefront of the herbal healthcare industry, showcasing the enduring legacy of Chinese family businesses.

With a diverse product range encompassing traditional remedies like chicken essence and bird's nest alongside innovative concoctions infused with local ingredients such as Snakehead fish and sea cucumber, Besfomec caters to a global audience. From its origins in Malacca, Malaysia, Besfomec has expanded its footprint across Southeast Asia and beyond, forging strategic partnerships and captivating markets in Singapore, China, Hong Kong, and Vietnam. Today, Besfomec stands as a paragon of success, embodying the essence of tradition, innovation, and family values in the ever-evolving landscape of herbal healthcare.

5.5.2 Stage One: Start-up

Besfomec Industries Sdn. Bhd.'s journey began with a profound dedication to traditional Chinese medicine (TCM) embodied by its founder, Lau Tin Shun. Rooted in Chinese cultural heritage and guided by principles of holistic healing, the business's inception as *Xin Chun Woh* (杏春和)[4] Chinese medical hall in Malacca in 1948 marked the convergence of ancestral wisdom with entrepreneurial vision. Lau's Hakka Chinese heritage, hailing from Dabu County in Guangdong Province, infused the business with a deep understanding of TCM practices dominant within the Malaysia landscape.

Figure 5.6 The Original Signboard Name of Xin Chun Woh Chinese Medical Hall, Written in Traditional Chinese Craft Style, Now Displayed Inside the Besfomec Shop as a Tribute to its Origins. Photograph by the author.

In its nascent stages, Besfomec operated as a family business, with Lau at the helm, passionately dedicated to infusing the market with exceptional traditional Chinese medicinal healthcare products. Despite the challenging socioeconomic landscape of the time, Lau's commitment to offering high-quality products at affordable prices garnered widespread acclaim, catapulting the brand, Besfomec, into the spotlight.

The second generation, Lau Poo Chin, the eldest son of Lau, who entered the business during his secondary school years, assisted his father in promoting pharmaceutical products, traveling across Malaysia to sell medicines. This experience allowed him to understand market trends and learn the principles of business management. At the age of 24, Poo Chin took over his father's Chinese medical hall. The father, meanwhile, stepped back from the forefront and managed the finances. This reflects the cultural norm in many Chinese family businesses, where the founder does not directly let go of control but instead entrusts authority to the successor, while observing, guiding, and assisting from the sidelines. This practice helps to pass down tacit knowledge and allows the successor to hone their skills through practical experience.

5.5.3 Stage Two: Expansion

In response to escalating consumer demand, the second generation transformed Besfomec into a corporate entity in 1974, marking a pivotal moment in its trajectory. The transition from traditional Chinese medical hall to the production of chicken essence under Poo Chin's leadership demonstrated their commitment to innovation while honoring its roots. Poo Chin's managerial style, characterized by a departure from his father's risk-averse approach, marked a significant shift toward embracing modernization and technological advancement to create an herbal healthcare brand with a *Nanyang* flair. Bolstered by substantial capital injection from Lau's family, the company embarked on an expansion and technological advancement. Leveraging state-of-the-art technology, Besfomec elevated the quality of its products, solidifying its status as a leader in the herbal healthcare industry.

With the collaborative efforts of six brothers, they expanded and enhanced the shop's operations. Subsequently, they also established a factory in Alor Gajah in 1993, marked a milestone in the firm's technological advancement. Embracing GMP standards and leveraging manufacturing processes, Besfomec positioned itself as a leader in the herbal healthcare industry, expanding its product offerings and market reach.

5.5.4 Stage Three: Maturity

Traditional Chinese Medicine[5] (TCM) and evidence-based medicine represent two distinct yet complementary approaches to healthcare. While TCM draws on centuries-old practices rooted in holistic healing and herbal remedies, evidence-based medicine relies on rigorous scientific research and clinical trials to assess the efficacy and safety of medical treatments. There has been increasing interest in integrating TCM with evidence-based medicine to harness the strengths of both approaches. This integration allows practitioners to leverage the wealth of knowledge and experience embedded in TCM while subjecting its treatments to the same rigorous scrutiny applied to modern medical interventions. By combining the principles of TCM with scientific evidence, healthcare providers can offer patients a comprehensive approach to wellness that addresses both the physical and holistic aspects of health. This synergy between traditional wisdom and modern scientific methods not only enhances patient care but also contributes to the ongoing evolution and validation of TCM practices in the contemporary medical landscape.

Besfomec's products, including chicken essence, bird nest essence, and fish and vegetarian essence, not only catered to market demands but also reflected a deep-seated connection to Chinese culture and history. Due to the presence of numerous traditional chicken essence brands in the market, Besfomec not only produces traditional chicken essence but also utilizes its tacit knowledge, integrates Chinese herbal ingredients into medicinal chicken essence formulations, such as ginseng chicken essence and cordyceps chicken essence. These products, which contain traditional Chinese medicine components, have gained significant favor among consumers. By meticulously selecting Chinese herbs from their homeland and adhering to stringent quality standards, Besfomec ensured that each product encapsulated centuries-old wisdom while embracing contemporary production methodologies.

In addition to its best-selling products such as chicken essence and bird's nest, Besfomec has also developed a variety of health products with a Southeast Asian twist by combining traditional Chinese medical knowledge and skills with Western pharmaceutical research technology. One particularly unique product is Traditional Essence of Fish, with its key ingredient, Snakehead fish (生鱼)[6], sourced from local Malaysian waters. This product is beneficial for aiding in surgical or postpartum wound healing, as well as relieving fatigue and enhancing the body's immune system. In their fish essence product line, they have further developed by incorporating precious marine resources from Malaysian waters, such as sea cucumber, into the fish essence, launching a product known as Essence of Fish with Sea Cucumber and Collagen. This not only showcases innovative product concepts but also effectively utilizes local resources.

As traditional Chinese herbal remedies gave way to a burgeoning demand for health tonics and supplements, Besfomec adeptly pivoted its product offerings to meet consumer preferences while staying true to its cultural heritage. Besfomec's evolution from a family-operated business to a globally recognized brand reflects its adaptive response to market changes across different historical eras. The firm's expansion into overseas markets, facilitated by strategic networking and distribution channels established by Low, exemplifies its commitment to sharing the benefits of TCM with diverse populations worldwide. By leveraging their expertise in TCM and embracing western-based pharmaceutical ideas, Besfomec positioned itself as a front-runner in the global herbal healthcare industry. The journey from a

Chinese medical hall in Malacca to an internationally renowned enterprise shows the transformative power of family entrepreneurship and the enduring appeal of TCM in an increasingly interconnected world.

Central to Besfomec's ethos is its dedication to product excellence and safety. All products undergo rigorous testing and formulation, blending advanced technology with professional pharmaceutical knowledge. Adhering to stringent GMP (Good Manufacturing Practice) standards and HACCP (Hazard Analysis and Critical Control Point) requirements, Besfomec's products are not only approved by the Malaysia Ministry of Health but have also received prestigious certifications including HALAL and VHM (Veterinary Health Mark).

5.5.5 Stage Four: Diversification

As Poo Chin's children matured into adults, each with their own strengths, they joined the group as a new force, becoming the third generation to take over the family business. The eldest son, Low Chew Ping, a pharmacy graduate from Australia, embraced an innovative approach by integrating western-based pharmaceutical ideas with traditional Chinese herbal remedies. He is responsible for managing production and promotion. His strategic move allowed Besfomec to conduct clinical research and develop health tonics and supplements backed by scientific evidence. Scientific evidence is crucial for developing health tonics and supplements as it validates their efficacy, safety, and potential health benefits. Rigorous research ensures that products meet regulatory standards, instills consumer confidence, and enables informed decision-making regarding their use for health and wellness purposes. Other than production development, given Malacca's status as a tourist destination, he previously proposed setting up specialty stores at the factory to allow tourists to purchase products as souvenirs, achieving remarkable results. The third son, Low Chih Bin, who graduated from the Department of Economics and Trade in Taiwan, is responsible for exploring foreign markets and has become an indispensable right-hand man. Following in his father's footsteps, Poo Chin allows his children to exercise their own initiative in market development. He personally oversees financial matters and provides guidance when needed.

In terms of marketing strategies, Besfomec initially offered complimentary gifts with chicken essence purchases to introduce customers to their products, gradually building a loyal customer base through word of mouth and establishing a foothold in the market. They further developed the concept of health product gift hampers, packaging products in the form of gift hampers as a gifting option, exporting them to other countries. Despite tapping into the Malay market, Malaysia's market remains relatively small. Therefore, Besfomec expanded internationally by participating in trade exhibitions and venturing into markets such as Singapore, China, Hong Kong, Macau, and Vietnam. With their products certified as halal, they targeted the markets in Islamic countries such as the Middle East and Indonesia as well.

In line with its diversification efforts, Besfomec embarked on a strategic expansion plan, culminating in the establishment of the Besfomec Boutique Hotel in 2014. Situated in the heart of the vibrant Jonker Walk, the hotel occupies a historically significant space, formerly a double-story pre-World War II building dating back to 1936, originally housing the *Xin Chun Woh*. With the burgeoning tourism industry in the state of Malacca, both domestic and international visitors have surged, presenting immense opportunities for the hospitality sector, particularly in the culturally rich enclave of Jonker Walk. The transformation of this heritage site into a modern boutique hotel symbolizes their commitment to innovation and leveraging emerging trends in the tourism sector.

5.5.6 Ownership Pattern and Financial Performance

Besfomec Industries Sdn. Bhd. operates as a private limited company, primarily owned and managed by members of the founding family. The balance sheet and income statement for Besfomec are currently unavailable, likely due to the firm's status as a private entity, which may not be required to disclose all financial information details publicly. Alternatively, it could be a strategic decision to maintain confidentiality regarding financial performance.

The pattern of ownership reflects a typical structure seen in Chinese family businesses, where key stakeholders often hold dual roles as directors and major shareholders. This alignment of ownership and leadership underscores the family's commitment to maintaining control and preserving the company's legacy across generations. The company's main shareholders, who also serve as directors, include Low Poo Chin, the founder's eldest son, along with his brothers Lau Pak Siong and Lau Pak Kong. Additionally, Low Poo Chin's elder son, Low Chew Ping, and third son, Low Chih Pin, hold significant shares in the company. This concentration of ownership within the family ensures a strong sense of unity and continuity

Table 5.7 List of Shareholders of Besfomec Industries Sdn. Bhd.

Name	*Shares*	*Percentage*
Lau Chaim Ping	135,556	13,56%
Lau Kai Pin	80,555	8,06%
Lau Pak Kong	90,001	9,00%
Lau Pak Siong	100,001	10,00%
Lau Siong Ping	35,555	3,56%
Lau Xuan Pin	45,000	4,50%
Lau Zhen Bin	35,555	3,56%
Low Chew Ping	100,000	10,00%
Low Chih Pin	85,556	8,56%
Low Chung Ping	35,555	3,56%
Low Poo Chin	100,001	10,00%
Low Kian Ping	35,555	3,56%
Low Wee Peng	35,555	3,56%
Low Yong Pin	85,555	8,56%

Total Issued Shares: 1,000,000
Source: Companies Commission of Malaysia (SSM).

in decision-making, aligning with the traditional values of family and collective responsibility often associated with Chinese family businesses.

Moreover, the close familial ties extend to the next generation, with nephews Lau Kai Pin and Lau Chaim Ping also holding directorship roles and substantial shares in the company. Together, these family members collectively hold the majority of shares, consolidating their control over Besfomec's strategic direction and ensuring that the company's operations remain closely intertwined with the family's values and aspirations.

5.6 Case Study Five: Hei Hwang Food Industries (M) Sdn. Bhd.

5.6.1 Introduction

Founded in 1965 amid the vibrant streets of Ipoh, Perak, Hei Hwang Food Industries owned rich heritage and entrepreneurial spirit of the *Huizhou* Hakka Chinese. Specializing in the production and distribution of a diverse range of coffee, health beverages, and organic foods, Hei Hwang epitomizes the fusion of traditional wisdom and modern innovation. With a strong emphasis on quality and authenticity, the company has become synonymous with excellence in the realm of Chinese herbal remedies and gourmet delights.

Figure 5.7 Exterior View of Hei Hwang Food Industries (M) Sdn. Bhd. Factory. Photograph by the author.

Hei Hwang's market presence extends across Malaysia, Singapore, and China, serving a diverse clientele through strategic distribution channels such as Chinese medical halls, provision shops, organic stores, supermarkets, and overseas Chinese markets. As a family-owned business, Hei Hwang is currently led by the second generation, including Lee Hock Nee, CEO and founder, along with his wife Chan Sau Leng, and their sons Lee Haw Yuan and Lee Haw Hwang, who oversee various aspects of operations. Despite facing challenges, including those brought about by the COVID-19 pandemic, Hei Hwang remains committed to upholding its legacy of quality, innovation, and customer satisfaction, positioning itself as a trusted name in the global food and beverage market.

Hei Hwang Food Industries embodies a harmonious blend of tradition and innovation. This transformative journey reflects Hei Hwang's commitment to innovation and quality, transitioning from its origins in Chinese herbal drinks to becoming a trailblazer in the realm of unique Ipoh instant coffee, health supplements, and organic foods.

5.6.2 Stage One: Start-up

Hei Hwang Food Industries traces its origins to Ipoh, Perak, where Lee Hock Nee, a Hakka descent founder, established a traditional herbal shop[7] in 1965. As mentioned previously, the Hakka Chinese community in Malaysia has long been prominent in the remedies and herbal shop business, drawing from generations of tacit knowledge and ancient traditions. From this beginning, Lee Hock Nee's vision expanded beyond herbal remedies, leading to the inception of Hei Hwang Food Industries in 1975, a pioneering enterprise in coffee. Recognizing the refined tastes of Ipoh residents, Lee Hock Nee embarked on a quest to redefine coffee, thus giving birth to the renowned Hei Hwang brand.

According to traditional Chinese medicine (TCM) theory, black-colored foods are believed to contribute to health due to their nourishing and therapeutic properties. Black foods are typically rich in nutrients which help to eliminate free radicals, boost immunity, slow down aging, and provide protective effects on the cardiovascular and digestive systems. Additionally, TCM theory states that black foods nourish the kidneys and replenish the liver's essence and blood, promoting blood circulation and thereby assisting in maintaining a healthy balance in the body. Common black foods include black sesame seeds, black beans, black fungus, black goji berries, and black rice. This concept is reflected in the name "Hei Hwang," where "Hei" means black in Mandarin, symbolizing the emphasis on health and wellness through the consumption of black-colored foods.

Driven by a commitment to quality and innovation, Hei Hwang swiftly gained renown for its signature Ipoh white coffee, meticulously crafted from 100% locally sourced beans. Embracing technological advancements, the company introduced instant coffee powder, revolutionizing the way coffee was consumed. With an eye on global markets, Hei Hwang ventured into international trade, exporting its beloved white coffee to China following the country's open-door policy in the 1990s. This strategic move not only solidified Hei Hwang's position as a leader in the coffee market but also underscored the commitment to embracing new opportunities and reaching broader horizons. The sales in China were exceptional, with demand so high that Hei Hwang's white coffee was often sold out, demonstrating its immense popularity and widespread acclaim among Chinese consumers in China. As a result, Hei Hwang became a household name and a renowned brand of Nanyang white coffee, symbolizing the rich heritage and exquisite taste of traditional coffee culture.

In that era, traditional herbal shops were highly popular due to economic and social conditions. Many Chinese people did not have the means to afford medical treatment, so when they felt unwell, their recourse was to visit herbal shops to purchase simple medicinal herbs to boil into soups at home or to buy ready-made herbal teas from the shops. Therefore, there was a high demand for herbal tea shops. As society progressed, Western medicine gradually replaced the role of traditional Chinese medicine shops and herbal tea shops. Additionally, since herbal tea is a liquid and has a short shelf life, it is prone to spoilage. Leveraging the tacit knowledge of coffee powder production, Hei Hwang began to transform herbal tea formulas and medicinal herbs into powdered form to create instant health beverages. This not only reduced storage costs and opened new sales markets but it also laid the foundation for subsequent product development.

5.6.3 Stage Two: Expansion

Due to historical background, crossing borders was not a novel concept for Lee family, even before the era of globalization. Malaysian Chinese ancestors migrated from China, engaging in transnational trade, which ingrained a natural inclination toward international commerce. This cultural predisposition, coupled with a deep-seated entrepreneurial spirit, equipped the Lee family with the mindset necessary for global expansion.

The Lee family's successful venture into the global market with the iconic Hei Hwang brand of instant Ipoh coffee and health beverages exemplifies the strategic fusion of tacit knowledge and Chinese networks. Building upon their ancestral roots and leveraging historical ties, Hei Hwang capitalized on their understanding of traditional Chinese business practices, which often emphasized expansive perspectives and cross-border ventures. They faced numerous challenges when running their operations in China, but their extensive network of kinship ties in the region proved invaluable in navigating unfamiliar territories and overcoming obstacles.

Moreover, the Lee brothers' astute management involved assigning Lee Haw Yuan and a team of food technologists to manage overseas operations, ensuring seamless coordination between international suppliers and Malaysian processing facilities. By codifying their tacit knowledge and expertise, the Lee family streamlined the global supply chain, optimizing efficiency, and maintaining product excellence.

In their pursuit of global expansion, the Lee family recognized the inherent value of Chinese networks in navigating unfamiliar territories. Drawing upon historical precedents, they tapped into existing commercial networks to forge strategic partnerships and secure advantageous expansion opportunities. Furthermore, the enduring connections with their ancestral communities provided invaluable resources for business expansion. Leveraging these kinship and communal ties, the Lee family gained access to enhanced commercial networks, facilitating market penetration in China and Southeast Asia.

5.6.4 Stage Three: Maturity

As the mantle passed to the second generation, Lee Hock Nee's sons, Lee Haw Yuan and Lee Haw Hwang infused the company with fresh vigor and vision. Expanding beyond coffee, they diversified the product line to include an array of organic health foods and supplements. Venturing further, Hei Hwang embraced the burgeoning demand for health-conscious products, introducing a range of organic health foods including black sesame seed, instant pumpkin soup, detox cleansing powder, whole grains energy soup, and soybean powder.

Harnessing their entrepreneurial acumen, Haw Yuan and Haw Hwang strategically utilized land acquired in Guangdong, establishing a factory warehouse to meticulously select premium organic beans and seeds ingredients such as sesame seeds, oats, soybeans, ginger, and walnuts, and sent the ingredients to Malaysia for further processing. After completing the manufacturing process in Malaysia, the products are exported to the Chinese market. With this approach, Hei Hwang's supply chain forms a closed loop that the company can effectively control, encompassing every stage from sourcing raw materials, through manufacturing, to marketing and sales. This move not only ensured quality control but also facilitated the company's expansion into international markets, with dealership assignments in China and Singapore. Hei Hwang's journey from retailing to wholesaling reflects the embodiment of Chinese wisdom, leveraging tacit knowledge and expansive networks to drive strategic growth. Rooted in Ipoh, the first generation of Hei Hwang pioneered the production of instant Ipoh coffee series and health drinks, initially focusing on retail distribution channels such as convenience stores, sundry shops, vegetarian restaurants, mini-marts, and organic shops.

Transitioning from retailing to wholesaling marked a strategic shift for Hei Hwang, orchestrated by the second generation. Building upon the foundation laid by their predecessors, they expanded the product line to include health supplements and beverage supplements. With a keen understanding of the market and a commitment to innovation, Hei Hwang strategically distributed its products across Malaysia, Singapore, and China. By establishing local distributors in Malaysia and securing sole distributorships in China and Singapore, Hei Hwang capitalized on existing commercial networks and familial connections. This approach facilitated seamless expansion into new markets while maintaining a competitive edge.

Hei Hwang's strategic decision to assign Singapore as its main distributor in the overseas market exemplifies its astute understanding of consumer preferences and market dynamics. By capitalizing on Singapore's vibrant multicultural landscape and well-established distribution channels, Hei Hwang effectively taps into diverse consumer segments and expands its reach beyond national borders. The choice of Singapore as the main distributor reflects Hei Hwang's recognition of the city-state's status as a regional hub for commerce and cultural exchange. Singapore's Chinese medical halls, provision shops, and organic stores serve as ideal platforms for showcasing Hei Hwang's products, catering to consumers seeking traditional remedies and natural health solutions. This strategic placement allowed Hei Hwang to reach diverse consumer segments and tap into the growing demand for health-conscious products. Partnering with established retailers such as Sheng Siong stores and Mustafa further enhances Hei Hwang's visibility and accessibility. Targeting other overseas Chinese markets in Singapore underscores Hei Hwang's strategic focus on leveraging cultural affinity and diaspora networks. By catering to the preferences of these overseas communities, Hei Hwang strengthens its brand presence and fosters a sense of connection with consumers who share a common cultural heritage.

5.6.5 Stage Four: Diversification

Hei Hwang stands as a beacon of cultural fusion, seamlessly integrating Chinese heritage into the areas of halal and frozen food industries. Founded on the principles of quality and innovation, Hei Hwang's journey reflects the dynamic interplay between tradition and modernity in Malaysia's multiracial society. In Malaysia, a nation characterized by its diverse ethnic makeup, the concept of halal food holds immense cultural significance, particularly within the Muslim community. Recognizing this, Hei Hwang embarked on a strategic pivot, infusing its Chinese heritage with the halal ethos to cater to a broader audience while respecting Islamic dietary laws. This strategic move not only expanded its market reach but also fostered inclusivity within Malaysia's multicultural landscape.

By embracing halal certification from JAKIM Malaysia in 2021, Hei Hwang demonstrated its commitment to meeting the dietary requirements of Muslim consumers without compromising on the authenticity of its Chinese-inspired offerings. This harmonious integration of Chinese culinary traditions with halal principles not only enriches Malaysia's culinary tapestry but also accentuates the company's ethos of cultural respect and adaptation.

Central to Chinese culture is the concept of harmony: harmony within oneself, with others, and with the natural world. These principles guide Hei Hwang's emphasis on balance and moderation in its products, aligning with the traditional Chinese belief in the interconnectedness of mind, body, and spirit. Drawing from the rich legacy of Chinese herbal medicine, Hei Hwang's tacit knowledge encompasses centuries-old remedies and healing practices passed down through generations. This heritage forms the bedrock of the company's commitment to natural ingredients and holistic health solutions. Through its range of health supplements and beverages, Hei Hwang promotes the cultivation of vitality and longevity, echoing the Chinese belief in the importance of preventive care and lifestyle moderation.

Figure 5.8 Products of Hei Hwang. Photograph by the author.

Furthermore, Hei Hwang's foray into the frozen food industry signifies a strategic expansion driven by a deep understanding of consumer preferences and market trends. Leveraging its tacit knowledge of Chinese culinary techniques and flavor profiles, the company developed a range of frozen food products that resonate with both Malaysian and international palates. Hei Hwang's frozen food offerings reflect its commitment to culinary and continuous innovation.

However, navigating the complexities of Malaysia's multiracial society presents both challenges and opportunities. While the incorporation of halal practices broadens Hei Hwang's consumer base, it also requires stringent adherence to Islamic dietary guidelines, which may necessitate adjustments to traditional recipes and production processes. Additionally, maintaining cultural authenticity while appealing to diverse tastes requires a delicate balance that demands a deep understanding of local customs and preferences. By honoring its roots while embracing the evolving needs of a diverse consumer base, Hei Hwang epitomizes the spirit of culinary exploration and cross-cultural exchange in Malaysia's vibrant gastronomic landscape.

5.6.6 Ownership Pattern and Financial Performance

Hei Hwang Food Industries (M) Sdn. Bhd. is a private limited company with a share capital of 1,733,000 ordinary shares. The company participates in various aspects of the coffee and beverage industry, including manufacturing, wholesaling, retailing, exporting, importing, distributing, and dealing in a wide range of products. Lee Hock Nee, the founder and CEO, leads the company, along with other key directors and officers, including Chan Sau Leng, Lee Haw Yuan, and Lee Haw Hwang.

Table 5.8 Hei Hwang Food Industries (M) Sdn. Bhd. Balance Sheet, 2018–2022

(RM)	*2022*	*2021*	*2020*	*2019*	*2018*
Non-Current Assets	4,220,287	4,295,133	3,549,831	3,450,857	3,514,432
Current Assets	4,968,519	4,420,771	4,236,963	4,558,614	4,462,251
Non-Current Liabilities	310,579	410,876	477,444	799,097	899,073
Current Liabilities	3,037,163	2,993,951	2,205,841	2,504,616	2,419,602
Share Capital	1,733,000	1,733,000	1,733,000	1,733,000	1,733,000
Reserve	0	0	0	0	0
Retain Earning	4,108,064	3,578,077	3,370,509	2,972,758	2,925,008

Source: Companies Commission of Malaysia (SSM).

The ownership structure of Hei Hwang reflects a typical Chinese family business model, characterized by close familial ties and involvement in key management roles. The founders, Lee Hock Nee and his wife Chan Sau Leng, maintain significant ownership stakes in the company, holding 22.12% and 17.74% of the shares, respectively. Their sons, Lee Haw Yuan and Lee Haw Hwang, also hold directorial positions and substantial shares, with each owning 29.99% of the company's shares. This familial ownership structure aligns with traditional Chinese values of family unity and intergenerational continuity, where family members work together to build and sustain the business. It fosters a sense of loyalty, trust, and mutual support within the company, contributing to its long-term success and stability. Moreover, the distribution of shares among family members reflects a balance of power and responsibility, with each member having a stake in the company's performance and growth. This arrangement promotes accountability and collaboration, ensuring that decisions are made with the collective interests of the family and the business in mind.

Over the five years from 2018 to 2022, Hei Hwang showed steady growth and stability. Non-current assets, reflecting long-term investments, grew to RM4.22 million in 2022 despite minor fluctuations. Current assets consistently increased, reaching RM4.97 million, indicating strong liquidity and the ability to meet short-term obligations. On the liabilities side, non-current liabilities notably decreased from RM899,073 in 2018 to RM310,579 in 2022, highlighting effective long-term debt management.

Additionally, Hei Hwang has maintained a stable share capital of RM 1,733,000 throughout the five-year period, indicating consistency in the company's ownership structure. Retained earnings have steadily increased from RM 2,925,008 in 2018 to RM 4,108,064 in 2022, reflecting the company's profitability and ability to generate earnings over time. Despite economic uncertainties and challenges, Hei Hwang has exhibited resilience and prudent financial management, positioning itself as a reliable player in the food industry.

Hei Hwang's income statement from 2018 to 2022 shows consistent growth despite fluctuations. Revenue peaked in 2022 at RM10.96 million, reflecting sustained expansion. Profit before tax also rose to RM577,987 in 2022, up from RM372,392 in 2018. The COVID-19 pandemic caused a dip in revenue and profits

Table 5.9 Hei Hwang Food Industries (M) Sdn. Bhd. Income Statement, 2018–2022

(RM)	*2022*	*2021*	*2020*	*2019*	*2018*
Revenue	10,964,488	10,041,170	8,903,956	8,522,576	9,611,674
Profit/(loss) before tax	577,987	207,740	496,267	61,786	372,392
Profit/(loss) after tax	529,987	207,568	397,751	+47,750	294,463
Net dividend	0	0	0	0	0

Source: Companies Commission of Malaysia (SSM).

in 2020, highlighting industry challenges, but the company quickly rebounded. Hei Hwang's ability to maintain profitability during uncertain times displays its strong business model and strategic resilience.

5.7 Case Study Six: Kam Lun Tai (Loy Kee) Sdn. Bhd.

5.7.1 Introduction

Kam Lun Tai (Loy Kee) Sdn. Bhd. (KLT) stands as a beacon of culinary excellence, blending tradition with innovation to offer a diverse range of gastronomic delights deeply rooted in the Cantonese sub-dialect group. With a rich history spanning generations, KLT has evolved from its beginnings as a local dim sum eatery to a multifaceted culinary empire renowned for its exquisite offerings.

At the heart of KLT's success lies its unwavering commitment to quality and craftsmanship. Specializing in Hong Kong and Malaysian fusion style Dim Sum, KLT has mastered crafting delectable delicacies that tantalize the taste buds and evoke a sense of nostalgia. Building upon this foundation, KLT has expanded its product range to include mooncakes, pastries, Japanese Mochi, egg rolls, sauces, and luxurious noodles, each meticulously made to perfection.

Operating in a diverse market landscape, KLT has established a strong presence in both local and international markets. From its roots in Kuala Lumpur's bustling streets to its expansion into regional and global markets, KLT's offerings have captivated the palates of discerning food enthusiasts worldwide. With a focus on embracing technological advancements and exploring new culinary frontiers, KLT remains at the forefront of the industry.

From beginnings in hawker stall cooking to expanding to restaurant chains, food processing, and catering services, KLT's journey shows the enduring strength of cultural heritage and the potential of culinary innovation. With each bite of KLT's creations, we taste not just the flavors but also the wisdom passed down through generations.

5.7.2 Stage One: Start-up

In post-Kapitan Kuala Lumpur, the Cantonese became the dominant Chinese group, surpassing the Hakkas and shaping the city's cultural fabric. Their influence extended beyond language, with the Cantonese dialect becoming the common

Figure 5.9 Exterior View of Kam Lun Tai (Loy Kee) Shop. Photograph by the author.

tongue within the Chinese community. Cantonese culture also permeated daily life, particularly through cuisine. Known for its delicate flavors and meticulous preparation, Cantonese food became a staple of Malaysian life, each dish reflecting the community's rich history and resilience.

Lum Tuck Loy, driven by a relentless pursuit of perfection, embodied this cultural tradition. Coming from a humble background with six siblings, his passion for learning was constrained by poverty. At age 13, Lum began his entrepreneurial journey in the world of Cantonese cuisine as a kitchen apprentice. He worked at several establishments, mastering the art of dim sum, noodles, and mooncakes. Over time, Lum's dedication and skill earned him a prominent place in the industry.

Kam Lun Tai's origins date back to a -pre-World War II double-story shop on Jalan Imbi, where it began as a travel agency and Western restaurant owned by Lee Hau Shik (H.S. Lee) and other businessmen from Gaozhou, Guangdong Province. Kam Lun Tai also provided currency exchange services, helping Chinese immigrants send money back home. While Lum did not establish Kam Lun Tai, his pivotal role in transforming it into a renowned restaurant and mooncake brand solidified his place in Kuala Lumpur‘s culinary history. His contributions marked the rise of Cantonese cuisine and culture in the city.

In 1971, initially leased the ground floor space by H.S. Lee and his partners, Lum Tuck Loy took a significant leap forward by opening Loy Kee Hong Kong

Dim Sum Restaurant. Impressed by Lum's diligence and dedication, H.S. Lee and his partners eventually leased the entire ground floor to him. As Lum saved up money, H.S. Lee and his partners eventually allowed Lum to take over the shop entirely. KLT was born, a golden brand synonymous with the fusion of Hong Kong and Malaysian Cantonese styles. With a commitment to quality and a keen eye for innovation. This historical account underscores how shared origins and the dialect group based social network fostered greater opportunities for development during that era.

5.7.3 Stage Two: Expansion

When Lum first took over, he endured a decade of hardship, often sleeping for only about three hours a day. However, not all his time was spent toiling away in the shop making dumplings, dim sum, and mooncakes. Despite being in his early 20s, he was determined to succeed, driven by his entrepreneurial spirit and a desire to success. One of his most groundbreaking decisions was purchasing the first machine in the country for making pastries and mooncakes at an exhibition in Hong Kong. In the 1980s, mooncakes were handmade, and the demand often exceeded the supply. Lum realized the limitations of manual production and saw an opportunity to increase efficiency. He immediately ordered the machine and brought it back to Malaysia. Lum's foresight was evident in his embrace of automation technology. He pioneered the introduction of automated machinery for mooncakes production, revolutionizing the process with speed, hygiene, and stringent quality control measures, sparking emulation among competitors. This visionary approach not only revolutionized production methods but also highlighted his readiness to embrace innovation in an era dominated by manual labor. KLT became the first Malaysian mooncake company to introduce automation and computerized production processes, revolutionizing the industry.

While buying machines to produce food is commonplace today, it was a pioneering move back then. The consistent quality and increased output of KLT's mooncakes attracted attention from competitors, who soon followed suit. However, KLT had already established itself as a leader in the industry. For Lum, the essence of Chinese culture lies in its depth and richness, even within the seemingly small mooncake. It embodies values of loyalty, respect, and unity. Lum Tuck Loy, revered as *"Loy Go"*[8]in the culinary and business communities, had an extensive network ranging from ordinary folks to ministers and businessmen. The KLT brand, which he single-handedly elevated, became widely recognized within the Chinese community in Malaysia.

Lum Tuck Loy's extensive network, which spanned the Chinese diaspora and international business circles, played a crucial role in Kam Lun Tai's success and its tacit knowledge transformation. In the food industry, success often depends on strong relationships, and Lum's connections extended beyond the Chinese community to include individuals from Europe and America. These networks, built on mutual assistance, allowed Lum to leverage his political connections to promote culinary associations like The Malaysia Selangor and Federal Territory Ku Su

Figure 5.10 The Author with Lum Tuck Loy, Founder of the Business. Photograph by the author.

Shin Choong Hung Restaurant Association, while his associates benefited from the exposure, fulfilling their governmental roles and boosting tourism.

Lum embraced the "give and take" philosophy (取之社会，用之社会)[9], actively participating in industry associations to promote local Chinese cuisine and mentor future chefs. His strong network laid the foundation for his family business's success, as seen in how his children effectively utilized these connections to continue the growth of KLT.

5.7.4 Stage Three: Maturity

Over the years, KLT has received numerous accolades, including the Superbrand award in 2003 and the Golden Eagle Awards in 2014, reflecting its dedication to quality and excellence. KLT's product innovation stands out, with offerings such as Black Sesame Bamboo Charcoal 1 Yolk Mooncake, Crystalline Matcha Red Bean Mooncake, and Durian Mooncake, blending traditional and contemporary flavors. By incorporating local ingredients like pandan and durian, KLT highlights the unique Nanyang style in its creations. The company has also catered to health-conscious consumers by producing low-sugar mooncakes, meeting the preferences of younger generations and older adults.

Under Lum Tuck Loy's leadership, KLT thrived. The second generation, led by Lum's children Lum Wai Yee and Lum Kah Seng, expanded the business through food processing and product innovation. Armed with academic expertise and tacit knowledge, they modernized production, ensuring efficiency while preserving KLT's heritage. They introduced new products like Japanese Mochi, egg rolls, and sauces, responding to changing market demands. This generational transition was marked by a strong focus on research and development, leveraging accumulated knowledge of raw materials and production techniques to maintain consistency and excellence. Their commitment to continuous improvement helped KLT maintain its reputation for culinary creativity and innovation, securing its position at the forefront of the food industry.

5.7.5 Stage Four: Diversification

Over the years, KLT evolved by embracing innovation while maintaining its cultural heritage. Under the second-generation leadership of Lum Wai Yee and Lum Kah Seng, KLT expanded its presence. Lum Wai Yee led the establishment of Guardian Catering Service, enhancing the brand's influence in the culinary landscape. Lum Kah Seng propelled KLT Food Industries to new heights, earning significant certifications like Halal and ISO 9001:2000 for mooncake and omochi production. These achievements facilitated the global distribution of KLT products, from Australia and Singapore to Vietnam and New Zealand, particularly in Chinatowns around the world. Despite its international expansion, KLT stayed true to its roots, preserving its commitment to tradition while diversifying its offerings with mooncakes, pastries, and dim sum.

The success of KLT can be attributed to the intricate dynamics of a Chinese family business and the tacit knowledge passed down through generations. Kam Lun Tai (Loy Kee) Sdn. Bhd. anchors a culinary empire that includes Kam Lun Tai Restaurant Sdn. Bhd., Kam Lun Tai Cake House, and Kam Lun Tai Dried Meat-Dried Meat Floss, all contributing to the brand's legacy with Cantonese delicacies. Lum Tuck Loy's journey, from a humble hawker stall operator to a respected restaurant owner, reflects the classic Chinese family business narrative of perseverance, hard work, and a strong connection to tradition.

As KLT transitions into its second generation, Lum Wai Yee and Lum Kah Seng carry forward their father's entrepreneurial legacy, blending traditional values with modern business practices to expand and innovate. This seamless transition ensures the continuity of KLT's essence and reflects the familial pride inherent in Chinese family businesses. The involvement of Lum's granddaughter, with experience in a Japanese food company in Taiwan, also promises a new chapter for KLT, potentially extending its legacy into future generations while preserving the family's rich culinary heritage.

5.7.6 Ownership Pattern and Financial Performance

KLT, a private limited company, exemplifies the core values of a Chinese family business, grounded in strong relationships and shared values. KLT's foundation in

Table 5.10 Kam Lun Tai (Loy Kee) Sdn. Bhd. Balance Sheet, 2019–2023

(RM)	*2023*	*2022*	*2021*	*2020*	*2019*
Non-Current Assets	18,600	11,495	57,252	109,214	163,568
Current Assets	308,374	234,264	126,563	167,313	263,456
Non-Current Liabilities	2,859	0	3,546	4,335	13,509
Current Liabilities	487,994	451,673	426,685	502,423	422,342
Share Capital	100	100	100	100	100
Reserve	0	0	0	0	0
Retain Earning	-163,979	-206,014	-246,516	-230,331	-8,927

Source: Companies Commission of Malaysia (SSM).

Table 5.11 Kam Lun Tai (Loy Kee) Sdn. Bhd. Income Statement, 2019–2023

(RM)	*2023*	*2022*	*2021*	*2020*	*2019*
Revenue	1,641,204,00	1,155,406,00	985,762,00	1,158,665,00	1,686,149,00
Profit/(loss) before tax	48,920,00	37,012,00	-16,974,00	-230,934,00	68,328,.00
Profit/(loss) after tax	42,035,00	40,502,00	-16,185,00	-221,404,00	48,417,00
Net dividend	0.00	0.00	0.00	0.00	0.00

Source: Companies Commission of Malaysia (SSM).

both the restaurant and bakery confectionery sectors is intertwined with kinship and close friendships. The company is led by Lum Wai Yee, the founder's daughter, and Yap Soon Choi, a close friend of the founder. Both directors have deep ties to the company's vision and founder. The shareholder structure reflects a close-knit network, with significant stakes held by individuals connected to the family. Both Lee Pooi Lin, the founder's wife, and Lum Wai Yee hold 20%, ensuring family involvement. Lim Choon Fatt, the founder's son-in-law, has 11%, reinforcing family integration in the business. Additionally, close friends of the founder, including Kow Mun Seng, Lim Kin Hua, and Yap Soon Choi, collectively hold significant shares, showcasing the importance of trust and friendship in KLT's development.

Between 2019 and 2023, KLT's balance sheet reveals notable changes. Non-current assets decreased from RM 163,568 in 2019 to RM 18,600 in 2023, likely due to asset depreciation or divestment. Current assets fluctuated, peaking at RM 308,374 in 2023, reflecting shifts in short-term investments or inventory strategies. Non-current liabilities dropped from RM 13,509 in 2019 to RM 2,859 in 2023, indicating successful debt repayment. However, current liabilities rose significantly, reaching RM 487,994 in 2023, could be due to rising short-term obligations or operational challenges.

Despite financial fluctuations, KLT's share capital remained steady at RM 100 from 2019 to 2023, signaling stable ownership. However, retained earnings showed volatility, with losses deepening from -RM 8,927 in 2019 to -RM 163,979 in 2023, reflecting ongoing profitability challenges. The lack of reserves further highlights the need for better financial management. The income statement shows declining revenue from RM 1,686,149 in 2019 to RM 1,641,204 in 2023, suggesting difficulties in maintaining sales. However, the company achieved a profit before tax in 2023, indicating a recovery from earlier losses, likely due to improved cost control or strategic adjustments.

KLT returned to profitability in 2023, but the profit after tax was modest at RM 42,035, indicating ongoing financial challenges. The absence of dividends throughout the period suggests a strategy of reinvesting profits or retaining earnings to bolster reserves. Overall, KLT's income statement highlights the need for adaptability and prudent management in navigating market volatility.

5.8 Summary

This chapter opens by identifying six key Chinese family-owned SMEs, detailing how these enterprises have used innovation to enhance their competitive advantage. For instance, companies such as Besfomec Industries Sdn. Bhd. have leveraged partnerships with foreign firms to develop new products, while London Biscuits Berhad advanced food technology through R&D for export-oriented products. Similarly, Hei Hwang Food Industries has upgraded its production capabilities, introducing health beverages like Ipoh coffee and organic drinks. The study highlights the role of tacit knowledge, innovation, and strategic partnerships in these companies' growth.

The industry background section traces the roots of Malaysian cuisine back to ancient times, linking its development to trade routes and colonial influences. The food industry, as a key contributor to Malaysia's economy, has evolved with the help of SMEs that have embraced modern technologies and market trends. However, challenges such as urbanization, environmental concerns, and globalization continue to shape the industry's landscape.

Following the background, the chapter presents case studies of the six companies mentioned, starting with London Biscuits Berhad. The company's journey from a small family-owned enterprise to a publicly listed company is documented, displaying its expansion through the acquisition of other food companies, such as Kinos Food Industries and Khee San Berhad. London Biscuits' diversification into new product lines, like confectionery and canned foods, reflects its adaptive strategies in a competitive market. However, recent financial struggles led to the sale of assets and a winding-up petition, marking a significant downturn in the company's history.

Other companies featured in this chapter include King's Confectionery Sdn. Bhd., which expanded from a small *kopitiam* business to a well-established brand known for its baked goods. The company's emphasis on innovation and franchising helped it cater to a broader market, including rural and urban areas, while adapting to cultural preferences through halal certification.

Leong Hup International Berhad and Baker's Cottage also demonstrate the evolution of a family business through vertical integration and diversification. Originally a poultry farming business, Leong Hup expanded into food processing and bakery retail chains, utilizing tacit knowledge from its farming operations to create new business opportunities in the confectionery sector.

Besfomec Industries and Hei Hwang Food Industries represent businesses that have successfully merged traditional Chinese medicine with modern technology to develop health-oriented products. Besfomec's transformation into a corporate entity and Hei Hwang's venture into international markets highlight their growth strategies through innovation, market diversification, and strategic partnerships.

In conclusion, this chapter provides a comprehensive analysis of how Chinese family businesses in the food industry have sustained growth through innovation, focusing on how these businesses have evolved through organizational changes and the transfer of tacit knowledge across generations.

Notes

1 The Chinese proverb translates to 'repair the roof before it rains,' which means to take precautions and plan ahead to avoid potential problems. Rooted in Chinese thought, it underscores the value of foresight, responsibility, and prudent preparation to ensure future stability and success, particularly in both personal life and business.

2 The phrase translates to 'to cater to someone's preferences or tastes.' It reflects the understanding of human nature and the importance of adapting one's actions or offerings to meet the desires and expectations of others. This concept is significant in Chinese culture, particularly in business and interpersonal relationships, where building rapport and fostering goodwill are essential for success.

3 The phrase translates to "Those who know when to fight and when not to fight are victorious." This concept emphasizes the importance of discernment and strategic thinking in conflict situations. Rooted in Sun Tzu's The Art of War, it highlights that true wisdom lies not just in the ability to engage in battle, but in understanding when to act and when to seek peace, a principle applicable in both military strategy and everyday decision-making.

4 The business name translates to 'Apricot Spring Harmony,' symbolizing renewal, beauty and peace of nature.

5 Traditional Chinese Medicine (TCM) is a comprehensive system of healthcare that has been practiced for thousands of years in China. It encompasses various modalities such as acupuncture, herbal medicine, dietary therapy, massage (推拿), and exercise (气功). TCM views the body as a holistic system and seeks to restore balance and harmony to the body's energies (气) and bodily functions. TCM involves a deeper understanding of the principles and practices of traditional Chinese medicine, including diagnosis and treatment techniques, which may not be available in a typical herbal shop.

6 In various Asian cuisines, particularly in Chinese culinary traditions, snakehead fish is prized for its firm texture and mild flavor. It is often used in soups and stews and is believed to have health benefits, such as promoting vitality and recovery from illness. In some cultures, it is also associated with auspiciousness, making it a popular choice for celebratory dishes.

7 A traditional herbal shop and a traditional Chinese medical hall both offer traditional Chinese herbal remedies, but they often differ in scope and focus. Traditional Chinese

Medical halls often provide a range of holistic healthcare services, including herbal consultations, acupuncture, cupping therapy, and moxibustion. Practitioners at medical halls are trained in traditional Chinese medicine (TCM) and can offer personalized treatment plans based on individual health needs. Herbal shops typically focus solely on the sale of herbal products and may not offer additional healthcare services. Customers can purchase raw herbs and herbal remedies for home use without the need for consultation or professional advice.

8 In Cantonese Chinese community, the seniors are usually addressed in kinship terms by others such as *go* (elder brother), *suk* (uncle) and *ze* (elder sister). The juniors are referred to as *zai* (son), *mui* (younger sister) or *neoi* (daughter).

9 The phrase translates to "take from society and give back to society." This philosophy emphasizes the reciprocal relationship between individuals and the community, highlighting the importance of social responsibility and mutual support. It underscores the idea that while individuals benefit from societal resources and opportunities, they also have an obligation to contribute positively to the community, fostering a sense of interconnectedness and collective well-being. This concept is often invoked in discussions of ethical business practices and social entrepreneurship in Chinese culture.

6 Ethnic Chinese Businesses in the Plastic Industry

The evolution of Chinese family businesses in the plastic manufacturing sector from 1929 to 1988 highlights key shifts in industry dynamics. During the immediate post-colonial period, infrastructure investments and fiscal incentives primarily benefited MNCs (multinational corporations) under ISI (import substitution industrialization) policies. By the 1960s, FDI accounted for 50% of total manufacturing sector investments. The influx of MNCs spurred domestic demand for value-added products, particularly in high-quality parts for knowledge-intensive industries. Tacit knowledge in this sector, whether embodied or innovation-driven, evolved differently. Most plastic manufacturing firms struggled to retain and develop the founders' tacit knowledge due to rapid technological changes, making it difficult to build upon original expertise. As a result, the products typically produced today differ significantly from the originals. However, exceptions exist in firms like SKP Resources Berhad, LH Plus Sdn. Bhd., and Syarikat Perniagaan Kemajuan, which operate in sectors like PVC industrial products, housewares, and brush manufacturing. This chapter provides a detailed chronological analysis of these companies, showing that only a few firms manage to successfully retain and build upon their founders' tacit knowledge in the evolving plastics industry.

6.1 Industry Background

Malaysia's plastic industry exemplifies the nation's economic strength and resource utilization. With roots linked to its abundant petroleum resources, the sector has become a key contributor to Malaysia's economy, significantly boosting export revenue (Malaysia Crude Oil: Exports, 1980–2024 | CEIC Data, n.d.). The industry began in the 1960s, when Malaysia leveraged its petroleum resources to drive economic development. As a global leader in natural gas and petroleum exports, Malaysia built a robust petrochemical sector, forming the foundation for its plastic industry (Lebdioui, 2022). This growth attracted both local enterprises and multinational corporations to establish manufacturing plants producing a wide range of plastic products (Yew & Gomez, 2014). By the 1960s, fewer than 100 plastics companies operated in Malaysia, primarily small-scale businesses serving

DOI: 10.4324/9781032705842-6

the domestic market (Othman Khairuddin & Yeoh, 1986). During this period, production focused on household and consumer goods.

The concentration of the Chinese population in urban centers like Kuala Lumpur, coupled with their expertise in tin mining, rubber processing, and the iron industry, gave them a comparative advantage in the plastics sector. The rapid growth of family-owned plastics manufacturing enterprises began in the late 1970s, driven by Malaysia's robust economic expansion. This growth was bolstered by the influx of multinational corporations (MNCs) from Japan and the U.S., which created a higher demand for high-quality precision parts (Felker, 2003; Hiratsuka, 2016). Among Southeast Asian nations, Malaysia and Brunei are both rich in petroleum resources. However, as discussed in the previous chapter, Brunei's smaller land area, limited population, and scarcity of skilled labor made Malaysia the preferred choice for MNCs.

In the 1990s, Malaysia's electronics and plastics industries underwent a transformation. Outsourcing and Malaysia's emergence as a regional hub for high-end electronics shifted the focus from component manufacturing to industrial electronics (Ernst, 2004; Liang & Lean, 2024). This development led to the expansion of new services such as integrated circuit design and testing. Large procurement contracts in plastics manufacturing awarded by MNCs increasingly required companies to have proven technology and established products. Before Malaysia developed its petrochemical industry, most plastic resin was imported to meet growing market demand.

To strengthen its plastics sector, Malaysia implemented favorable policies that attracted significant foreign investment. The industry thrived due to factors such as abundant feedstock, robust infrastructure, and competitive costs. These advantages drew investments from Japan and the U.S. (Tanaka & Kenney, 1996), boosting Malaysia's exports, with key markets being the European Union, ASEAN (Association of Southeast Asian Nations), and Japan. The Comprehensive and Progressive Agreement for Trans-Pacific Partnership (CPTPP) further expanded export opportunities for Malaysia's plastics manufacturing industry.

The packaging segment dominates Malaysia's plastics sector, primarily supporting the semiconductor and electronics industries. However, many companies opted to resell international products rather than risk bidding for tenders. Malaysian plastics manufacturers emerged from the MNC ecosystem, which initially fostered a strong network of Original Equipment Manufacturing (OEM) suppliers. Despite this supportive environment, many SMEs remained OEM suppliers and did not transition to original design manufacturing (ODM) or original brand manufacturing (OBM) due to barriers like insufficient R&D investment and workforce challenges. With increasing competition from lower-cost countries like China and Vietnam, Malaysian manufacturers have shifted focus toward value-added and high-quality production.

This chapter will examine three prominent Chinese family-owned businesses in Malaysia's plastics industry: LH Plus Sdn. Bhd., SKP Resources Berhad, and Syarikat Perniagaan Kemajuan International Sdn. Bhd.

Figure 6.1 Exterior View of LH Plus Sdn. Bhd. Factory. Photograph by the author.

6.2 Case Study Seven: LH Plus Sdn. Bhd.

6.2.1 Introduction

LH Plus specializing in plastic injection molding, exemplifies the entrepreneurial spirit of the Chen family, renowned for their expertise in the manufacturing industry spanning generations. Nestled within the bustling city of Kuala Lumpur, LH Plus caters to a diverse clientele across various sectors including food, healthcare, medical, electrical, and automotive industries. With a focus on producing high-quality plastic goods, the company has carved a niche for itself as a trusted OEM manufacturer for esteemed brands such as Mattel, Tupperware, and Rubbermaid.

Led by a multi-generational of family members, LH Plus embraces a culture of innovation and adaptability. From the pioneering leadership of Tony Chen in 1969 to the astute guidance of third-generation CEO, Callum Chen, the company has continually evolved to meet the ever-changing demands of the market. Moreover, the involvement of the fourth generation, represented by Caryn Chen and Clement Chen, signals a commitment to diversification, sustainability and growth in an increasingly competitive landscape.

Amid global challenges and opportunities, LH Plus remains poised for continued success, driven by a steadfast dedication to excellence, a tradition of familial collaboration, and a forward-thinking approach to business. With a solid foundation built on decades of experience and a relentless pursuit of innovation, LH Plus stands ready to embrace the future and redefine the standards of plastic manufacturing excellence.

6.2.2 Stage One: Start-up

LH Plus was founded by the late Chen Kow Fatt, a Henghua Chinese in Kuala Lumpur around 1947 after the Japanese Occupation, where it started as "Lee Huat," a bicycle repair workshop specializing metal parts for bicycle stands. The Henghua people's engagement in the transportation industry in Malaysia can be attributed to historical and economic factors. Historically, the engagement of Henghua people in the transportation industry in Malaya stems from their arrival later than other sub-dialect groups, which resulted in many industries already being occupied. This situation prompted Henghua individuals to seek new opportunities, leading them to become rickshaw pullers. As time progressed, they gradually transitioned to becoming key players in the transportation industry. The transportation industry offers various opportunities for entrepreneurship, with many Henghua individuals establishing their own businesses, such as taxi services or logistics companies.

Over the next two decades, the business steadily grew. In 1969, Kow Fatt's elder son, the late Tony Chen Kwok Ming took over the reins of the family business and relocated it to Kepong. When the demand for bicycles declined due to economic development and improvements in the transportation industry, the family decided to pivot their business toward plastics manufacturing. Instead of staying in the same industry and transitioning to manufacturing motorcycle or automobile parts, they chose the plastics industry for its higher potential and lower capital requirements. Leveraging their tacit knowledge, the shift to plastics was a strategic and realistic choice, especially given the promising opportunities as first-mover in the burgeoning plastics sector at that time. Under Tony Chen's leadership, LH Plus shifted its focus to manufacturing plastic housewares and catering to customization orders from local multinational corporations (MNCs).

This period saw significant growth and development, with Lee Huat becoming the main supplier for producing innovative plastic wares targeted toward other brands during the 1980s and 1990s. This strategic shift propelled Lee Huat into prominence, positioning it as a primary supplier of innovative plastic wares for Nestle, Milo, and Glaxo Smith Kline, and catering to renowned brands OEM manufacturing such as Mattel, Tupperware, Rubbermaid. This era coincided with the rise in popularity of Tupperware-style products, further propelling LH Plus's success.

6.2.3 Stage Two: Expansion

In 1990, LH Plus embarked on a transformative journey by expanding beyond its origins as a bicycle repair workshop and entering the Australian market with its housewares under the 'LH' brand. This venture marked the company's evolution into an export-based houseware production firm, generating additional revenue and offering critical insights into cross-border trade. By focusing on procedural knowledge and detailed information in international business dealings, LH Plus steadily built its global presence. The company actively participated in international conferences and exhibitions, aided by the Malaysia External Trade Development Corporation (MATRADE), furthering its knowledge base and industry connections. Collaborating with international clients for product development and obtaining ISO and other quality certifications strengthened LH Plus's reputation as a premier supplier to global multinational conglomerates.

Recognizing the importance of technology in enhancing productivity and quality, LH Plus invested significantly in smart automation, supported by the Malaysian Investment Development Authority (MIDA) through initiatives like the Domestic Investment Strategic Fund (DISF), Accelerated Capital Allowance (ACA), Smart Automation Grant (SAG), and Industry4WRD schemes. This allowed the company to restructure its plastic technology, reducing workforce needs while increasing output. The strategic implementation of automation not only improved efficiency but also positioned LH Plus as an industry leader in innovation.

In October 2000, LH Plus faced a major setback when a devastating fire destroyed its factory, leaving the company under-insured and with a backlog of orders. Despite the challenges, the leadership remained resilient, seizing the opportunity to restructure. With support from bankers, suppliers, customers, and team members, LH Plus rebuilt a larger, more advanced factory in Shah Alam by 2002. This new facility, equipped with cutting-edge machinery, allowed the company to continue producing high-quality housewares, further solidifying its market position. LH Plus's ability to transform a crisis into an opportunity for growth and expansion underscored its resilience and commitment to excellence.

6.2.4 Stage Three: Maturity

By 2007, under the leadership of third-generation CEO Callum Chen Kok Seng, LH Plus continued its journey of modernization and expansion. Callum, who joined the family business as an apprentice in 1971 after completing his secondary education, initially worked as a factory operator and technician before moving into sales and marketing. Eventually, he took over the company's management and introduced Western management practices to professionalize and streamline its operations. Since becoming CEO in 1998, Callum has overseen LH Plus's transition from Original Equipment Manufacturing (OEM) to Original Design Manufacturing (ODM) and Original Brand Manufacturing (OBM), significantly enhancing its role in the plastics industry.

Callum's influence extends beyond LH Plus. He served as President of the Malaysian Plastics Manufacturers Association (MPMA) from 1998 to 2004 and remains its Honorary President. He also chairs the Malaysian Plastics Design

Centre (MPDC), promoting a design culture within the plastics sector. As Secretary General of the Asia Plastics Forum (APF), he leads a coalition of 12 member countries, fostering collaboration and knowledge exchange within the industry. His involvement with the Global Plastics Alliance, which includes organizations like the American Chemistry Council and Plastics Europe, allows LH Plus to stay competitive globally by leveraging market insights and resources.

Callum champions sustainable growth for mid-tier companies through strategic alliances and knowledge-sharing initiatives, driving continuous learning and innovation. He is also an advocate for changing public perceptions about plastics, actively dispelling myths about the material's safety. Through talks and forums, he educates the public on advancements in plastic manufacturing technology, ensuring plastics are viewed as safe and sustainable for everyday use.

Nicknamed "Fo Chieh Tau" (the train's front carriage), Callum is recognized for his relentless drive and leadership in pushing both LH Plus and the broader plastics industry forward. His commitment extends beyond profit, as he actively works to improve the industry's reputation and inspire the next generation of entrepreneurs.

6.2.5 Stage Four: Diversification

In 2008, LH Plus diversified by establishing Clover Design and Halo+ Agency, consultancy firms managed by Callum Chen's children (Caryn and Clement). These ventures allowed the family to utilize their design expertise and tap into new markets, showcasing their ability to leverage tacit knowledge for innovation and growth. Caryn, as Sales and Marketing Manager of Clover Design, focuses on expanding LH Plus's premium and gift division by forming new partnerships and enhancing the brand's presence. Meanwhile, Clement, as Product Development Manager at Halo+ Agency, drives forward LH Plus's design initiatives, incorporating advanced technologies to create innovative products.

LH Plus produces a wide range of items, including food storage containers, water bottles, household organizers, and medical products. Exporting 90% of its output to markets in the USA, Japan, Germany, Australia, and Asia, the company serves as the core of its divisions: Halo+ Agency provides design consultation, and Clover Design handles the premium and gift division. LH Plus remains focused on global expansion, targeting leading multinational conglomerates while also strengthening its domestic presence. The company is also committed to corporate social responsibility (CSR), contributing to various community needs.

One of the company's key strengths is its long-standing workforce, with many employees having served for over a decade, including one who has been with LH Plus for more than 40 years. This reflects the effectiveness of the company's business strategy and management style. Evolving from a bicycle repair workshop to a global leader in plastic household products, LH Plus demonstrates its adaptability and dedication to quality, innovation, and design excellence, further solidifying its presence in the competitive global marketplace.

6.2.6 Ownership Pattern and Financial Performance

LH Plus Sdn. Bhd. is a private limited company operating under the legal framework of being limited by shares. Established with a core focus on manufacturing plastic injection molding goods, LH Plus caters to a diverse array of industries including food, healthcare & medical, electrical, and automotive sectors. The company's share capital comprises a total of 5,000,000 ordinary shares, indicating a solid foundation for growth and investment.

At the helm of LH Plus's leadership are a team of dedicated directors and officers who steer the company toward its strategic objectives. Callum Chen serves as both the manager and director of the company, leveraging his expertise and vision to drive operational excellence and strategic growth initiatives. Joining him on the board of directors are Chen Zhilunn and Ng Chee Yaw, each bringing valuable insights and experience to guide LH Plus's decision-making processes and corporate governance practices.

Over the past five years, LH Plus has shown financial fluctuations. Non-current assets decreased slightly from RM44.49 million in 2021 to RM41.85 million in 2022 but remain significantly higher than in 2018, suggesting long-term investment for growth. Current assets fluctuated, rising from RM39.51 million in 2021 to RM50.72 million in 2022, indicating enhanced liquidity and potential expansion efforts.

LH Plus's non-current liabilities have trended upward, indicating increased reliance on long-term financing for growth. Meanwhile, current liabilities decreased from RM32.10 million in 2021 to RM27.59 million in 2022, reflecting better management of short-term obligations. The share capital has remained stable at RM5 million, and the company consistently held zero reserves. Retained earnings peaked at RM42.13 million in 2022, highlighting strong profitability and reinvestment potential. Despite fluctuations in some metrics, LH Plus remains financially stable with growth prospects.

From 2018 to 2022, LH Plus showed steady growth in revenue, increasing from RM41.39 million to RM59.79 million, indicating consistent business expansion and market share gains. Profits before and after tax also improved, reflecting effective cost management and operational efficiency. While net dividends fluctuated,

Table 6.1 LH Plus Sdn. Bhd. Balance Sheet, 2018–2022

(RM)	*2022*	*2021*	*2020*	*2019*	*2018*
Non-Current Assets	41,853,666	44,486,396	46,485,571	34,352,506	27,332,413
Current Assets	50,718,736	39,506,038	42,244,736	40,875,493	36,762,894
Non-Current Liabilities	17,852,346	7,925,061	6,202,030	2,699,840	3,498,650
Current Liabilities	27,592,045	32,104,512	36,176,534	28,073,201	14,655,522
Share Capital	5,000,000	5,000,000	5,000,000	5,000,000	5,000,000
Reserve	0	0	0	0	0
Retain Earning	42,128,011	38,962,861	41,351,743	39,454,958	40,941,135

Source: Companies Commission of Malaysia (SSM).

Table 6.2 LH Plus Sdn. Bhd. Income Statement, 2018–2022

(RM)	*2022*	*2021*	*2020*	*2019*	*2018*
Revenue	59,787,522	62,716,231	60,904,030	46,125,094	41,392,300
Profit/(Loss) Before Tax	6,447,285	2,480,035	3,104,427	873,065	687,397
Profit/(Loss) After Tax	6,165,150	1,607,118	2,528,785	313,823	256,185
Net Dividend	-3,000,000	-3,996,000	-632,000	-1,800,000	-12,000,000

Source: Companies Commission of Malaysia (SSM).

including negative values after 2018, this likely reflects a strategy to reinvest profits for future growth. Overall, LH Plus's financial performance demonstrates positive revenue trends, enhanced profitability, and a focus on long-term sustainability.

6.3 Case Study Eight: SKP Resources Berhad

6.3.1 Introduction

SKP Resources Berhad (SKP) stands as a titan in the realm of plastics contract manufacturing, boasting over half century of unparalleled expertise within the electrical and electronics plastics industry. This part explores the illustrious journey of SKP, tracing its beginnings as Sin Kwang Plastics to its status as a public-listed company on the main board of the Bursa Malaysia.

SKP originated as a plastic injection workshop in Singapore, initially focusing on the production of plastic household products. Transitioning to Johor and rebranding as Vital Conglomerate Sdn Bhd., the company expanded its operations and diversified its portfolio to cater to a broader market. Subsequently, in 2002, the company solidified its position as a key player in the industry. SKP capitalized on opportunities such as the acquisition of a License Manufacturing Warehouse (LMW) and participation in the ASEAN Free Trade Area (AFTA) to enhance its business prospects. This shift marked the second generation of leadership, characterized by a commitment to industry diversification and sustainable growth.

SKP's ascendancy to prominence is attributed to its broad-based expertise and full-service capabilities. From precision mold design and fabrication to meticulous finishing processes and final assembly, SKP sets the bar high in a fiercely competitive marketplace. It has emerged as the preferred supplier for an extensive and diverse clientele, spanning continents and renowned MNCs and OEM. The company's sterling reputation and strategic positioning have cemented its status as the go-to partner for all plastics and contract manufacturing needs. Notable clients include industry titans such as Sharp, Pioneer, Dyson, Sony, and Panasonic, among others.

6.3.2 Stage One: Start-up

The story of SKP Resources Berhad is one of remarkable evolution and relentless pursuit of excellence. The Gan family, leveraging their hands-on experience from

Figure 6.2 Exterior View of SKP Resources Berhad. Photograph by the author.

the pawn business, ventured into the plastics manufacturing industry with a keen understanding of market dynamics and operational efficiency. This strategic shift allowed them to apply their business acumen to a new sector, from its modest origins as a plastic injection workshop, to its current stature as a global leader in plastics manufacturing.

In the 1960s, SKP commenced its journey as Syarikat Sin Kwang Plastic, primarily catering to plastic housewares. Mostly working on same repeated orders of local consumption. Founded by Gan Kim Huat, a Hokkien Chinese, the business started as a plastics injection workshop in Singapore. However, recognizing the advantages of lower operational costs and more expansive land availability in Johor, Gan relocated the operations there and focused on plastic housewares and light industry parts manufacturing.

Living in Johor Bahru, an area with a high density of Chinese populations, Gan was acutely aware of the negative stereotypes associated with "Chinaman Business"[1]. Determined to dispel these prejudices, he worked intensively to eliminate the Chinese characteristics from his family business. This involved fostering a culture of integrity, fairness, and quality, which became the cornerstone of SKP's ethos and contributed significantly to its longstanding reputation and success.

6.3.3 Stage Two: Expansion

Policy that has positively affected SKP is the implementation of the foreign business culture such as Look East policy (LEP), has resulted in an important structural shift within the family firm where Japanese model of organization, technical or training programs, work ethics, cultural influence, education and MNCs, are promoted. SKP cultivated the Japanese *takumi* spirit, which emphasizes meticulous craftsmanship and dedication to quality. This cultural shift transformed the working environment and instilled a commitment to excellence and continuous improvement.

The cultivation of the Japanese *takumi* spirit at SKP stands in stark contrast to the negative stereotypes associated with "Chinaman Business." While the latter is often characterized by opportunism, profit-centric approaches, and a lack of emphasis on quality, the *takumi* spirit embodies principles of meticulous craftsmanship, dedication to excellence, and a deep-seated commitment to delivering superior products and services. This cultural shift within SKP not only reshapes the working culture but also redefines the company's identity, emphasizing integrity, innovation, and collaboration over outdated stereotypes.

By embracing Japanese manufacturing technology, SKP underwent a transformative journey, emerging as a prominent plastic OEM player in the market. This strategic shift not only bolstered their technical prowess but also cultivated enduring partnerships with Japanese MNCs. The incorporation of Japanese business practices and technologies proved instrumental in enhancing operational efficiency, elevating product quality, and ultimately, fostering greater customer satisfaction. Consequently, SKP solidified its position as the preferred partner for Japanese firms and other global clients, embodying a commitment to excellence and innovation in the competitive landscape of plastics manufacturing.

6.3.4 Stage Three: Maturity

Gan Poh San, son of the founder, contributes significantly to the growth of SKP Resources Berhad. After graduating with a Bachelor of Arts (Honours) in Accounting and Finance from Staffordshire University and a Master of Science in Finance from Imperial College Management School in 1998, that same year, he joined SKP as a management trainee. To enhance his expertise, Poh San studied Japanese language and plastic engineering at Kai Japanese School and Nissei Plastics School in Japan. His fluency in Japanese has strengthened SKP's relationships with Japanese multinational clients, giving the company a competitive edge in securing and maintaining international contracts. This linguistic proficiency facilitates smoother negotiations, builds deeper client relationships, and improves the company's understanding of cultural nuances.

The importance of linguistic adaptability in business is deeply rooted in Malaysian Chinese history, where different dialect groups often conducted business by speaking each other's dialects. Poh San's ability to speak Japanese reflects this tradition and enhances SKP's international collaboration. The company's strategic partnership with Audio Pioneer Visual underscores its rising reputation in the audiovisual sector, further establishing its global presence.

At the turn of the millennium, SKP shifted its focus toward Japanese multinationals in the semiconductor industry, reflected in its partnership with Vital Conglomerate in 2001. This pivot, driven by lessons from past experiences, was supported by Gan Poh Ling, Poh San's sister, who emphasized continuous improvement and technological adaptation. Poh Ling holds a Bachelor of Arts (Honours) in Business Administration from South Bank University, London, and a Master of Science in Information Management and Finance from the University of Westminster, London.

Under the leadership of the first generation and the second-generation's enthusiasm—led by Poh San and Poh Ling—SKP flourished, culminating in its public listing as SKP Resources Berhad in 2002. The company's evolution from a modest business to a leading contract manufacturer highlights its adaptability and forward-thinking mindset. By embracing innovation and leveraging academic knowledge, technical training, and linguistic skills, SKP has expanded its market reach and cemented its position as a prominent player in the global manufacturing industry.

6.3.5 Stage Four: Diversification

Gan Chia Siang, the son-in-law of Gan, joined SKP to contribute to the family business, further leveraging its dynamics. The second generation capitalized on opportunities like acquiring License Manufacturing Warehouse (LMW) status and actively participating in the ASEAN Free Trade Area (AFTA), reflecting SKP's commitment to seizing enhanced business opportunities, particularly in the automobile sector.

SKP's generational journey in product development showcases its adaptability and forward-thinking approach. Initially focusing on housewares, the company advanced its technology to meet the stringent demands of multinational corporations in the audiovisual and semiconductor industries. Serving as an OEM contractor for renowned brands across various sectors, from home appliances, IT equipment, automotive components, audio and visual equipment, medical equipment, office automation equipment, and computer peripherals including Audio Pioneer Visual, Panasonic, Philips, Fujitsu, Sony, Sharp and Dyson, SKP solidified its reputation for innovation and reliability.

Having the longest service in plastic contract manufacturing for the AV and semiconductor industry, SKP's marketing strategy is highly diversified, with distribution channels tailored to MNC partnerships. Management incorporates a formal board structure with high family involvement and centralized professional management, supplemented by outsourcing. The company has also created new tacit knowledge in producing automobile parts and focuses on industry specifications.

Today, SKP remains a stalwart in the region, listed on the main board of the Bursa Malaysia as an electrical and electronics plastics manufacturer. With over 1 million combined square feet of manufacturing facilities in Johor Bahru, housing more than 250 of the latest injection molding machines and a growing workforce of 2,500, SKP continues to expand operations to meet client needs. With the expertise spans three principal areas: tool and dye fabrication, injection molding and cosmetic finishing, as well as contract manufacturing and component assembly, SKP positioning it as a one-stop plastics solutions provider.

6.3.6 Ownership Pattern and Financial Performance

Based on the provided information, SKP Resources Berhad operates as a public limited company. The company is governed by a board of directors and officers, including key persons such as Gan Poh San, Koh Chin Koon, Chua Siew Chuan, Pan Seng Wee, Goh Kah Im, Anita Chew Cheng Im, Tan Sri Datuk Hussin bin Haji Ismail, and Yau Jye Yee. Gan Poh San serves as both a director and manager within SKP, embodying a dual role that emphasizes his multifaceted leadership and operational responsibilities.

The shareholding structure reveals significant ownership by the Gan family, notably Gan Kim Huat and Gan Poh San. Gan Kim Huat holds 70,856,647 shares (≈ 23.93%), while Gan Poh San owns 78,118,000 shares (≈26.38%). These significant stakes indicate their substantial influence within SKP. It's evident that the Gan family plays a pivotal role in shaping the company's direction and strategic decisions. With a diversified board of directors and officers, SKP maintains a robust governance structure aimed at driving sustained growth and value creation for its shareholders and stakeholders alike.

The financial data provided offers a snapshot of SKP's performance over the past five years. Over the specified period, there is a noticeable upward trajectory in both non-current and current assets. Non-current assets have steadily increased from RM204,539,000 in 2019 to RM37,503,000 in 2023, indicating substantial investments in long-term assets such as property, plant, and equipment. Similarly, current assets have also experienced growth, reaching RM856,039,000 in 2023, reflecting healthy liquidity and potentially increased inventory or cash reserves to support operations.

From 2019 to 2023, SKP's non-current liabilities increased slightly from RM17,278,000 to RM31,494,000, suggesting effective management of long-term debts for strategic investments. Current liabilities peaked at RM416,667,000 in 2022 but decreased to RM393,727,000 in 2023, indicating balanced short-term obligations. Share capital remained stable at RM296,126,000, indicating no significant dilution of ownership, while reserves were consistently negative. Retained earnings grew significantly from RM386,528,000 in 2019 to RM668,793,000 in 2023, reflecting SKP's strong profit generation and accumulation.

From 2019 to 2023, SKP showed consistent revenue growth, rising from RM1,654,215,000 to RM2,515,038,000, reflecting strong market expansion. Profit before tax increased from RM124,596,000 to RM177,184,000, indicating improved operational efficiency. Profit after tax also grew steadily, demonstrating sustained profitability. However, net dividends declined from RM-63,347,000 in 2019 to RM-86,711,000 in 2023, suggesting a focus on reinvesting profits rather

Table 6.3 SKP Resources Berhad Balance Sheet, 2019–2023

(RM'000)	*2023*	*2022*	*2021*	*2020*	*2019*
Non-Current Assets	437,503	362,952	303,997	284,551	204,539
Current Assets	856,039	889,200	744,769	718,058	668,569
Non-Current Liabilities	31,494	20,971	16,142	20,857	17,278
Current Liabilities	393,727	416,667	324,793	370,542	267,166
Share Capital	296,126,	296,126	296,126	296,126	296,126
Reserve	-96,598	-96,598	-96,598	-96,598	-95,002
Retain Earning	668,793	614,986	508,303	411,682	386,528

Source: Companies Commission of Malaysia (SSM).

Table 6.4 SKP Resources Berhad Income Statement, 2019–2023

(RM'000)	*2023*	*2022*	*2021*	*2020*	*2019*
Revenue	2,515,038	2,321,428	2,251,182	1,826,733	1,654,215
Profit/(Loss) Before Tax	177,184	222,383	171,322	96,128	124,596
Profit/(loss) After Tax	140,518	173,396	133,243	72,136	96,004
Net Dividend	-86,711	-66,713	-36,622	-48,007	-63,347

Source: Companies Commission of Malaysia (SSM).

than distributing them. Overall, SKP's financial performance highlights growth and effective cost management, with a strategic emphasis on long-term development over immediate shareholder returns.

6.4 Case Study Nine: Syarikat Perniagaan Kemajuan Int. Sdn. Bhd.

6.4.1 Introduction

Syarikat Perniagaan Kemajuan Int. Sdn. Bhd. (Kemajuan) was established in 1973 by Hakka and Cantonese Chinese. Initially starting as a metal fabrication and contracts firm, the company has evolved significantly over the decades. Today, Kemajuan is a private limited company renowned for its manufacturing and marketing of PVC profiles for electronic IC packing and other related plastic products. The company's journey from metal fabrication to becoming a leading force in the electronic packaging industry showcases its commitment to innovation and adaptability.

The company's product range is extensive, catering to the diverse needs of the electronic and semiconductor industries. Kemajuan manufactures shipping tubes, stoppers, carrier tapes, and cover tapes, providing a one-stop solution for component packaging. The firm has continually expanded its technological capabilities, adopted advanced manufacturing processes and maintained a focus on quality. This dedication has earned Kemajuan numerous certifications, including ISO 9002, ISO

Figure 6.3 Exterior View of Syarikat Perniagaan Kemajuan Sdn. Bhd. Photograph by the author.

14001, and QS 9000, highlighting its commitment to excellence and environmental sustainability. With a strategic presence in Malaysia, Thailand, and formerly in Casablanca, Kemajuan has positioned itself as a key player in the global market, supplying multinational semiconductor companies and establishing a reputation for reliability and precision.

Currently, Kemajuan is managed by the second generation of the founding families, the Chia and Chan family members steering the company toward continued growth and innovation. This division of responsibilities ensures a balanced approach to management, fostering an environment of trust and collaboration. As Kemajuan moves forward, it remains committed to leveraging its expertise, ensuring its products meet the highest standards of quality, and supporting its customers' needs worldwide.

6.4.2 Stage One: Start-up

From its inception in 1973 as a metal fabrication and contracts firm in Jinjang, Kepong, Kemajuan embarked on a path that intertwined familial values with business acumen, navigating through the intricate landscapes of the electronic and semiconductor industries. The founder sought partnerships within the intra-ethnic network to access capital and expertise, evident in Kemajuan's strategic collaborations beyond family boundaries. Kemajuan's founders, Chan Wee Koon and the late Chia Kiu, leveraged their expertise in metal fabrication to supply stainless steel cabinets to local MNCs. This initial foray into the industry laid the foundation for Kemajuan's subsequent evolution. The tacit knowledge acquired during this phase served as a guiding light, illuminating the path toward innovation and adaptation.

A pivotal moment in Kemajuan's history occurred when Chan and Chia coincidentally met a Korean plastic manufacturer. Recognizing an opportunity for growth, the Korean businessman proposed selling them plastic injection machines, a move that would diversify their manufacturing capabilities and open new avenues in the electronic packaging industry. This unexpected encounter marked the beginning of Kemajuan's transition from metal to plastic fabrication, significantly enhancing its product offerings and technological prowess.

The familial structure within Kemajuan's organizational hierarchy exemplified the profound influence of Chinese culture. The sustainability of Kemajuan hinged on the division of job tasks between the Chia and Chan family members, with the Chia family managing external operations and the Chan family overseeing internal operations. The symbiotic relationship between Chia and Chan family members fostered a sense of unity and cohesion, enabling Kemajuan to navigate through turbulent waters with resilience and fortitude. This balance of responsibilities ensured that Kemajuan could maintain its high standards of quality and customer satisfaction, reinforcing its reputation as a trusted supplier in the global market.

6.4.3 Stage Two: Expansion

In 1987, Kemajuan embarked on a transformative journey by assimilating knowledge from a Korean plastic manufacturer to venture into plastic packaging for electronic devices. This strategic pivot showcased Kemajuan's agility and willingness to embrace change, reflecting a core tenet of Chinese ideology—the concept of adaptability in the face of adversity (穷则变，变则通，通则久)[2]. This transition not only diversified Kemajuan's product offerings but also marked a significant milestone in its evolution from metal fabrication to a leader in plastic packaging technology.

Additionally, Kemajuan developed an inter-ethnic network by inviting Bumiputera directors with strong backgrounds in government affairs. This strategic move enabled the company to gain opportunities in the manufacturing and marketing of PVC profiles for electronic IC packing. By fostering these relationships, Kemajuan was able to navigate the complexities of the business environment and leverage governmental support, which was crucial for its growth and expansion. The inter-ethnic network also provided Kemajuan with diverse perspectives and enhanced technological competency, enabling the company to better understand and serve a broader market, fostering inclusive growth and reinforcing its competitive edge in the industry.

From 1989 to 1997, Kemajuan provided OEM capabilities to produce metal fabricated storage equipment and plastic injection and built a robust network targeting local MNCs in the electronics sector, including prominent companies such as Toshiba, Epson, Mohita, Hitachi, and Sanyo. This period was marked by significant growth as Kemajuan established itself as a reliable supplier to these major players. The company's ability to adapt and innovate, combined with its strategic partnerships and inter-ethnic collaborations, underpinned its success and solidified its position in the industry.

6.4.4 Stage Three: Maturity

As Kemajuan expanded its footprint, the second generation, led by Chia Jiunn Shyong, ushered in a new era of growth and innovation. Armed with a background in telecommunication engineering, Jiunn Shyong propelled Kemajuan into the semiconductor industry, forging partnerships with global giants like Fairchild and Motorola. This strategic expansion not only demonstrated Kemajuan's resilience but also epitomized the essence of the Chinese entrepreneurial spirit, characterized by seizing opportunities with determination. Jiunn Shyong's leadership heralded a transformative period for Kemajuan, positioning the company as a key player in the semiconductor sector and paving the way for further growth and success.

Kemajuan capitalized on its tacit knowledge by venturing into OEM plastic production after partnering with Malaysia's MNCs, particularly in the semiconductor and electronics sectors. Kemajuan codified its tacit knowledge by transitioning from metal fabrication to OEM plastic injection molding, subsequently emphasizing plastic packaging technology in the electronics sector. This strategic shift enabled Kemajuan to align its operations with industry trends and capitalize on emerging opportunities. This strategic move enabled Kemajuan to diversify its product offerings and cater to the needs of its clientele. Furthermore, Kemajuan demonstrated openness to innovative ideas by investing in in-house research and development in carrier tape technology, aiming to achieve recognition in Southeast Asia. By producing carrier tapes compliant with international standards and implementing advanced manufacturing techniques, there was consequently success in welding and ultrasonic processing on customized plastic reels.

The company's commitment to excellence was underscored by its attainment of ISO 9002, ISO 14001, and QS 9000 certifications, reflecting Kemajuan's dedication to quality management and environmental sustainability. Additionally, Kemajuan's establishment of an overseas manufacturing plant in Thailand facilitated prompt delivery to international MNCs, aligning with the Just in Time (JIT) production model and enhancing its competitiveness on the global stage.

In essence, Kemajuan exemplified the resilience, adaptability, and innovation inherent in Chinese entrepreneurial endeavors. Through strategic partnerships, technological advancements, and a commitment to excellence, these companies not only weathered challenges but also thrived in dynamic and competitive markets, leaving an indelible mark on the semiconductor and electronic packaging industries.

6.4.5 Stage Four: Diversification

Kemajuan targeted OEM contract manufacturing for the electronics and semiconductor sectors, focusing on Japanese, European, and American multinational corporations. Their aim was to build a solid reputation and establish Kemajuan as a one-stop service solution for electronic packaging components, catering specifically to the needs of the electronic and semiconductor industries.

In parallel, Kemajuan entered Casablanca, Morocco, as a strategic move to collaborate with ST Microelectronics, a multinational corporation and global semiconductor company with strong roots in France and Italy. With major customers including Apple, Seagate, Bosch, HP, Continental, Tesla, Delta Electronics, Huawei, Samsung, and Intel, ST Microelectronics presented a significant opportunity for Kemajuan to expand its market presence and technological expertise. Casablanca, known for its French-speaking environment and bustling business connections, provided an ideal platform for Kemajuan to establish fruitful collaborations with ST Microelectronics, aligning with their strategic goals.

Kemajuan developed and innovated its tacit knowledge by leveraging the insights and experience gained from its collaboration with ST Microelectronics. The decision to improve its carrier-tape packaging process after adopting ideas from ST Microelectronics exemplified its commitment to innovation and continuous improvement. With the largest in-house R&D in carrier tape technology and plastic packaging components in Malaysia and Southeast Asia, Kemajuan positioned itself as a leader in electronic packaging solutions. By leveraging insights from global industry leaders like ST Microelectronics, Kemajuan not only enhanced its product offerings but also strengthened its competitive advantage in the market.

Furthermore, Kemajuan's embrace of a blended Japanese and Western management style, characterized by hierarchical leadership and autonomy for managers, facilitated seamless operations across its global footprint. While the closure of the packaging facility in Casablanca, due to escalating costs and a lack of skilled labor marked a strategic decision, it further highlighted Kemajuan's strategic acumen, as the main purpose of collaborating with ST Microelectronics had already been achieved, demonstrating their focus on core products.

As Kemajuan continue to navigate the dynamic landscape of the electronic and semiconductor industries, they remain steadfast in their commitment to nurturing tacit knowledge and fostering a culture of innovation and collaboration. Kemajuan remained committed to its values of collectivism. The active involvement of family members across all facets of the business underscored a shared commitment to success and prosperity.

6.4.6 Ownership Pattern and Financial Performance

Kemajuan is a private limited company primarily engaged in the manufacturing and marketing of PVC profiles for electronic IC packing and other related plastic products. It operates under the governance structure of a limited by shares entity, with a total issued share capital of 25,000,000 ordinary shares. The board of directors comprises of individuals holding key positions in the company's management and decision-making processes. Chan Wee Koon, Chan Wei Yen, Song Kwee Fong, and Chia Jiunn Shyong serve as directors, overseeing strategic direction and operational activities.

Table 6.5 Syarikat Perniagaan Kemajuan Int. Sdn. Bhd. Balance Sheet, 2015–2019

(RM)	*2019*	*2018*	*2017*	*2016*	*2015*
Non-Current Assets	N/A	42,063,618	42,823,587	N/A	N/A
Current Assets	N/A	284,980	1,906,968	N/A	N/A
Non-Current Liabilities	N/A	17,129,005	19,190,689	N/A	N/A
Current Liabilities	N/A	25,000,000	25,000,000	N/A	N/A
Share Capital	N/A	3,881,242	3,610,230	N/A	N/A
Reserve	N/A	13,713,668	13,713,668	N/A	N/A
Retain Earning	N/A	16,312,733	17,783,410	N/A	N/A

Source: Companies Commission of Malaysia (SSM).

Table 6.6 Syarikat Perniagaan Kemajuan Int. Sdn. Bhd. Income Statement, 2015–2019

(RM)	*2019*	*2018*	*2017*	*2016*	*2015*
Revenue	N/A	N/A	N/A	-3,382,695	-1,562,922
Profit/(Loss) Before Tax	N/A	N/A	N/A	-1,470,677	-942,394
Profit/(loss) After Tax	N/A	N/A	N/A	27,013,412	29,686,142
Net Dividend	N/A	N/A	N/A	0	0

Source: Companies Commission of Malaysia (SSM).

In terms of shareholding, the company's ownership is distributed among several shareholders, each holding varying proportions of shares. Notable shareholders include Chan Wei Yen, who holds the largest stake of 8,750,000.00 shares, followed by Chia Jiunn Shyong with 5,000,000.00 shares. Other shareholders, such as Chan Pei Siew, Chia Jin Bing, Chia Jin Ling, Chia Jin Ting, Chia Jin Wei, Saap Ken Yong, and Song Kwee Fong, also hold significant shares in the company, fostering collaboration and shared interests among them.

From 2015 to 2019, Kemajuan's balance sheet shows stability in its financial position with fluctuations in key metrics. Although specific data for some years is missing, the available information indicates consistent investment in assets and effective management of liabilities. Share capital and reserves remained steady, reflecting cautious financial management. Retained earnings varied slightly, suggesting changes in profitability or reinvestment strategies. Overall, the balance sheet highlights Kemajuan's stable financial health and strategic decision-making during this period.

The income statement for Kemajuan spanning from 2015 to 2019 illustrates fluctuations in revenue and profitability, with specific data unavailable for certain years. Revenue was negative in 2015 and 2016, indicating operational losses, while subsequent years lack available revenue figures. Profit before tax similarly reflects negative figures in 2015 and 2016, with profitability recovering in later years but specific details remain undisclosed. Profit after tax experienced a substantial increase in 2016, rebounding from previous losses, yet no data is provided for subsequent years. Net dividend remains consistent at zero across all reported years, suggesting reinvestment of profits or other financial strategies.

6.5 Summary

This chapter explores the evolution of Chinese family-owned enterprises in Malaysia's plastics manufacturing sector. The chapter focuses on key companies, including LH Plus Sdn. Bhd., SKP Resources Berhad, and Syarikat Perniagaan Kemajuan International Sdn. Bhd., detailing their organizational strategies, growth trajectories, and their ability to adapt to industry demands.

The chapter begins with a background on Malaysia's plastic industry, highlighting its origins tied to the country's petroleum resources and its development into a key contributor to the national economy. With the influx of MNCs during the post-colonial period, domestic demand for value-added products surged, particularly in sectors requiring high-quality, precision plastic parts.

The section on LH Plus Sdn. Bhd. traces the company's transformation from a small bicycle repair shop into a major player in plastic injection molding. The Chen family, starting with the founder, successfully pivoted from metal works to plastic manufacturing, expanding into international markets and securing contracts with leading global brands like Mattel. LH Plus exemplifies the importance of adaptability and innovation within family-run businesses, particularly in embracing technology and automation.

SKP Resources Berhad's journey from a modest plastic injection workshop to a publicly listed company on the Bursa Malaysia is also explored. This case highlights how the Gan family integrated Japanese business practices, particularly the *takumi* spirit of craftsmanship, to transform their operations. SKP's partnerships with global brands like Dyson and Panasonic are a testament to their emphasis on quality and long-term strategic planning.

Syarikat Perniagaan Kemajuan International Sdn. Bhd.'s story demonstrates a similar trajectory, from metal fabrication to a leader in plastic packaging for the electronics and semiconductor industries. Strategic partnerships, particularly with MNCs in the semiconductor sector, propelled the company into a globally competitive space.

The chapter concludes by reflecting on the resilience, innovation, and strategic foresight of these family-owned Chinese businesses, emphasizing how they have navigated challenges and capitalized on opportunities in Malaysia's plastic manufacturing industry.

Notes

1 The term "Chinaman Business" refers to a stereotype historically used to describe Chinese business practices perceived as deceitful, exploitative, and focused solely on profit. This characterization often arises from cultural misunderstandings and prejudices, painting Chinese entrepreneurs as lacking ethical standards. As Yeung (2006) proclaims, the advantage of the network perspective rests in its capacity to incorporate the "different

loci of power and control within specific firms (intra-firm dimension) and significant bargaining and cooperative relationships between business firms and other institutions." However, this advantage can also be interpreted negatively, as it may lead to the concentration of power in a few hands, fostering an environment where dominant players can manipulate market conditions, marginalize smaller firms, and potentially engage in anti-competitive practices that stifle innovation and limit market diversity.

2 The phrase translates to "When in a difficult situation, adapt; when you adapt, you will find a way; and when you find a way, you will endure." This concept emphasizes the importance of flexibility and resilience in overcoming challenges. It reflects the idea that those who can adapt to changing circumstances are more likely to succeed and thrive in the long term. Rooted in Chinese philosophy, this principle underscores the value of innovation and perseverance in the face of adversity, applicable not only in personal life but also in business and social contexts.

7 Ethnic Chinese Businesses in the Rubber Industry

In one decisive move, new Chinese capitalists and progressive members of the old Malacca Straits-born families transitioned from network-based family firms to professionalized corporate enterprises within Malaysia's rubber industry, gaining control of the booming local economy. However, Chinese family businesses in this sector still face challenges in adapting to the rapidly evolving business environment. The younger generations are increasingly enhancing their competitiveness in regional and global markets by improving skills and leveraging rubber technology to transform rubber into innovative products. Innovation capacity—resulting in new products, services, or technological processes—has enabled these family businesses to create distinctive product lines, designs, and brands, differentiating them from their founders' generation. Generational evolution in Chinese family businesses significantly influences the professionalization of tacit knowledge and innovation capacity, shaping organizational outcomes and objectives. For instance, companies like Top Glove Corporation Berhad, Fun Keong Rubber Manufactory (M) Sdn. Bhd., and Aerofoam Manufacturing (1969) Sdn. Bhd. have successfully navigated first-mover advantages and secured a position in an oligopoly. They achieved this by strategically leveraging economies of scale and fostering "innovation capabilities" within Malaysia's rubber industry.

7.1 Industry Background

Malaysia was one of the world's largest rubber producers by the early 20th century (Gordon, 2004). The roots of Malaysia's rubber industry stretch back to the colonial era, dating back to the late 19th century when British colonizers introduced rubber tree cultivation to the Malay Peninsula (Hill, 2013). During the late 19th and early 20th centuries, as Europe and North America underwent rapid industrialization, rubber became essential in automotive, textile, and machinery sectors, increasing demand significantly (Herbert, 2007). The British needed vast quantities of rubber to fuel their industrialization and economic interests. Recognizing the country's favorable climate and fertile land, the British aggressively developed rubber plantations and manufacturing facilities, laying the groundwork for what would become one of Malaysia's most vital industries.

DOI: 10.4324/9781032705842-7

During British colonial rule, rubber plantations became ubiquitous across Malaya. Plantation owners, predominantly British colonial administrators and investors, established vast estates primarily using migrant workers, including Indian and Chinese people (Kaur, 2004). This marked the beginning of a racially diverse workforce that would characterize the industry for decades to come. Some Chinese immigrants were employed as rubber tappers on rubber estates established by the British. This prompted some of them within social networks engaged in industrial work to later seize opportunities to enter rubber cultivation and the rubber industry.

Following Malaysia‘s independence in 1957, the rubber industry underwent significant transformation. The newly formed government recognized the strategic importance of rubber as a key export commodity and enacted policies to support its development (Lim, 1987; Mohamed, 2009). Initiatives such as the Rubber Research Institute of Malaysia (RRIM) aimed to enhance productivity, improve rubber varieties, and strengthen the industry's competitiveness on the global stage.

One of the major public policies that influenced Malaysia‘s rubber industry was the Look East Policy in the 1980s. This policy aimed to emulate the economic successes of East Asian countries such as Japan and South Korea. As part of this policy, Malaysia focused on enhancing its manufacturing capabilities, including the rubber processing industry. Under the Look East Policy, Malaysia sought to modernize its rubber industry by adopting advanced technologies and improving productivity (Lebdioui, 2022). Furthermore, the Look East Policy emphasized human capital development, encouraging Malaysians to acquire skills and expertise in rubber technology and management. This led to the establishment of specialized institutions and training programs aimed at equipping individuals with the knowledge and skills needed to drive innovation and competitiveness in the rubber industry. Subsequently, led to the flourish of the original equipment manufacturer (OEM) in Malaysia.

Today, the Malaysian Rubber Export Promotion Council (MREPC) have played an important role in identifying and expanding new export markets for Malaysian rubber products (Lebdioui, 2022). MREPC was established in 2000 to promote Malaysia made rubber products and identify new export opportunities. Malaysia remains one of the leading producers and exporters of rubber products globally, with a diversified industry including natural rubber cultivation, rubber processing, and manufacturing of value-added rubber goods. The historical legacy of the rubber industry, coupled with forward-looking entrepreneurs and government policies continues to shape Malaysia's economic.

7.2 Case Study 10: Top Glove Corporation Berhad

7.2.1 Introduction

Top Glove Corporation Berhad has a rich history that spans several decades, owned by a Hokkien Chinese family, and becoming a global leader in the glove manufacturing industry. Top Glove began its journey with just one factory in Malaysia. Initially, it focused on producing latex gloves for the healthcare industry.

Figure 7.1 Photograph of the Interior of Top Glove. Photograph by the author.

Throughout the 1990s and early 2000s, Top Glove aggressively expanded its production capacity and diversified its product range. It invested in advanced manufacturing technologies and processes to enhance efficiency and quality. This strategic approach enabled Top Glove to capture a larger share of the global glove market. As the company continued to grow, it ventured into new geographical markets and established a presence in key regions worldwide. Top Glove's commitment to innovation and continuous improvement further solidified its position as the world's largest manufacturer of gloves with 26% of the global market share. By the mid-2000s, the company had become synonymous with reliability, quality, and scale in the industry.

The COVID-19 pandemic, which began in late 2019, brought unprecedented challenges and opportunities for Top Glove. As the demand for personal protective equipment surged worldwide, particularly for gloves, the company experienced a dramatic increase in orders. Top Glove played a crucial role in supplying gloves to frontline workers, healthcare facilities, and various industries battling the pandemic. However, the pandemic also exposed vulnerabilities in Top Glove's operations, particularly concerning labor practices and working conditions. In 2020, the company faced allegations of labor rights violations, including issues related to migrant worker recruitment, living conditions, and workplace safety. These issues led to regulatory scrutiny and international attention, prompting Top

Glove to address and improve its practices. To overcome these challenges, the company has implemented various initiatives to improve labor standards, invest in worker welfare programs, and strengthen corporate governance.

In the year 2021, Top Glove was included the Forbes Global 2000 and is the only Malaysian glove company on the prestigious list. As of the current situation, Top Glove continues to be a dominant force in the global glove market. It remains committed to meeting the growing demand for gloves while upholding high standards of quality, ethics, and corporate responsibility.

7.2.2 Stage One: Start-up

Top Glove's journey began in 1991 when Dr. Lim Wee Chai, a Malaysian-born Hokkien Chinese, who raised in the Chinese New Village of Titi, Jelebu, Negeri Sembilan, founded the company. Lim grew up immersed in the rubber trading business operated by his family. He helped out in business activities during weekend and gained firsthand experience in business.

In the early 1990s, Lim recognized the opportunity in the rubber glove industry due to the prosperous economy. He observed that there was a good demand for rubber gloves, which resulted in high profit margins. Lim's diverse educational background, including a Bachelor of Science Degree in Physics, a Master of Business Administration, and a Doctor of Philosophy in Management, coupled with his Hokkien business family heritage, endows him with exceptional business expertise. This blend of academic qualifications and cultural insight empowers Lim to leverage his tacit knowledge effectively, enabling him to venture into the rubber glove manufacturing industry with foresight and strategic planning.

Additionally, his brother, Lim Hooi Sin, has been an Executive Director since the company's establishment. Hooi Sin brings over two decades of expertise in the insurance and financial services sector as had a distinguished career with MetLife Financial Services. Prior to his appointment, he held various positions, where he excelled in product development, marketing, recruitment, training, and supervision. With over 20 years of experience in the USA glove market, he founded TG Medical (U.S.A.), Inc. in 1994, and served as its Executive Vice President from 2001 to 2005 and President since 2005, showcasing his entrepreneurial abilities and leadership qualities.

Top Glove's early success stemmed from its commitment to innovation and quality, leveraging the rubber resources available in Malaysia, one of the world's largest exporters of rubber. By harnessing these resources efficiently, Top Glove maximizes production capabilities while maintaining stringent quality standards, positioning itself as a leader in the global market for rubber gloves.

7.2.3 Stage Two: Expansion

Innovation is the crucial element that guarantees the growth of family businesses. When founders prioritize innovation, particularly in transforming tacit knowledge into implicit knowledge, there is significant changes occur in the quality of products and services. This, in turn, brings about alterations in the management approach of the business.

Top Glove is deeply rooted in family involvement, with founder Dr. Lim serving as Executive Chairman since September 2000. His spouse, Tong Siew Bee, played a crucial role as co-founder and former Executive Director, currently serving as a Non-Independent Non-Executive Director. During the early stage of business, the big glove manufacturers in Malaysia were the foreign MNCs. Dr. Lim and his spouse envisioned that it was possible to compete with the MNCs by consistently manufacturing high quality gloves at an efficiently low cost. Since then, they have turned this vision into Top Glove corporate mission: "To be a world-class glove manufacturer providing top quality products with excellent services through continuous improvement and innovation."

Traced back to few decades ago, the implementation of The New Economic Policy (NEP) motivated the emergence of new Chinese business conglomerates that built corporate empires through inter-ethnic connections by partnering with Bumiputera capitalists and politicians. During the 1990s, this group of Chinese entrepreneurs, which included Dr. Lim, became prominent by operating within the frameworks of the NEP and National Development Policy (NDP).

Top Glove has emphasized in R&D to manufacture a diversified range of high-quality glove products to fulfill the demands of its consumers. Through the connection of the former and current board members such as Tan Sri Dato' Seri Utama Arshad Bin Ayub, Tan Sri Mohd Sidek Bin Haji Hassan, Tan Sri Rainer Althoff and Martin Giles Manen, Top Glove collaborates with numerous agencies like the Malaysian Rubber Board (MRB), Malaysian Rubber Export Promotion Council (MREPC), Federation of Malaysian Manufacturers (FMM), Sirim Bhd., Plantation Industries and Commodities Ministry, Ministry of International Trade and Industry (MITI), and Malaysia External Trade Development Corp (MATRADE) to keep itself updated with the latest development in rubber research technology.

7.2.4 Stage Three: Maturity

Top Glove began with one factory and grew quickly to one of the world largest rubber glove manufacturers with 19 factories located in Malaysia, China, and Thailand by increasing production and expanding product range. Apparently, the growth of certain major companies owned by ethnic Chinese in Malaysia can be attributed to business connections within the ethnic group. The intra-ethnic collaborations facilitated ethnic resources such as capital and knowledge.

Subsequently, the social network impacted the development and transformation of tacit knowledge. According to Tsoukas (2005), "Tacit and explicit knowledge are not two ends of a continuum but two sides of the same coin: even the most explicit kind of knowledge is underlain by tacit knowledge". Undeniably, Top Glove's excellent quality control, innovation and R&D for its products is the explicit result of the tacit knowledge. The extensive social network fosters the changes of tacit knowledge, driving innovation and the creation of new knowledge within the company.

As the founder and Executive Chairman of Top Glove, Dr. Lim has been actively involved in many Chinese associations and organizations in Malaysia, including:

1. Honorary President of the Associated Chinese Chambers of Commerce and Industry of Malaysia (ACCCIM) since 2017
2. Life Honorary Advisor of the Federation of Chinese Associations Malaysia since 2011
3. Life Honorary President of the Federation of Hokkien Associations of Malaysia since 2017
4. Honorary President of the Malaysia-China Chamber of Commerce since 2012
5. Honorary President of the Lim Association of Malaysia since 2018.

Through connections within the Chinese community, Top Glove found opportunities for cross-industry collaborations, marked the new knowledge gained. In October 2017, Dr. Lim became the shareholder and director of Malaysian property developer Tropicana Corporation Berhad, acquiring a 10.24% stake. This marked his initial venture into the real estate industry. Tropicana was founded by another notable Hokkien businessman, Tan Sri Dato' Tan Chee Sing. The announcement of their collaboration led to an increase in Tropicana's share price. Although Dr. Lim resigned from his position as Non-Independent and Non-Executive Director at Tropicana in 2022 due to commitment issues as Top Glove rapid growth after the pandemic. Today, Dr. Lim still retains 162,208,937 direct ordinary shares.

One of the pivotal collaborators is Dr. Chong Su-Lin, the current Independent Non-Executive Director, who commenced her career in 1984 as a medical practitioner in the National Health Service in the United Kingdom. She has held prominent roles such as CEO of Sunway Medical Centre, CEO of Prince Court Medical Centre, and Executive Director of Beacon Specialist Hospital. Additionally, she served as the CEO of the Healthcare arm of the International Medical University. Dr. Chong's leadership extends to national initiatives, including being the leader for the healthcare National Key Economic Areas blueprint planning by the Malaysian Government in 2010. Furthermore, she was appointed as a member of the task force by the Minister of Health to examine workplace culture in the Ministry of Health hospitals. Her extensive network and experience within the healthcare industry, both locally and internationally, bring invaluable knowledge to Top Glove's strategic direction and governance.

The rubber industry in Malaysia has undergone a remarkable evolution, transforming itself into a multibillion-dollar industry, controls a large portion of the global rubber gloves market with significant contributions from companies like Top Glove. This transformation has been fueled by advancements in R&D, particularly in rubber cultivation, harvesting, and processing. The advent of technically specified rubber (the SMR) in 1965 and strategic initiatives like the three Industrial Master Plans (IMP) (1986–2020) have propelled Malaysia's rubber processing and manufacturing sectors to global prominence. Amidst this evolution, Top Glove has emerged as a key player in the global rubber gloves market, reflecting Malaysia's dominance in this sector.

7.2.5 Stage Four: Diversification

Top Glove's main operations involve the manufacturing and trading of rubber gloves, synthetic gloves, and surgical gloves (see Figure 7.2). Additionally, they are involved in machinery trading, property investment, investment holding, latex

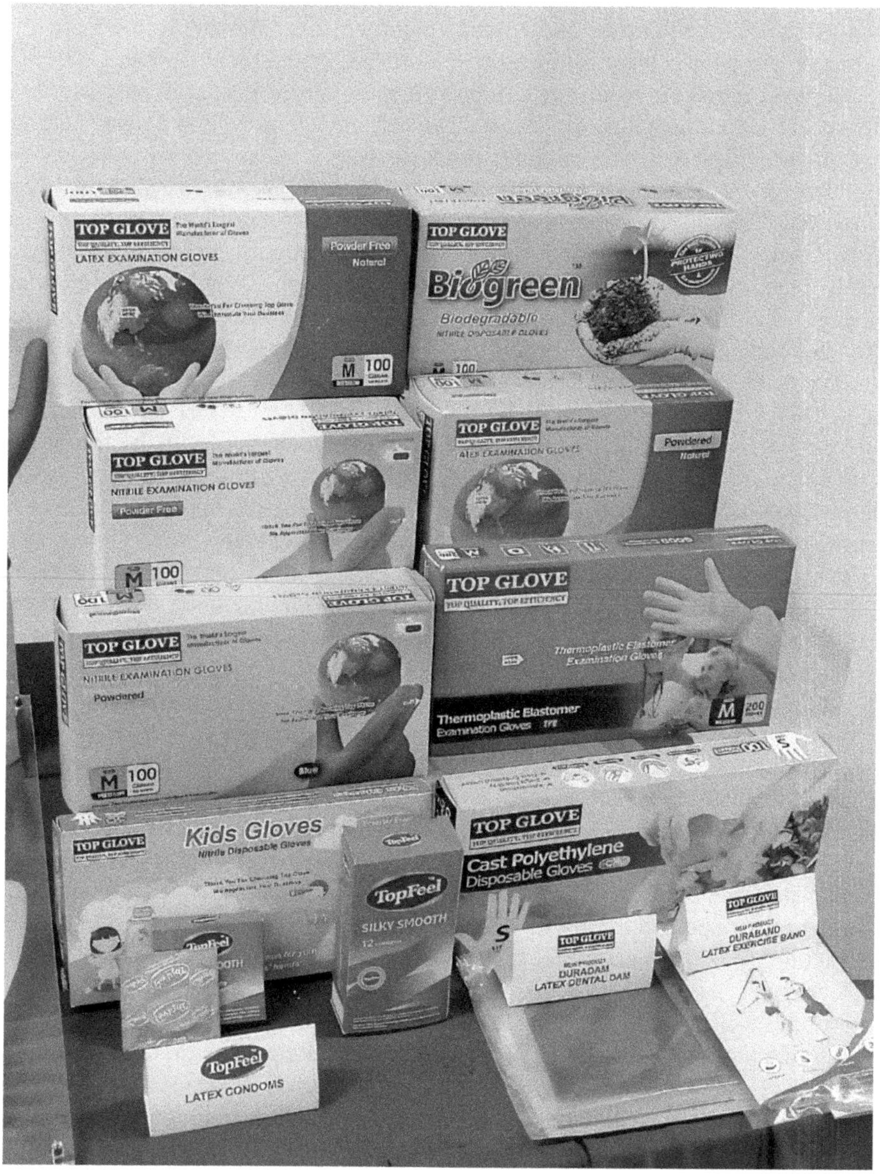

Figure 7.2 The Products of Top Glove. Photograph by the author.

concentrate production and sales, and management services provision. As the business continued to expand, it needed more formalized structures and processes. The company focused on streamlining operations, implementing efficient supply chain management systems, and enhancing production capabilities. Investments in technology and automation played a crucial role in increasing productivity and ensuring consistent quality standards across its operations. Top Glove as a domestic player, possesses competitive advantages stemming from its deep understanding of culture, local knowledge, and working environments, allowing it to effectively compete with MNCs that manufacture in Malaysia.

The success of the local glove industry can be attributed to the collaborative efforts between local glove makers and government agencies. Top Glove's aim to become a world-class, cost-effective producer with a wide range of high-quality glove products is supported by the upgrading and collaborations in R&D. Top Glove has obtained a long list of certifications and accreditations that cover various critical stages of production, such as raw material control, processing control, product quality control, and pre-shipment quality control. These include important standards like the Standard Malaysian Glove (SMG), ISO 9001, TUV for Germany, the US Food and Drug Administration (US FDA) Quality System Regulation, and the US ADA, ASTM, and EN455 Standards. Additionally, Top Glove has also achieved certifications like CGSB for Canada and the latest ABNT for Brazil.

The entrepreneurial journey is like riding a rollercoaster, with its fair share of highs and lows. Top Glove's management has shown a resilient and professional approach, particularly in addressing the US ban issued by the United States Customs and Border Protection (CBP) in July 2020. The company's commitment to worker welfare, extensive audits, and operational adjustments reflects its dedication to ethical practices. The lifting of the ban by the United States of America on September 10, 2021, after 16 months underscores Top Glove's responsive management and commitment to corporate responsibility.

The familial connection currently extends to the next generation, with Lim Jin Feng, Dr. Lim's son, taking on the role of General Manager of Marketing since January 2022. Armed with a Bachelor of Science in Business Administration with a focus on International Business, Jin Feng brings a wealth of knowledge and expertise to his role. With over a decade of experience in the glove manufacturing industry, Jin Feng has demonstrated his ability to navigate the complexities of the market and drive strategic initiatives forward. His dedication, coupled with his academic background and extensive industry experience, positions him as a key asset in driving Top Glove's continued success and innovation in the global marketplace.

Currently, Top Glove continues to evolve by embracing collaboration and knowledge sharing both internally and externally. The company actively engages in intra-ethnic and inter-ethnic partnerships with research institutions, industry associations, and other stakeholders to drive innovation, enhance sustainability, and address challenges collectively. By fostering a culture of continuous learning and tacit knowledge creation, Top Glove remains at the forefront of the global rubber gloves industry.

7.2.6 Ownership Pattern and Financial Performance

Top Glove Corporation Berhad is a is a public limited liability company incorporated and domiciled in Malaysia, and is listed on the Main Market of Bursa Malaysia Securities Berhad and Main Board of Singapore Exchange Securities Trading Limited, with a total issued ordinary share capital of 1,829,084,215.16. The company is governed by a board of directors (see Figure 7.3) and officers who oversee its operations and strategic direction. The current board members include:

Each director brings a wealth of experience and expertise to the company, contributing to its continued success and growth. With its diverse leadership team and robust governance structure, Top Glove is well-positioned to navigate challenges and capitalize on opportunities in the global glove market.

The provided financial information in Table 7.1 reveals significant ownership stakes in Top Glove, with the founder, Dr. Lim Wee Chai, his spouse, Tong Siew Bee, his brother, Lim Hooi Sin and his son, Lim Jin Feng holding substantial direct and indirect interests. It highlights the complex network of ownership, with certain shareholders deemed to have interests in shares held by related individuals and entities.

The structure of ownership in Top Glove reflects characteristics often observed in Chinese family businesses, where family members play key roles in both ownership and management. The concentration of ownership among family members, such as the founder, spouse, brother, and son, is a common feature in Chinese business culture, emphasizing continuity and unity within the family. This tight-knit network fosters a sense of loyalty and shared vision, facilitating long-term strategic planning and decision-making. These familial and business ties create a

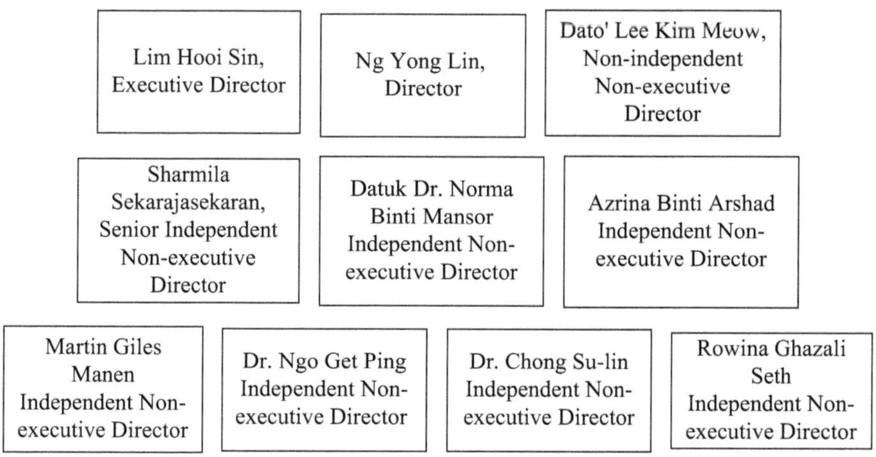

Figure 7.3 Top Glove Corporation Berhad Board of Directors.

Source: Top Glove Integrated Annual Report 2023.

Table 7.1 The Substantial Shareholders of the Company: Based on the Register of Substantial Shareholders of the Company and their Respective Shareholdings

No. of Ordinary Shares Held					
No.	*Name of Substantial Shareholders*	*Direct*	*% ^*	*Indirect*	*% ^*
1.	Tan Sri Dr Lim Wee Chai	2,231,043,256	27.86	692,691,448 *	8.65
2.	Puan Sri Tong Siew Bee	17,562,876	0.22	2,906,171,828 **	36.29
3.	Lim Hooi Sin	100,061,244	1.25	2,823,473,460 ***	35.26
4.	Lim Jin Feng	200,000	0.00	2,823,473,460 ***	35.26
5.	Firstway United Corp	554,966,328	6.93	-	-

Note:

^ Calculated based on 8,008,160,534 Ordinary Shares (Issued share capital of 8,207,924,834 Ordinary Shares less Treasury Shares of 199,764,300)

* Deemed interested by virtue of the shareholding of Puan Sri Tong Siew Bee, Mr Lim Hooi Sin, Mr Lim Jin Feng, Firstway United Corp, Top Fortress Ventures Limited and TS Dr Lim WC (L) Foundation in Top Glove

** Deemed interested by virtue of the shareholding of Tan Sri Dr Lim Wee Chai, Mr Lim Hooi Sin, Mr Lim Jin Feng, Firstway United Corp, Top Fortress Ventures Limited and TS Dr Lim WC (L) Foundation in Top Glove

*** Deemed interested by virtue of the shareholding of Tan Sri Dr Lim Wee Chai, Puan Sri Tong Siew Bee, Firstway United Corp, Top Fortress Ventures Limited and TS Dr Lim WC (L) Foundation in Top Glove

Source: Top Glove Integrated Annual Report 2023.

Table 7.2 Top Glove Corporation Berhad Balance Sheet, 2018–2022

(RM'000)	*2022*	*2021*	*2020*	*2019*	*2018*
Non-current assets	5,373,545	6,005,593	5,436,667	4,418,311	4,149,514
Current assets	1,688,025	2,111,117	4,345,757	4,287,653	1,538,691
Non-current liabilities	211,588	326,987	363,777	382,557	1,542,273
Current liabilities	923,867	996,488	2,198,487	2,132,524	1,591,791
Share capital	1,843,271	1,842,189	1,841,654	1,675,704	788,326
Reserve	-1,262,966	-1,304,637	-16,349	63,521	-3,334
Retain earning	4,134,229	5,041,670	5,342,360	3,131,530	1,751,963

Source: Companies Commission of Malaysia (SSM).

solid foundation for Top Glove's governance and operations, reinforcing trust and stability within the company.

Tables 7.2 and 7.3 illustrate significant fluctuations in Top Glove's financial performance over the past five years. Revenue peaked at RM16.36 billion in 2020 before plummeting to RM2.26 billion in 2022. Similarly, profit before and after tax showed substantial declines, with significant losses reported in 2022. This downturn is largely due to factors such as the global decrease in demand for gloves during post-COVID-19 pandemic period, increased market competition, and volatile raw material prices. Additionally, the company's decision to withhold dividends

Table 7.3 Top Glove Corporation Berhad Income Statement, 2018–2022

(RM'000)	*2022*	*2021*	*2020*	*2019*	*2018*
Revenue	2,257,221	5,572,349	16,361,443	7,237,427	4,801,139
Profit/(loss) before tax	-900,415	358,424	10,033,813	2,165,551	423,588
Profit/(loss) after tax	-925,218	281,590	7,823,992	1,788,830	367,546
Net dividend	0.00	-5,862	-113,665	-10,641	-2,868

Source: Companies Commission of Malaysia (SSM).

in recent years underscores its focus on conserving cash flow and stabilizing financial performance amid challenging market conditions.

The company's balance sheet reveals financial strain, with both non-current and current assets declining compared to the previous year. Non-current assets fell from RM6.01 billion in 2021 to RM5.37 billion in 2022, possibly reflecting divestment or impairment of long-term investments. Additionally, reserves decreased from -RM1.26 billion in 2021 to -RM1.30 billion in 2022, indicating potential financial challenges or restructuring efforts. These indicators highlight the urgency for Top Glove to adopt strategic measures aimed at improving profitability, optimizing operations, and boosting shareholder value amid tough market conditions.

7.3 Case Study 11: Fung Keong Rubber Manufactory (M) Sdn. Bhd.

7.3.1 Introduction

This section explores the pivotal role of tacit knowledge innovation in the business trajectory of Chinese entrepreneurs, with a focus on Fung Keong Rubber (FKR) Manufactory (M) Sdn. Bhd. As a significant player within the Cantonese Chinese family business landscape specializing in rubber products. FKR's journey from its founding in Canton in 1920 to its eventual acquisition by N.D. Rubber Public Company Limited showcased the critical influence of tacit knowledge in fostering business resilience and growth. The case study highlights how the acquisition, adaptation, and application of tacit knowledge have been instrumental in enabling FKR to navigate changing market conditions and maintain success over the decades.

Initially focused on manufacturing and selling rubber shoes, Fung Keong's product range has evolved over the decades to encompass a diverse array of offerings. From its beginnings in Canton, the company expanded its operations to Hong Kong and Malaya, catering to a burgeoning market across Southeast Asia. Its product portfolio includes bicycle and motorcycle tires, alongside other related accessories and lubricants.

Amidst shifting market dynamics and evolving consumer preferences, Fung Keong has demonstrated remarkable adaptability and foresight. Led by successive generations of the Fung family, the company has remained at the forefront of innovation and industry leadership. Leveraging its deep-rooted knowledge in rubber

Figure 7.4 Exterior View of Fung Keong Rubber Manufactory (M) Sdn. Bhd. Photograph by the author.

manufacturing and strategic market positioning, Fung Keong continues to thrive, serving a loyal customer base across various regions.

7.3.2 Stage One: Start-up

Chinese entrepreneurs have long been acknowledged for their astute business acumen and adeptness at navigating complex socio-economic landscapes. Mr. Fung Keong's migration from *Wan Fou* in Canton, Guangdong to Sungai Ujong (Seremban), Negeri Sembilan in Malaya at the age of 11, in 1902, coupled with his study of machinery, endowed him with tacit knowledge that formed the cornerstone of his entrepreneurial venture. Additionally, his involvement in politics, particularly as the general secretary and vice chairman of the Seremban branch of the Chinese Nationalist Party (KMT), equipped him with invaluable insights into regional dynamics and networks. With the knowledge and experience gained, Fung returned to Canton to establish Fung Keong Rubber (FKR) Manufactory in 1920, concentrating on the manufacturing and sale of rubber shoes and related products. Fung chose to name his business after himself, a practice commonly observed among Chinese entrepreneurs.

Founded by Fung in 1920, FKR embarked on its journey in Canton, expanded to Hong Kong, focusing on the manufacturing and sale of rubber shoes and related products. However, the company faced significant challenges due to the Japanese invasion in 1938. Anticipating the obstacles ahead, Fung made the crucial decision to relocate the entire factory to Klang in Malaya, leading to the establishment of Fung Keong Rubber (FKR) Manufactory (M) in 1939.

After World War II, FKR resumed operations in Hong Kong. The post-war period saw an influx of refugees from mainland China, many of whom found employment with FKR, including people from Fung's origin, *Wan Fou*. Despite facing difficulties in Hong Kong during the late 1940s and early 1950s, the company remained focused on the city, while operations in Malaya continued without interruption.

7.3.3 Stage Two: Expansion

In the expansion stage, FKR relocated its operations to Klang, in the aftermath of World War II, the company experienced substantial expansion. The adoption of advanced technologies, such as electrically driven Singer Sewing machines, exemplifies FKR's innovative approach to manufacturing, propelled by tacit knowledge acquisition and application. This phase marks a transition from manual labor to mechanization, reflecting the company's adaptability to technological advancements and its commitment to efficiency and productivity.

FKR starting in Canton and later expanding to Hong Kong and Malaya. Fung Keong's rubber sole canvas shoes gained immense popularity due to their affordability, particularly during tough economic times. Their cost-effectiveness made them a favored choice among consumers, solidifying their presence in the market. Fung Keong's rubber sole canvas shoes became memorable for people growing up in Hong Kong and Southeast Asia during that period.

Fung smartly noticed that there was more demand for rubber shoes in the mass market. Also, because of new trade policies and tariffs within the British Colonial Empire, there was a higher demand for rubber shoes made in Hong Kong. Places like the Malaya, Singapore and North Borneo became important markets, as Chinese immigrant workers there earned higher wages, had greater purchasing power compared to those in China. Moreover, it was not just the Chinese immigrant workers who bought their shoes. The affordable rubber shoes also appealed to Malay and Indian workers in these regions.

Hong Kong and Malaya were good places to set up the factory because they had the materials needed to make shoes. For example, Malaya produced crepe rubber which can be used to make shoe soles. The way they made the soles made them strong and long-lasting, which was important to customers. FKR's success came from making good products and promoting them well. They also came up with new ideas, like using aluminum to make the shoes last longer. By making good shoes and promoting them cleverly, FKR became a leader in the industry by meeting the needs of customers.

7.3.4 Stage Three: Maturity

During the maturity stage of Fung Keong Rubber Manufacturing, Fung began the essential task of cultivating his successors, a common practice among Chinese business founders. This strategic grooming process was not merely about handing over the reins but involved a profound transfer of tacit knowledge accumulated over decades of experience in the industry. This period of succession planning and leadership development was crucial in ensuring the company's continued stability and growth.

Fung's strategic choice of successors reflected his foresight and understanding of the importance of leadership in family businesses. His only son, Fung Che-yee, and his eldest son-in-law, Ignatius S. W. Tang, were pivotal figures in the company's operations. Che-yee, who took on the role of general manager at the Hong Kong factory, was instrumental in maintaining and enhancing the company's manufacturing capabilities. His leadership ensured that the Hong Kong operations ran smoothly, contributing significantly to the company's overall stability.

Tang, who married Fung's eldest daughter, played an equally crucial role. With a solid educational background, having graduated from Saint Joseph College in Hong Kong and earning a Bachelor of science in engineering from the University of Hong Kong, Tang brought a wealth of technical knowledge and expertise to the business. His engineering background proved invaluable in overseeing the operations in Canton and later in Malaya, where his skills in optimizing production processes and implementing innovative manufacturing techniques greatly benefited the company.

Tang's political acumen also enriched FKR's leadership. His involvement in community and political activities provided the company with a broader perspective on market dynamics and regulatory environments, allowing FKR to navigate complex socio-political landscapes effectively. This blend of engineering proficiency and political insight helped solidify the company's foundation during its maturity stage, characterized by stable operations and thoughtful succession planning.

Unfortunately, both Che-yee and Tang passed away before Fung, marking a poignant chapter in the company's history. Their untimely deaths were a significant loss to the company, as both had been groomed meticulously to lead FKR into the future. However, their contributions during their tenures were substantial, leaving a lasting impact on the company's operational strategies and leadership culture.

Fung's efforts to cultivate his successors highlighted the importance of intergenerational knowledge transfer in Chinese family businesses. By embedding his tacit knowledge and values in his chosen successors, Fung ensured that FKR's core principles and innovative spirit would endure, guiding the company through subsequent challenges and market evolutions. This strategic approach to succession planning underscored the vital role of leadership in maintaining the legacy and continuity of family businesses.

As the saying goes: "when it rains, it pours." As the economies of Asian countries experienced rapid growth in the 1970s and 1980s, consumer preferences shifted toward Western brands like Bata, Nike, and Adidas, affecting the demand for FKR's affordable shoes. Consequently, FKR had to adjust its focus to manufacturing bicycle and motorcycle tires, adapting to changing market trends.

7.3.5 Stage Four: Diversification

In response to shifting consumer preferences, FKR diversified its product portfolio from shoes to bicycle and motorcycle tires, by leveraging its tacit knowledge in rubber manufacturing. Transitioning from the manufacturing of shoes to the production of bicycle and motorcycle tires was motivated by the substantial market opportunities present in Southeast Asia's burgeoning tire industry, driven by high demand. This strategic pivot enabled the company to maintain its market leadership amidst evolving market dynamics, showcasing the adaptability and innovation inherent in tacit knowledge.

In the face of changing market dynamics, FKR's agile response and foresight have been pivotal in sustaining its relevance and dominance. By shifting focus to meet the growing demand for bicycle and motorcycle tires, the company not only capitalized on emerging trends but also diversified its product portfolio to cater to the evolving needs of consumers. This strategic expansion into related sectors, such as motorcycle parts and lubricants, further solidified FKR's foothold in the industry. Their enduring success over the decades highlights their mastery in exploring and nurturing a niche market, ensuring their continued resilience and prominence in the tire and motorcycle accessories sector.

Since the 1970s, FKR demonstrated astute responsiveness to market shifts. With a decline in demand for affordable shoes, the company keenly recognized the emerging need for bicycle and motorcycle tires. They made a decisive move to transition from shoe manufacturing to tire production, subsequently expanding into motorcycle parts, lubricants, and related products. Despite half a century passing, FKR remains steadfast in the tire and motorcycle accessories industry. From the global perspective, the use of motorcycles is particularly high in Southeast Asian countries (Kitamura, Hayashi, & Yagi, 2018), an indication of their adeptness in penetrating and developing a specific market segment, underscoring the significance of FKR's strategic pivot.

Following Fung's passing in 1973 and the absence of a suitable successor, the family opted to disengage from FKR. Consequently, the company was sold to General Corporation Berhad (GCB), a prominent construction and property development group, in 1983. Later in 2018, FKR was acquired by N. D. Rubber Public Company Limited, a distinguished Thai-listed tire manufacturer. This transition of ownership underscored the enduring competitiveness, value and tacit knowledge of FKR in the market.

Currently, FKR has rebranded as FKR Malaysia Sdn. Bhd. It stands as Malaysia's leading supplier of motorcycle and bicycle tires under the FKR brand. The firm handles domestic marketing and distribution, utilizing a well-positioned extensive dealer network across Malaysia to ensure widespread availability of FKR products nationwide. Additionally, FKR motorcycle tires hold certifications for selected sizes from both the Malaysia Standard MS: 1394: 2008 and the European Standard ECE - R75, showcasing the company's dedication to quality and compliance.

7.3.6 Ownership Pattern and Financial Performance

Currently, FKR is a private limited company, operating under the business type of limited by shares. The company's total issued share capital consists of 20,000,000 ordinary shares with all 20,000,000 shares of FKR Malaysia are owned by N.D. Rubber Public Company Limited from Thailand. This indicates complete ownership of the company by N.D. Rubber Public Company Limited. The company's board of directors and officers include Chaiyasit Samrittivanicha, Pornpoj Swadwan, and Lee Yew Wah, who serve as directors.

The financial data for Fung Keong Rubber (FKR) from 2018 to 2022 reveals key insights into the company's financial performance. First, FKR's non-current assets remained stable over this period, indicating consistent investment in long-term assets such as equipment, plant, and property, vital for sustained operations and growth. Meanwhile, current assets fluctuated within a narrow range of RM 27 million to RM 31 million, reflecting stable short-term liquidity. Notably, the company successfully reduced its current liabilities from RM 14.89 million in 2018 to RM 4.79 million in 2022, signaling improved financial stability and lower risk exposure. The share capital remained constant at RM 20 million, indicating a stable ownership structure, while retained earnings increased from RM 12.86 million in 2018 to RM 17.03 million in 2022, highlighting enhanced profitability.

Following a significant loss in 2018, FKR, acquired by N.D. Rubber Public Company Limited, achieved positive profitability from 2019 onward. This suggests successful efforts by the firm to address the issues that led to the loss and implement corrective measures to restore profitability, as evidenced by the positive profit before tax and profit after tax figures in the last four years. The company improved its profit before and after tax, reflecting effective cost management and

Table 7.4 Fung Keong Rubber Manufactory (M) Sdn. Bhd. Balance Sheet, 2018–2022

(RM)	*2022*	*2021*	*2020*	*2019*	*2018*
Non-current Assets	18,953,583	18,666,605	21,953,965	21,372,859	22,466,790
Current assets	27,595,370	31,613,065	29,113,105	28,395,451	31,682,109
Non-current liabilities	261,812	715,428	1,266,428	1,200,206	1,223,108
Current liabilities	4,786,036	7,544,876	9,616,653	9,618,131	14,893,227
Share capital	20,000,000	20,000,000	20,000,000	20,000,000	20,000,000
Reserve	4,466,219	4,466,219	6,141,182	4,931,182	5,169,451
Retain earning	17,034,886	17,553,147	14,042,807	14,018,791	12,863,113

Source: Companies Commission of Malaysia (SSM).

Table 7.5 Fung Keong Rubber Manufactory (M) Sdn. Bhd. income statement, 2018–2022

(RM)	*2022*	*2021*	*2020*	*2019*	*2018*
Revenue	48,058,445	51,537,919	52,240,742	54,952,283	65,478,118
Profit/(loss) before tax	1,337,468	3,065,478	2,573,872	2,059,103	-62,873,22
Profit/(loss) after tax	1,481,739	2,835,377	1,524,016	1,435,471	-64,424,872
Net dividend	48,058,445	51,537,919	52,240,742	54,952,283	65,478,118

Source: Companies Commission of Malaysia (SSM).

operational efficiencies. Overall, FKR demonstrates stable financial fundamentals with prudent asset management, enhanced liquidity, consistent profitability, and stable dividend payments, positioning it well for continued success. Overall, FKR appears to possess stable financial fundamentals, characterized by prudent asset management, improved liquidity, consistent profitability, and stabilized dividend payments.

7.4 Case Study 12: Aerofoam Manufacturing (1969) Sdn. Bhd.

7.4.1 Introduction

Aerofoam is a prominent player in the bedding industry, specializing in the manufacturing and distribution of latex foam mattresses and bedding accessories. Aerofoam traces its roots back to the entrepreneurial spirit of its founder, who was raised in the Jinjiang Selatan, Kepong, and brought up within the Hakka family engaged in pawn business that influenced his journey into the business world.

Over the years, Aerofoam has evolved into a multifaceted entity, encompassing three separate entities: Aerofoam Industries, Aerofoam Bedding, and Aerofoam Manufacturing. This diversification emphasizes Aerofoam's adaptability and commitment to meeting the diverse needs of its customers. Its product range includes latex mattresses, divans, pillows, cushions, spring mattresses, and other bedding accessories, catering to both domestic and international markets.

While Aerofoam's primary market area remains rooted in Malaysia, its reach extends far beyond national borders. With a strategic focus on international expansion, Aerofoam has successfully penetrated overseas markets, particularly in the hospitality sector. Under the leadership of the second generation, Aerofoam has strategically expanded its reach to cater to an international clientele, exporting 80% of its total output overseas.

As Aerofoam embraces the challenges and opportunities of the modern business landscape, the company remains committed to upholding its legacy of excellence and innovation. With the involvement of the third parties, who acquired Aerofoam entirely, Aerofoam continues to chart a path toward sustainable growth and market leadership. The visionary leadership has propelled Aerofoam to new heights, solidifying its position as a global leader in the bedding industry.

Figure 7.5 Exterior View of Aerofoam Manufacturing (1969) Sdn. Bhd. Photograph by the author.

7.4.2 Stage One: Start-up

Aerofoam Industry (1969) Sdn. Bhd. was founded in 1969 by Choo Fook Yen. Originally from Jinjiang Selatan, Kepong, Choo was born and raised in a Hakka family in Malaya. Early Hakka settlers arrived as workers for the gold and tin mines due to historical reasons. When the mining industry faced an economic decline, these settlers redirected their attention toward other sectors. As the family initially worked as mine workers, and later involved in the pawn business, it was from this historical context that Choo was inspired by his upbringing to venture in business world.

Choo embarked on his professional journey in the ironworks and construction sectors before delving into entrepreneurship. The success of Chinese business can be determined by several factors, and the network has been proved as a key business determinant on enterprise performance. In 1969, Choo received support from two influential business tycoons affiliated with YTL Cement and Sun Complex, which laid the groundwork for Aerofoam Industry (1969) Sdn. Bhd. Choo leveraged his knowledge and experience in ironworks and manufacturing to develop Aerofoam's initial products, the latex foam bedding accessories. Through his visionary outlook and determination, he propelled the company to great heights, solidifying its position as a prominent player in the industry.

Since its establishment, Aerofoam has been manufacturing latex foam mattresses. In the early 1980s, the company expanded its operations by establishing another factory dedicated to producing spring mattresses. Since then, the name "Aerofoam" has grown in popularity. As a pivotal latex producer, Aerofoam plays a crucial role in supporting Malaysia's primary natural commodity sector by exclusively utilizing 100% pure Malaysian rubber as its primary raw material. This strategic decision not only enhances the company's commitment to local sourcing but also aligns with broader national economic objectives, fostering sustainability and promoting the country's natural resources.

7.4.3 Stage Two: Expansion

Aerofoam's journey toward excellence is characterized by its commitment to R&D, which serves as the cornerstone of its success. Recognizing the importance of innovation in driving growth and competitiveness, Aerofoam has made substantial investments in R&D initiatives aimed at advancing manufacturing processes and product innovation. By harnessing state-of-the-art machinery and maximizing technological advancements, the company has achieved remarkable operational efficiency while upholding uncompromising quality standards. The proactive approach to R&D adopted by Aerofoam ensures that the company remains at the forefront of industry innovation. Through continuous experimentation and improvement, Aerofoam continually refines its manufacturing techniques and explores new avenues for product development. This relentless pursuit of excellence enables Aerofoam to surpass customer expectations and outpace competitors.

Aerofoam's dedication to manufacturing excellence is further exemplified by its prestigious certifications and accolades. One notable achievement is the SIRIM certificate, awarded to the company for its adherence to stringent quality standards as outlined in the Malaysian Award for Product Quality (MS679:1999). Remarkably, Aerofoam has received this esteemed certification every consecutive year since 1991, a demonstration of its commitment to quality assurance and customer satisfaction.

Moreover, Aerofoam's latex products have garnered certification from the ECO Umwelt Institute of Germany, further validating the company's commitment to environmental sustainability and product integrity. This certification underscores Aerofoam's proactive approach to environmental stewardship, ensuring that its products meet the highest standards of eco-friendliness and sustainability. By prioritizing environmental considerations in its manufacturing processes, Aerofoam not only demonstrates corporate responsibility but also enhances its brand reputation as a socially conscious and environmentally responsible organization.

In addition to its focus on R&D and quality assurance, Aerofoam places a strong emphasis on customer-centricity and market responsiveness. By closely monitoring consumer trends and feedback, Aerofoam can tailor its products and services to meet customer needs and preferences. This customer-centric approach enables Aerofoam to maintain a competitive edge in the marketplace and foster long-term relationships with its clientele.

Overall, the expansion stage of Aerofoam is characterized by a multifaceted strategy encompassing R&D, quality assurance, environmental sustainability, and customer-centricity. Through its proactive approach to innovation and commitment to superior quality, Aerofoam has established itself as a trusted leader in the industry.

7.4.4 Stage Three: Maturity

If the succession is not managed effectively, it can lead to fractures within the family that may require several years to mend. Succession planning is an integral component of a comprehensive strategy that encompasses the development of leadership skills and training to adequately prepare the incoming successor. In preparation for grooming his elder daughter, Florence Choo Suit Ling to assume leadership within the family firm, Choo made a strategic decision to send her abroad for education. Florence assumed the role of leader at Aerofoam in February 2000, following a successful tenure within the company upon her return. With a degree in Business Studies from London Metropolitan University, she dedicated an impressive 33 years to Aerofoam. Started as an Executive Director, she progressively ascended the ranks to become the Chief Executive Officer, leaving an enduring mark on the company's growth trajectory and strategic direction.

During her time as leader, Florence led various strategic initiatives that propelled Aerofoam to new levels of success. Aerofoam serves as an original equipment manufacturer (OEM), producing a wide range of bedding products for various brands and clients. One notable achievement was the establishment and development of the company's export division. She also expanded Aerofoam's footprint in government procurement and local retail sectors, while ensuring high quality standards by initiating ISO certification for the factory. Her visionary leadership also fostered key international partnerships, such as the collaboration with Therapedic Inc. USA, which enhanced Aerofoam's brand recognition and technical expertise. This is a remarkable outcome that demonstrates the new insights generated by Florence, based on the tacit knowledge she acquired. More precisely, it indicates that local consumers prefer European brands.

The change from one generation to another has a substantial impact on a family business's capacity to enhance its structure of ownership, knowledge innovation, and firm's visions. Florence's emphasis on building a robust sales and marketing team ensured that Aerofoam became a preferred supplier of bedding products to prestigious hotel chains. Her tenure marked a period of significant innovation, expansion, and market dominance for the firm. Consequently, Aerofoam established two distinct entities: Aerofoam Industries and Aerofoam Bedding.

Under the leadership of Florence from 2000 to 2012, the company strategically expanded its reach to cater to international clientele, particularly in the hospitality sector. Under her leadership, Aerofoam exports 80% of its total output overseas. By offering premium bedding accessories, the company has successfully penetrated overseas markets, capitalizing on its reputation for quality and reliability. This strategic diversification not only strengthens Aerofoam's market position but also positions it as a global leader in the bedding industry.

7.4.5 Stage Four: Diversification

Upon Florence's retirement, her siblings and relatives showed little interest in inheriting the family business, prompting her to make the decision to sell the company. In 2011, Ji Kim Chuan and Francis Ng Boon Toung seized the opportunity to acquire Aerofoam's business, recognizing its bright prospects and market potential. Under their stewardship, Aerofoam has flourished, becoming a leading producer of Therapedic and Mylatex, an all-latex line of mattresses, pillows, and other bedding accessories. Currently, Aerofoam ranks among the top three manufacturers of 100% natural latex bedding in Malaysia, boasting a dedicated team of 220 skilled and experienced staff members.

Ji and Francis shared a vision of expanding Aerofoam's business internationally. They strategically focused on tapping into the burgeoning Chinese market, establishing distribution channels such as Beijing Mylatex Technology Co., Ltd and Guangdong Sweetnight Home Co., Ltd. This proactive approach enabled Aerofoam to gain a foothold in China, a key milestone in its journey toward global expansion.

In 2020, Aerofoam embarked on a transformative partnership with Eclipse International, a leading bedding producer in America. This collaboration saw Aerofoam acquiring the Eastman House and Chittenden & Eastman licenses in Malaysia, positioning them as the company's high-end luxury brands in Malaysia and Singapore. This strategic move not only bolstered Aerofoam's product portfolio but also solidified its presence in the luxury bedding segment.

Furthermore, Aerofoam's partnership with Maeda Matsu Co. PPE Ltd., the former operator of Eastman House of Southeast Asia, further strengthened its position in the Malaysian and Singaporean markets. With Peter Yau's recommendation and retirement from the business, Aerofoam was entrusted as his successor, reflecting the trust and confidence placed in Aerofoam's capabilities.

Aerofoam's success can be attributed to its relentless pursuit of innovation, quality, and market penetration within the Malaysian bedding industry. By strategically leveraging locally sourced materials, investing in research and development, expanding into international markets, and prioritizing customer satisfaction, Aerofoam has established itself as a shining example of industry excellence and resilience.

7.4.6 Ownership Pattern and Financial Performance

According to the Companies Commission of Malaysia (SSM), Aerofoam falls within the category of a private limited company engaged in manufacturing and distributing rubber foam products and spring mattresses. The analysis of the provided financial information offers valuable insights into the performance and capabilities of the company over recent years.

The summary of share capital indicates a total issued capital of RM 7,800,003.00, solely consisting of ordinary shares. Notably, there have been no discernible changes in the capital shares as outlined in the provided report. Delving into the shareholder composition, it is evident that the company is primarily owned by four individuals, each holding varying proportions of shares. Chung Chow Cheang, Ji Kim Chuan, and Ng Boon Toung hold an equal stake of 2,340,001.00 shares each, signifying a shared ownership structure among these key stakeholders. Meanwhile, Ji Lee Chen possesses a smaller shareholding of 780,000.00 shares, indicating a minority ownership position within the company's ownership hierarchy. From an ownership pattern perspective, the equal distribution of shares among Ji Kim Chuan, Ng Boon Toung, and Chung Chow Cheang suggests a collaborative decision-making framework among these major shareholders. Their equal stake in the company signifies a balanced distribution of power and influence in strategic decision-making processes. Conversely, Ji Lee Chen's minority stake may imply a less significant role in shaping the company's direction, potentially necessitating a deeper examination of the dynamics within the boardroom and shareholder interactions.

From 2018 to 2022, the company experienced significant revenue fluctuations, peaking at RM 62,648,020 in 2019 but declining to RM 35,618,458 and RM 35,531,084 in 2020 and 2021, respectively. These variations, especially during the COVID-19 pandemic, indicate challenges in sustaining sales. The company's profitability also suffered, with negative profit figures before and after tax in 2021 and 2022, suggesting difficulties in managing expenses or generating revenue. Meanwhile, the company maintains a stable capital structure with consistent levels of share capital and reserves over the years, there is a noticeable increase in current liabilities compared to non-current assets. This suggests potential liquidity concerns or short-term debt obligations that require effective management to avoid financial strain. In conclusion, while the company demonstrates stability in its capital structure and ownership dynamics, its recent financial performance highlights challenges in profitability and revenue generation.

Table 7.6 Aerofoam Manufacturing (1969) Sdn. Bhd. balance sheet, 2018–2022

(RM)	*2022*	*2021*	*2020*	*2019*	*2018*
Non-current Assets	46,980,858	46,092,733	48,071,329	49,763,605	46,482,174
Current assets	42,450,996	41,038,031	42,357,537	56,891,022	49,606,037
Non-Current Liabilities	28,730,671	25,394,820	23,204,460	30,306,782	27,980,377
Current Liabilities	37,793,652	37,933,802	37,110,440	40,722,558	43,799,114
Share Capital	7,800,003	7,800,003	7,800,003	7,800,003	7,800,003
Reserve	14,842,792	14,842,792	14,842,792	14,842,792	0
Retain Earning	293,729	1,195,344	7,426,350	13,332,476	16,329,767

Source: Companies Commission of Malaysia (SSM).

Table 7.7 Aerofoam Manufacturing (1969) Sdn. Bhd. income statement, 2018–2022

(RM)	*2022*	*2021*	*2020*	*2019*	*2018*
Revenue	55,158,307	35,531,084	35,618,458	62,648,020	46,482,174
Profit/(loss) before tax	-209,766	-5,748,211	-5,519,103	-2,543,519	925,490
Profit/(loss) after tax	-894,611	-6,311,824	-5,509,322	-3,526,225	765,697
Net dividend	0	0	0	0	0

Source: Companies Commission of Malaysia (SSM).

7.5 Summary

This chapter focuses on the evolution and impact of Chinese family-owned businesses in Malaysia's rubber industry. The chapter explores how these businesses have adapted over time to changes in the global market, maintaining their competitiveness through innovation and leveraging tacit knowledge across generations.

The chapter begins by detailing the historical context of Malaysia's rubber industry, which dates to the colonial era. British colonizers introduced rubber cultivation in the late 19th century, recognizing the region's climate and land as ideal for rubber production. Over time, Malaysia became one of the world's leading rubber producers. Chinese immigrants, initially employed as rubber tappers, gradually entered the rubber business, and some established successful enterprises.

The chapter highlights key Chinese-owned companies such as Top Glove Corporation Berhad, Fung Keong Rubber Manufactory (M) Sdn. Bhd., and Aerofoam Manufacturing (1969) Sdn. Bhd. These businesses have thrived by leveraging generational knowledge, first-mover advantages, and innovation in rubber-related products. For example, Top Glove has grown into the world's largest glove manufacturer, driven by strong family leadership and a focus on R&D. Similarly, Fung Keong's transition from shoe manufacturing to tire production showcases the ability to adapt to shifting market demands. Aerofoam Manufacturing's diversification into latex foam bedding and mattresses also reflects the adaptability of Chinese family businesses in the rubber industry. These companies have successfully transformed their operations, navigating global challenges by developing new products and entering international markets.

Overall, the chapter reflects how Chinese family businesses in the rubber industry have evolved by building on their founders' tacit knowledge, professionalizing their operations, and innovating to remain competitive in the global market.

8 From Familyrizing to Evolutionizing Chinese Businesses in Malaysia

This chapter presents the findings of the study through two key lenses: empirical analysis and theoretical synthesis. The first part focuses on generational shifts in Chinese family businesses in Malaysia, dissecting crucial themes: class resources, ethnic resources, knowledge factors, Chinese networks, local markets, and the role of the state. The second part compares and synthesizes these themes to offer deeper insights into the evolution of these businesses. A comparative analysis of 12 businesses in the food, plastics, and rubber industries highlights the role of tacit knowledge innovation as leadership transitions across generations. This exploration uncovers socio-economic dynamics often overlooked, illustrating how generational entrepreneurship unfolds within Malaysia's Chinese community. Drawing from the case studies, the chapter showcases the journeys of these entrepreneurs, revealing how past legacies influence present strategies and how today's decisions shape the future. Ultimately, it offers a comprehensive view of the resilience and transformation of Chinese family businesses across generations in Malaysia.

8.1 Introduction

The evolution of CFBs in Malaysia presents a unique narrative of adaptability and strategic innovation. They navigate through generational changes, shifting market dynamics, and state policies. This chapter aims to explore the intricate process of transformation from "familyrizing"—where businesses are predominantly family run—to "evolutionizing," signifying their adaptation and growth into modern, competitive entities.

Through an integrated thematic analysis, we explore the multifaceted factors influencing this evolution, including class and ethnic resources, knowledge transfer, market dynamics, and state influence. Comparative analyses will further illuminate how these businesses have balanced traditional values with modern business practices, leveraging ethnic enclaves, targeting diverse markets, and evolving their products and business identities. By examining these elements, we aim to uncover the strategic pathways that have enabled CFBs in Malaysia to sustain growth and achieve prominence over generations.

DOI: 10.4324/9781032705842-8

This chapter not only highlights the successes but also the challenges and strategic responses of these businesses, offering valuable insights into their enduring legacy and future potential in a rapidly changing economic environment.

8.2 Integrated Thematic Analysis on the Evolution of Chinese Family Businesses in Malaysia

8.2.1 Generational Change and Resources

To construct a comprehensive analysis of the 12 CFBs in Malaysia, it is essential to navigate their strategic evolution through the lenses of class resources, ethnic resources, impact of networks, and the transfer of tacit knowledge across generat ions.

8.2.1.1 Class Resources

Across the cases studies, education emerges as a pivotal class resource in all three industries, evident in most of the cases such as London Biscuit, King's Confectionery, Besfomec, LH Plus, SKP Resources, Top Glove, Fung Keong, and Aerofoam stand out with their second or subsequent generation leaders educated abroad, bringing back insights into modern management and technology. In Top Glove's case, even the founder, Lim Wee Chai himself gained a PhD in Management. The educational advantage not only empowered them to adopt cutting-edge practices but also facilitated strategic decision-making and adaptation to global market trends. Besides education, initial capital accumulation through family savings or strategic partnerships from the same social class played a pivotal role in establishing these businesses, illustrating their ability to leverage financial resources for growth and expansion, exemplified by London Biscuits' strategic acquisitions and market expansions. This financial acumen enables resilience during economic downturns and facilitates pivots into new markets or product lines, ensuring long-term sustainability amidst competitive pressures. Education and financial literacy facilitate the transfer of tacit knowledge from experienced family leaders to the next generation, preparing them to innovate and lead effectively in a dynamic business environment.

8.2.1.2 Ethnic Resources

The ethnic resources, cultural heritage and values form another significant pillar for these businesses, shaping their operational ethos and market strategies. CFBs in food industry demonstrates how adherence to traditional values fosters consumer trust and authenticity in their products. These 6 CFBs in food industry have adeptly integrated cultural elements into their product development, branding and operations, maintaining a competitive edge while catering to diverse consumer preferences within Malaysia's multicultural society when the market and generations changed. Baker's Cottage and Kam Lun Tai innovated mooncakes by

Table 8.1 London Biscuit: Generational Shifts in Resources, Knowledge, and Networks

Generation	*Class Resources*	*Ethnic Resources*	*Tacit Knowledge*	*Networks*
First	Began as a family business in timber industry dealing with construction and furniture trading	The family business leader, Low Nam Hui was a reputational icon in Hakka community	Developed knowledge in management and operation of family business	Low Nam Hui utilized his connections within the local business, Hakka community and the World Low Family Reunion Association to sustain his business
Second	The transition of leadership to the son, Liew Kuek Hin, who graduated from Nanyang University	Ventured into food industry after acquiring London Biscuits (Johor) Sdn. Bhd.	Leveraging local resources and traditional methods with implementing advanced technologies for corn-based snacks and biscuit cup products with different flavors, introducing London Pie Cakes and Swiss roll cakes	Leveraging familial and business networks and gained Disney character licensing in London Swiss roll to penetrate the Southeast Asian market
Third	Kuek Hin's children, Liew Yew Chung, Liew Yew Cheng, Liew Yet Lee and Liew Yet Mei joined the family businesses after graduated from university	Expansion into snack foods and cakes catering to local tastes and preferences	Gained different tacit knowledge through acquisition and implementing professional management strategies while retaining the core family values and traditional business practices	Establishing strong relationships with suppliers and distributors, as well as expanding local and international market presence through strategic partnerships

Source: Compiled by the author.

Table 8.2 King's Confectionery: Generational Shifts in Resources, Knowledge, and Networks

Generation	*Class Resources*	*Ethnic Resources*	*Tacit Knowledge*	*Networks*
First Part I	Opened a Hainanese style Kopitiam in a small town with small capital	Operated as ethnic enterprise through their expertise in Hainanese style foods and coffee	Utilized founder's profound knowledge of Hainanese traditional food recipes and brewed coffee to attract customers who love Hainanese foods	Family-oriented business model with significant involvement of family members
First Part II	Transition of leadership from the founder to the next generation, Wong Yoke Khing, who was well-trained in professional culinary skills	Successfully integrating traditional Hainanese bakery techniques with modern baking practices to cater to local markets	Accumulated and transferred bakery knowledge such as the Portuguese egg tart from Macau, allowing the business to innovate	Active engagement with the local and regional bakery industry, leveraging family and business connections to expand market presence and build a trusted brand
Second	Wong Lei Hoy, graduated from overseas university in Australia, majored in business administration	Preserving the Hainanese cultural influence in their products while adopting contemporary baking techniques and international standards	Implementing professional management strategies Focus on R&D to produce many different products with different packaging	Transformation into franchising powerhouse, *Kopitiam* lifestyle cafes and opens outlets in Dhaka, Bangladesh through their business connections

Source: Compiled by the author.

Table 8.3 Leong Hup and Baker's Cottage: Generational Shifts in Resources, Knowledge, and Networks

Generation	*Class Resources*	*Ethnic Resources*	*Tacit Knowledge*	*Networks*
First	Gained initial capital from their father's vegetable wholesale business, ventured into day-old chicken rearing and poultry farming activities	Leveraged traditional Chinese methods in poultry farming and food processing, integrating these with modern agricultural techniques	Utilized profound knowledge of poultry farming to establish Leong Hup Enhanced feedmill technology and established overseas plants and prepared for food processing	Large number of family members involved in the business, leveraged their network in Teochew community that are experts in agriculture
Second	Generated profit rapidly and listed on the Malaysian main board, improve the social status of the family	Integrated traditional Chinese methods with scientific expertise and modern agricultural practices to cater to local and regional markets	Accumulated and transferred knowledge of poultry farming and food processing, allowing for innovation and adaptation	Leveraging networks with Emivest Berhad, Teo Seng Capital Berhad, Lee Say Group, PT Malindo Feedmill TBK etc. to expand their market reach, including Malaysia, Indonesia, Vietnam, Singapore, and the Philippines
Third	Further diversification and expansion into new product lines through investment capital	Diversified into the confectionery business, acquired Baker's Cottage and transformed it from bakeries to a renowned mooncake brand	Drawing inspiration from traditional Teochew mooncake recipes and adapted new techniques to meet the evolving tastes Established "Farm-to-Plate" concept	

Source: Compiled by the author.

Table 8.4 Besfomec: Generational Shifts in Resources, Knowledge, and Networks

Generation	*Class Resources*	*Ethnic Resources*	*Tacit Knowledge*	*Networks*
One	Lau Tin Shun worked as a traditional Chinese medicine (TCM) practitioner; his profession placed him at a higher social level compared to laborers	Began with Xin Chun Woh Chinese medical hall to serve the Chinese community	Leveraging profound knowledge of TCM and deep-seated cultural heritage	Imported traditional Chinese herbs such as ginseng and cordyceps from China through the Hakka network
Second	The transition of leadership from Mr. Lau Tin Shun to his son, Low Poo Chin who joined the business during his secondary school years	Introduced products that resonates with the Chinese culture and preferences	Strategic use of local ingredients, such as Snakehead fish and sea cucumber, to build a Nanyang-style healthcare brand based on tacit knowledge in remedies passed down by the founder	Active engagement with the Chinese community, participation in local cultural and social activities such as Malacca Hakka Association Forging strategic partnerships and gaining markets in Singapore, China, Hong Kong, and Vietnam
Third	The third generation, including Low Chew Ping, a pharmacy graduate from Australia and joined the family business	Diversified the business into tourism industry based on heritage culture, including developed the concept of health product as gift hampers and established the Besfomec Boutique Hotel	Integrating traditional Chinese herbs with modern pharmaceutical practices has enabled the products to meet the market demand	

Source: Compiled by the author.

Table 8.5 Hei Hwang: Generational Shifts in Resources, Knowledge, and Networks

Generation	*Class Resources*	*Ethnic Resources*	*Tacit Knowledge*	*Networks*
First	Began as a traditional herbal shop in Ipoh The family business grew continuously, diversified into coffee powder manufactured and health beverages	Served the Chinese community with home-based herbal drinks, especially those who fall sick but are not able to afford to consult TCM practitioner.	Possessed deep expertise in traditional Chinese herbs Codified knowledge in coffee and herbal production Processed quality soybean powder, nut powder and Detox cleanse powder with fruit ingredients	Strong community ties in Ipoh, and expanding networks through the Hakka clan and kinship such as their relatives in homeland, the *Huizhou* Hakka Chinese in China
Second		Explored opportunities to bring Ipoh white coffee series in instant packaging within Chinese community in Ipoh		Kinship and commercial networks in China, enabling market expansion and distribution. Ties with local communities in Malaysia and international partners
Third	Lee Haw Yuan and Lee Haw Huang joined the family business after graduated from university	Maintained authenticity of Chinese herbal traditions while meeting halal principles, global health standards and consumer trends	Continued to innovate traditional Chinese herbal remedies, further diversified into health drinks and wellness products with modern packaging and marketing techniques	Local distributors in Malaysia and sole distributorships in China and Singapore. Strong presence in organic shops, Chinese medical halls, and convenience stores in the region. Partnered with retailers like Sheng Siong

Source: Compiled by the author.

Table 8.6 Kam Lun Tai: Generational Shifts in Resources, Knowledge, and Networks

Generation	*Class Resources*	*Ethnic Resources*	*Tacit Knowledge*	*Networks*
First	Began as a dim sum eatery Invested Malaysia's first automated mooncake production machine, increasing efficiency and quality control	Utilized traditional Chinese recipes and culinary techniques in food preparation and processing Bought over the "Kam Lun Tai" name from HS Lee, transformed Kam Lun Tai into renowned brand	Founder gained extensive knowledge and skills in Cantonese culinary through hands on experience, mastery of Cantonese cuisine, especially dim sum, noodles and mooncakes Continued commitment to Cantonese culinary traditions while integrating automation to enhance production	The founders and key associates were from Gaozhou, Guangdong, reflecting the importance of dialect group connections within the Cantonese community. The strong community presence, building a loyal customer base through quality and consistency in traditional food offerings
Second	Diversified into catering services and food processing, receiving halal certification and expanding product offerings internationally	Introduced flavors with local influences (e.g., pandan, durian) while maintaining Cantonese culinary heritage, appealing to both traditionalists and modern consumers	Leveraged family knowledge passed down across generation to maintain high standards while expanding into new areas, including frozen dim sum and OEM production	Expanded network to include international connections and culinary associations, which boosted Kam Lun Tai's market presence and credibility. Broadened distribution channels through partnerships in Singapore, Chinatowns globally, and OEM services

Source: Compiled by the author.

Table 8.7 LH Plus: Generational Shifts in Resources, Knowledge, and Networks

Generation	*Class Resources*	*Ethnic Resources*	*Tacit Knowledge*	*Networks*
One & Second	Chen Kow Fatt started a bicycle workshop with small capital The elder son, Tony Chen took over the reins in 1969	Henghua people initially dominated the rickshaw pulling occupation, then transitioned to dominating the bicycle and transportation industry Retained entrepreneurial adaptability inherent in Henghua culture while branching into a new industry (plastics)	Expertise in metalwork and bicycle part manufacturing Shifted expertise from metalwork to plastics wares manufacturing and catering to customization orders from MNCs Leveraged first-mover advantage in the emerging plastics sector	Built connections within the local community, catering to transportation needs and gaining customers in the bicycle industry. Extensive collaborations with international brands (Nestle, Mattel, Tupperware and Rubbermaid) Participated in global exhibitions with MATRADE's guidance, establishing global connections
Third	Under the leadership of third-generation CEO Callum Chen, who joined the family business after completed his secondary education, LH Plus enhanced its production capabilities further	Embraced modern management practices while preserving family-driven business culture	Expansion to OEM, OBM, and ODM MNCs, leading in plastic manufacturing	Extensive global network through leadership in Malaysian Plastics Manufacturers Association (MPMA), Asia Plastics Forum (APF), and collaboration with global industry leaders
Fourth	Caryn and Clement who earned university degrees joined the family business	Diversification initiative led to the establishment of Clover Design and Halo+ Agency, supported by Google Inc., in promoting Nanyang Malaysia branded products	Complementing the family business with their design expertise for consultancy services and product development Expanded offerings to include premium and gift products	Strengthened domestic and international business through new partnerships, CSR involvement, and maintaining employee loyalty. Continued participation in industry forums and knowledge-sharing networks

Source: Compiled by the author.

Table 8.8 SKP Resources: Generational Shifts in Resources, Knowledge, and Networks

Generation	*Class Resources*	*Ethnic Resources*	*Tacit Knowledge*	*Networks*
First	Established as Sin Kwang Plastic in Singapore, focusing on plastic injection molding	Leveraged cultural understanding of local Chinese communities and moved operations to Johor to improve their costs	Accumulated significant expertise in high-precision plastic injection molding Focus on integrity and quality to counter negative stereotypes	Developed strong relationships with local suppliers and customers, leveraging community connections in the Johor Bahru area to build a robust business network
Second	The second- generation family members are highly educated Gan Poh San completed his bachelor's and master's degree in overseas and was sent to Kai Japanese School and Nissei Plastics School in Japan	Leveraged linguistic adaptability for collaboration, speaking Japanese to facilitate smoother negotiations	Continued knowledge transfer from the first generation, adapted Japanese working culture, learned plastics engineering from Japan and strategic pivot toward semiconductors and continuous technological adaptation	Formed strategic partnerships with MNCs, such as Audio Pioneer Visual, fostering strong international relationships and leveraged international trade agreements like AFTA Strengthened global supply chain relationships, enhancing market position and fostering international collaborations

Source: Compiled by the author.

Table 8.9 Kemajuan: Generational Shifts in Resources, Knowledge, and Networks

Generation	*Class Resources*	*Ethnic Resources*	*Tacit Knowledge*	*Networks*
First	Founded by Chan and Chia families as a metal fabrication and contracts firm in Kuala Lumpur	Intra-ethnic collaborations leveraged to access capital and technical expertise	Profound knowledge of metal fabrication and contract work, developed through hands-on experience and family expertise	Established local industry connections and clientele, building a reputation for quality and reliability in metal fabrication
Second	Bought plastic injection machines, expanding into plastic packaging for electronic devices	Adapted traditional Chinese values to create unity and cohesion between two families	Expanded expertise in plastic packaging Codified plastic injection molding knowledge and invested in in-house R&D for carrier tape technology Diversified into OEM manufacturing	Developed relationships with Japanese and, European, and American MNCs. Expanded overseas operations, including a plant in Thailand Strategic collaboration with ST Microelectronics in Casablanca, Morocco, leading to key insights for technological advancement

Source: Compiled by the author.

Table 8.10 Top Glove: Generational Shifts in Resources, Knowledge, and Networks

Generation	*Class Resources*	*Ethnic Resources*	*Tacit Knowledge*	*Networks*
First	Educational background in Physics, MBA, and PhD in Management Leveraged family business experience in rubber trading Strong family members with high educational level involvement in leadership roles	Hokkien Chinese family business heritage Family and Chinese community support in initial business setup Collaborations with Chinese business community	Accumulated knowledge from rubber trading and manufacturing Strategic foresight in glove industry Hands-on experience from family business Advanced R&D in glove production technologies and quality control measures Diversification into specialized glove products and sustainable manufacturing practices	Partnerships with local rubber resource suppliers, leveraged personal business connections and rubber trading network. Built intra- and inter- ethnic connections within the local rubber industry and began exporting globally, establishing early market presence. Expanded global distribution channels and formed strategic alliances with distributors, healthcare institutions, suppliers and international regulatory bodies for compliance and market expansion.
Second	Lim Jin Feng graduated from university and currently taking on the role of General Manager of Marketing		Jin Feng demonstrated ability to navigate the complexities of the market and drive strategic marketing initiatives and build up the brand name of Top Glove	Collaborations with government agencies and industry associations (e.g., Malaysian Rubber Board, MREPC, FMM). Extensive involvement in Chinese associations and organizations

Source: Compiled by the author.

Table 8.11 Fung Keong Rubber: Generational Shifts in Resources, Knowledge, and Networks

Generation	*Class Resources*	*Ethnic Resources*	*Tacit Knowledge*	*Networks*
One	Background in machinery and rubber trading Early focus on manufacturing rubber shoes Cultivated highly educated successors, but regrettably passed away before founder	Community connections from Canton and leveraged Chinese immigrant networks in Malaya and Hong Kong	Tacit knowledge from studying machinery and rubber production Transition from manual to mechanized production Experience in political and regional dynamics	Network established through political involvement and early business operations. Involvement in regional business networks, market networks in Hong Kong, Malaya, Singapore, and North Borneo
Second	Sale to General Corporation Berhad (GCB) in 1983 Acquired by N.D. Rubber Public Company Limited in 2018	Integration into new ownership structures Maintaining market presence and adapting to new ownership dynamics	Shift in focus to bicycle and motorcycle tires, continued application of tacit knowledge in rubber manufacturing Expansion into related sectors such as motorcycle parts and lubricants	Leveraged extensive dealer network in Malaysia. Established relationships with regional and international business partners

Source: Compiled by the author.

Table 8.12 Aerofoam: Generational Shifts in Resources, Knowledge, and Networks

Generation	*Class Resources*	*Ethnic Resources*	*Tacit Knowledge*	*Networks*
First	Support from influential business tycoons (YTL Cement, Sun Complex)	Choo Fook Yen's background as a Hakka and his experience in ironworks and manufacturing	Accumulated knowledge from ironworks and manufacturing Developed deep knowledge in latex foam manufacturing processes and product quality	Established strong connections with suppliers, distributors, and key industry stakeholders in Malaysia. Industry certifications and collaborations with international partners for quality assurance and market expansion
Second	Florence Choo's education and leadership, including business studies and strategic initiatives Investment in R&D, advanced machinery, and certifications (SIRIM, ECO Umwelt Institute)	Collaborated with the Chinese business community as they dominated the rubber industry	Enhanced knowledge in OEM manufacturing and product diversification strategies	Expanded market presence through partnerships with global brands and OEM manufacturing contracts
Third	Acquisition by Ji Kim Chuan and Francis Ng Boon Toung	Continuation of the legacy and expansion into international markets (e.g., China)	Expertise in R&D for manufacturing processes and product innovation Expansion into luxury bedding market	Partnerships with Eclipse International and Maeda Matsu Co. PPE Ltd. for market expansion and luxury segments

Source: Compiled by the author.

introducing modern flavors and healthier ingredients, maintaining cultural relevance while appealing to contemporary consumers. London Biscuits' utilization of tacit knowledge of corn flour to produce Nanyang-style snack food, King's Confectionery's creation of pandan layer cake, Besfomec's integration of traditional Chinese herbal ingredients into chicken essence, and Hei Hwang's development of health drinks incorporating traditional Chinese medicinal herbs showcases how tacit knowledge innovation led to unique product developments tailored to local tastes and cultural preferences.

In plastic and rubber industry, we find that it is difficult to recognize that they are CFBs by the products only. This is due to the nature of the industry which is closely tied with technology. However, they retained the cultural values within their operations, successor planning and the "jia" family concept remained unchanged as the base of the business. Family governance models, anchored in cultural values, drive decision-making processes and intra-family dynamics. The Liew family of Leong Hup and Baker's Cottage, the Chia and Tan family of Kemajuan, and the Lim family of Top Glove exemplify cohesive family governance, fostering continuity and resilience to navigate market challenges and capitalize on growth opportunities through strategic alignments and decisive leadership.

8.2.1.3 Tacit Knowledge Transfer and Generational Adaptation, Intra-ethnic, and Inter-ethnic Collaborations Networks

Networks provide CFBs with access to diverse resources and expertise critical for tacit knowledge innovation. Intra-ethnic resources, such as the Chinese Chambers of Commerce, dialect groups, and clanship networks, play a crucial role in facilitating tacit knowledge transfer and generational adaptation among CFBs. These organizations provide a support system, fostering business collaborations, mentorship, and cultural continuity. The Chinese Chambers offer a platform for advocacy and networking, while dialect groups and clanships create trust-based relationships that promote knowledge sharing and mutual assistance. Even though these organizations were founded in the early stage of migration, they remain functional are an effective network for CFBs. Among all 12 cases, we can find that they are good in utilizing the intra-ethnic network through generations. For instance, Hei Hwang adopted a strategy where they leveraged their network of kinship ties to collaborate with community in *Huizhou*, China is remarkable.

Aerofoam's journey began with collaborations with influential business figures associated with YTL Cement and Sun Complex, similar to Kam Lun Tai that was sold to Lum Tuck Loy by Tun HS Lee. The success of these 12 CFBs can be attributed to its strategic use of networks. The founders, through their extensive connections within the Chinese business community, were able to access critical market information, resources, and expertise. These networks not only provided a support system but also facilitated the transfer of tacit knowledge. As the business expanded, the integration of new members into these networks ensured that the flow of tacit knowledge continued, enabling the company to innovate and maintain its competitive edge.

Illustrated by several examples among the 12 cases, inter-ethnic networks. Examples of this are the with governmental bodies, like the Malaysia External Trade Development Corporation (MATRADE) or the Malaysian Investment Development Authority (MIDA) and MNCs, that offer access to market insights, funding opportunities, and technological support. This network enhances businesses' ability to innovate by providing crucial resources that may not be available in class or ethnic resources.

CFBs like Top Glove have expanded globally through partnerships with international entities, leveraging diverse networks to enhance their technological capabilities in the rubber glove manufacturing. Similarly, SKP Resources has forged alliances with MNCs and foreign investors, enriching its business strategies with global perspectives and fostering innovation in manufacturing and distribution. Leong Hup's with non-Chinese board members and business partners exemplify how inter-ethnic collaborations enable businesses to diversify their product offerings and penetrate new markets. Fung Keong's success story also highlights the significance of inter-ethnic networks in its business evolution. Initially operating in British colonies like Hong Kong and Malaya, Fung Keong leveraged its strategic presence to build relationships with diverse communities and business partners.

Interactions within networks facilitate knowledge exchange and learning, and are foundational to tacit knowledge development. Intra-ethnic and inter-ethnic networks, such as those within family businesses like Top Glove or Leong Hup, foster a culture of shared experiences and insights. This informal sharing of tacit knowledge among family members, board members, and long-term employees enables the refinement and adaptation of business practices, promoting continuous improvement and innovation. Strategic alliances and innovation partnerships enhance the innovation capabilities of CFBs by pooling complementary expertise and resources. For instance, collaborations between LH Plus and international organizations for R&D initiatives illustrate how strategic partnerships leverage external expertise to develop new technologies and improve product offerings. These alliances accelerate innovation cycles, enhance product differentiation, and strengthen market competitiveness.

Networks contribute to risk management and resilience by diversifying business relationships and reducing dependency on singular markets or suppliers. Inter-ethnic collaborations, such as those seen in partnerships with Bumiputera directors, navigate regulatory landscapes and mitigate geopolitical risks. This network diversity enhances business continuity and resilience against external shocks, safeguarding tacit knowledge assets and sustaining long-term innovation efforts.

8.2.2 Market Dynamics and State Influence

The motion of local market shifting was intertwined with the macro environment. It can be observed through the condition of CFBs in Southeast Asia countries, that state policies are the strongest force that unleashed and restricted the market potential. Thus, in this part, we discuss how market dynamics and state policies impacted the growth strategies and adaptations of CFBs across generations in Malaysia. This discussion integrates insights from various cases, emphasizing how businesses navigated local markets and leveraged state policies to achieve growth and sustainability.

8.2.2.1 Influence and Support of State Policies

Among all 12 cases in three industries, it was difficult to find out if there are any initiatives that benefit the CFBs, however, they are actively aligned to the state policies. Focusing on the technological advancement, the issue of innovation plays a vital role in every development or transformation policy agenda. By institutionalizing the innovation processes within innovation systems, policymakers endeavor to nurture and develop entrepreneurial capacity to produce new products and services, including supporting firms, as shown in case studies, of attempts to transform tacit knowledge into codified forms toward a knowledge-based economy. In the food, plastic, and rubber manufacturing industry, fostering innovation to nurture a knowledge-based economy challenged the government to implement policies related to industry specification, product differentiation, benchmarking, branding management, and industry transformation.

Government initiatives such as the Look East Policy (LEP) and Industry4WRD have provided crucial support in terms of technology adoption, skills development, and market expansion. For example, SKP Resources and Kemajuan benefited from the LEP, which encouraged the adoption of Japanese business practices and enhanced the company's operational efficiency and product quality. This policy alignment enabled the family businesses to gain a competitive edge in the global plastics manufacturing industry, illustrating how state interventions can foster business growth and innovation.

Moreover, policies under the Malaysian Rubber Export Promotion Council (MREPC), Malaysia External Trade Development Corporation (Matrade) and Malaysian Investment Development Authority (MIDA), such as the Domestic Investment Strategic Fund (DISF) and Smart Automation Grant (SAG), have incentivized businesses like Leong Hup, LH Plus, and Top Glove to invest in technology upgrades and automation. These initiatives not only enhanced operational capabilities but also facilitated market expansion and international competitiveness. State support has thus been instrumental in shaping the strategic directions of these businesses, enabling them to navigate challenges and capitalize on growth opportunities.

In food industry, the halal certification from JAKIM Malaysia significantly influences CFBs by expanding their market reach to Muslim consumers, both locally and internationally. Obtaining this certification ensures compliance with Islamic dietary laws, as well as enhancing product credibility and trust among Muslim customers. Among all 6 cases in the food industry, London Biscuit, King's Confectionery, Baker's Cottage, Besfomec, Hei Hwang, and Kam Lun Tai have strategically sought halal certification to access a larger consumer base, fostering brand loyalty and boosting sales. Additionally, the certification opens opportunities for export to predominantly Muslim countries, driving business growth and competitive advantage in the global market.

8.2.2.2 Local Markets: Adaptation and Evolution

The 12 cases for this study have demonstrated remarkable adaptation to local market dynamics over decades. Initially starting with niche products or services catering to specific community needs, these businesses evolved to capture broader market segments.

From the 1930s, Malaysia's economy was largely colonial, dominated by rubber and tin industries under British control. Large plantations and mines thrived, with minimal local industrial activity. It was in this context that Fung Keong relocated its factory to Klang in Malaya. The 1940s brought disruption due to the Japanese occupation during World War II, leading to a period of economic disarray followed by reconstruction efforts to restore infrastructure and revitalize the rubber and tin sectors. Understanding the economy and societal conditions, it is reasonable that Besfomec was founded as *Xin Chun Woh* Chinese medical hall in Malacca in 1948, and LH Plus was established in Kuala Lumpur around 1947 as a bicycle repair workshop. Businesses established after the war were relatively low-cost and required low technology skills.

The 1950s marked Malaysia's independence in 1957, spurring economic diversification beyond rubber and tin to include agriculture and manufacturing. This era saw significant infrastructure development. The 1960s introduced import substitution industrialization policies, fostering the growth of manufacturing industries like textiles and electronics. Leong Hup was founded in this era, transitioning from a small-scale chicken farm to a leading integrated poultry producer in response to increasing local demand for poultry products. Similarly, SKP Resources began as a plastic injection workshop and expanded its operations in response to industrialization and the manufacturing boom in Malaysia. Hei Hwang established a traditional herbal shop and produced home-based herbal drinks to cater to the local community. Aerofoam was founded in 1969, focusing on manufacturing latex foam mattresses. That same year, LH Plus pivoted its business toward plastics manufacturing.

In the 1970s, the New Economic Policy (NEP) aimed to restructure wealth distribution and reduce poverty. It resulted in significant advancements in education and employment for Bumiputera, and expanded the public sector. The 1980s shifted focus toward export-oriented industrialization, leading to rapid growth in electronics and electrical industries, with free trade zones attracting substantial foreign direct investment (FDI). As a result, consumer purchasing power increased gradually, and demand for foreign brands surged. As consumer preferences shifted toward Western brands, affecting the demand for affordable shoes, Fung Keong adjusted its focus to manufacturing bicycle and motorcycle tires, motorcycle parts, and lubricants. Concurrently, Lum Tuck Loy opened Loy Kee Hong Kong Dim Sum Restaurant and eventually bought over the Kam Lun Tai brand name, pioneering automated machinery for mooncake production. Kemajuan, established in 1973 as a metal fabrication and contracts firm, embarked on a transformative

Table 8.13 A Historical Overview of Economic Trends and Business Innovations in CFBs

Economic Context and Decade	*Business Developments and Adaptations*
1930s: Colonial economy dominated by rubber and tin industries.	Fung Keong relocates its factory to Klang, Malaya, adapting to colonial economic conditions.
1940s: Japanese occupation, economic disruption, post-war reconstruction.	Besfomec founded as *Xin Chun Woh* Chinese medical hall; LH Plus starts as a bicycle repair workshop.
1950s: Independence in 1957, economic diversification beyond rubber and tin.	Leong Hup begins as a small-scale chicken farm. SKP Resources starts as a plastic injection workshop.
1960s: Import substitution policies, growth in manufacturing industries.	Hei Hwang starts traditional herbal shop. Aerofoam founded in 1969, focusing on latex foam mattresses.
1970s: New Economic Policy (NEP), focus on wealth distribution and Bumiputera advancement.	King's Confectionery expands retail presence. Besfomec transitions to producing chicken essence.
1980s: Export-oriented industrialization, growth in electronics and FDI.	Fung Keong shifts to manufacturing bicycle and motorcycle tires. Kemajuan transitions to plastic packaging for electronics.
1990s: Economic liberalization, globalization, boom in construction and services.	SKP Resources diversifies into global plastics manufacturing. Top Glove enters rubber glove industry.
2000s: Transition to a knowledge-based economy, emphasis on technology and innovation.	London Biscuit diversifies into snack foods. Aerofoam becomes OEM for bedding products.
2010s: Emphasis on sustainable development, expansion into renewable energy and technology.	Leong Hup acquires Baker's Cottage. King's Confectionery innovates with modern flavors and healthier ingredients.
2020s: Digital economy acceleration post-pandemic, growth in e-commerce and fintech.	All 12 CFBs involved in cross-border markets; plastic industry pivotal in semiconductor production for AI development.

Source: Compiled by the author.

journey into plastic packaging for electronic devices. Besfomec transitioned from a traditional Chinese medical hall to producing chicken essence, embracing modernization and technological advancement to create a Nanyang herbal healthcare brand. In 1975, King‘s Confectionery started its first shop house in Kepong and established a factory warehouse in 1977 to distribute pastries across Malaysia. Recognizing retail sales potential, Hei Hwang launched an Ipoh white coffee series as an instant product using different packaging.

The 1990s brought economic liberalization and globalization, with Malaysia integrating into the global economy, experiencing a boom in construction and infrastructure projects, and expanding its services sector. By diversifying its product offerings and embracing technological advancements, SKP positioned itself as a key player in the plastics manufacturing sector, catering not only to local demands but also to global markets. Top Glove, founded in 1991, recognized the opportunity in the rubber glove industry amid a prosperous economy. The Liew family diversified their business by venturing into the food industry, marked by the acquisition of London Biscuit. In 1995, King's Confectionery expanded from 25 to 90 outlets, becoming the largest retail confectionery chain in Malaysia.

The company's ability to innovate and adapt to changing consumer preferences ensured its sustainability and growth. The 2000s saw a transition to a knowledge-based economy, with technology and innovation driving growth in ICT, biotechnology, and higher education sectors. For example, London Biscuit leveraged its local market knowledge to diversify into snack foods and cakes, maintaining its market position. Aerofoam served as an original equipment manufacturer (OEM), producing a wide range of bedding products for various brands and clients.

In the 2010s, Malaysia continued to diversify its economy, emphasizing sustainable development, with expansion into renewable energy, green technology, and sustainable agriculture. In this period, observed that all of the 12 CFBs featured in the case studies involved in cross border markets and strong effort of diversification in their family business. Influenced by the macro environment, Leong Hup acquired Baker's Cottage and created their "Farm-to-Plate" concept as a strategy to diversify and sustain the family business. King's Confectionery also evolved by incorporating modern flavors and healthier ingredients into traditional products, appealing to a broader consumer base while maintaining cultural relevance. The 2020s accelerated the shift toward a digital economy, driven by the need for post-pandemic recovery. Digital transformation, growth in e-commerce, fintech, and digital services became prominent, supported by government stimulus packages aimed at economic resilience and futureproofing against disruptions. The biggest winners included the plastic industry, which played a significant role in semiconductor production, crucial for artificial intelligence development.

In summary, these adaptations reflect the businesses' strategic responses to local market dynamics, driving growth and market prominence over successive generations. The strategic navigation of market dynamics and state policies has been crucial for the growth and sustainability of CFBs in Malaysia. By leveraging government support and adapting to local market conditions, these businesses have achieved significant growth and market prominence across generations.

8.2.3 From Familyrizing to Evolutionizing

Based on the cases, tacit knowledge in different industry evolved differently. In food industry, tacit knowledge was retained but developed in new ways to create innovative food products. In the plastic and rubber industry, most of the firms did not retain and develop the founders' tacit knowledge for product development. As plastic and rubber manufacturing technology evolved rapidly, this put a strain for the founders to build their tacit knowledge. In fact, tacit knowledge was deemed irrelevant as technology transfer happened through distributed learning, business intelligence, and collaboration. As a result of product development, the current manufactured products differ greatly from the original.

As these businesses matured, they diversified their product portfolios and expanded geographically, driven by increasing consumer demand and competitive pressures. The businesses capitalized on its strong brand reputation and local market insights to expand regionally, catering to diverse consumer preferences within Malaysia and neighboring countries. This expansion phase marked a strategic shift toward scalability and market penetration, supported by strategic alliances and enhanced distribution networks. In later growth stages, businesses embraced globalization and technological advancements to consolidate their positions as industry leaders. Strategic investments in research and development, coupled with the proactive approach to regulatory compliance and market expansion, exemplify how businesses leverage state policies drive innovation and sustainable growth. Similarly, adopting advanced manufacturing techniques and international market strategies underscore its evolution from a regional player to a global exporter, propelled by state-supported initiatives and strategic partnerships.

The integration of local market dynamics with the role of state influence highlights the dynamic interplay that shapes the growth and evolution of CFBs. From adapting to changing consumer preferences and competitive landscapes to leveraging state policies for technological advancement and market expansion, these businesses have demonstrated resilience and strategic foresight across generations. Moving forward, navigating evolving market dynamics and aligning with supportive state policies will remain critical for sustaining growth, fostering innovation, and maintaining competitive advantage in an increasingly globalized economy.

8.2.4 Summary

As time progressed, the accumulated class and ethnic resources provided a robust internal foundation for CFBs in Malaysia, making them resilient to short-term challenges. These resources, deeply embedded in cultural and community networks, reinforced the businesses' stability and continuity. The foresighted and effective leverage of networks, coupled with the strategic alignment of state policies, served as powerful external forces that CFBs could utilize to their advantage. These external elements facilitated market adaptability and expansion, complementing the internal strengths.

The success of CFBs in Malaysia hinges on a blend of educational advantages, cultural heritage, strategic network engagements, and effective tacit knowledge management. Education abroad equips leaders with global perspectives, while cultural values foster authenticity and consumer trust. Networks significantly impact tacit knowledge innovation within CFBs in Malaysia by providing access to resources, facilitating knowledge exchange, offering market insights, fostering strategic alliances, enhancing risk management, upholding cultural values, and supporting leadership development. Leveraging these networks enables businesses to adapt, innovate, and sustain competitive advantage ensuring long-term success.

Tacit knowledge, transferred across generations, fuels innovation and adaptive strategies, ensuring these businesses thrive economic uncertainties and technological disruptions.

Class and ethnic resources, networks, and state policies each function as core influencing factors in their respective dimensions. Together, they catalyze the transfer and innovation of tacit knowledge, ensuring that vital skills and insights are passed down through generations. This dynamic interplay between internal and external factors highlights their ability to navigate and thrive amidst market conditions and socio-political landscapes.

8.3 Comparative Analysis

The comparative analysis of Chinese family businesses in Malaysia serves as a crucial examination of how these enterprises navigate and adapt to various business themes, reflecting their unique paths to success. By analyzing themes such as ethnic enclaves, target markets, product evolution, business identity, commodifying ethnicity, international business expansion, tacit knowledge, and knowledge transfer, we gain insight into the intricate dynamics shaping their operations. This analysis not only highlights the strategies employed by these businesses but also provides a broader understanding of their contributions to the Malaysian economy and their responses to global market trends.

8.3.1 Ethnic Enclaves, Target Markets, Product Evolution, and Business Identity

8.3.1.1 Ethnic Enclaves as Market Foundations

In the food industry, the influence of ethnic enclaves is evident across generations. Chinese family businesses began in areas predominantly occupied by Chinese communities, leveraging their cultural knowledge and community ties effectively. For instance, Kam Lun Tai, renowned for its dim sum and mooncakes, capitalized on the trust and loyalty of the local Chinese community, built on shared cultural values and a deep understanding of consumer preferences within the enclave. Similarly, King's Confectionery gained popularity by offering traditional Chinese pastries and cakes, which resonated well with the local community. This foundation provided a stable platform for expansion. Besfomec and Hei Hwang also thrived due to their roots in the Chinese community, where they marketed Chinese medicine and traditional herbal drinks, aligning with local values and preferences for traditional remedies. London Biscuit and Leong Hup began their operations in Johor, a region with a high concentration of Chinese people, further benefiting from the ethnic enclave's support.

In contrast, ethnic enclaves have had a relatively low influence on product development and marketing in the plastic and rubber industries. However, they played a crucial role in providing access to a network of suppliers and skilled labor, which facilitated business operations and market entry. This support was instrumental in sustaining these family businesses across generations.

In the context of CFBs in Malaysia, ethnicity has not only been a marker of identity but also a strategic asset leveraged for business expansion. The commodification of ethnicity involves using cultural symbols, practices, and values to market products and create a unique brand identity that appeals to both local and international markets. This strategy has been particularly effective in differentiating businesses in competitive industries and establishing a loyal customer base rooted in shared cultural heritage. Ethnicity has played a crucial role in business strategies by providing cultural narratives that can assist with marketing innovation and product development. These enclaves provided a culturally familiar environment, community support, and a ready market for their products. CFBs often use their ethnic identity to emphasize qualities such as reliability, quality, and tradition, which resonate strongly with both local Chinese communities and broader markets that value cultural authenticity. This approach not only reinforces the business's brand identity but also enhances its appeal in diverse markets.

8.3.1.2 Target Markets

The target markets of CFBs in Malaysia demonstrate evolution from focusing primarily on local ethnic communities to expanding into broader regional and international arenas. Initially, companies such as London Biscuit and King's Confectionery concentrated on serving the local Chinese community. London Biscuit, founded in Johor, began by offering traditional biscuit products to the local Chinese market. Over time, the company diversified its product range to include snacks and cakes, which helped it expand beyond the local demographic to reach a wider Malaysian audience and eventually international markets. Similarly, King's Confectionery started by providing traditional Chinese pastries and cakes to the local community. The company's ability to adapt its offerings to both traditional and contemporary tastes facilitated its expansion into broader Malaysian and international markets, such as Bangladesh.

In contrast, Leong Hup and Baker's Cottage exhibit a strategic shift from local to regional and international markets. Leong Hup, initially a small-scale poultry supplier catering to the local Chinese community, responded to increasing demand driven by Malaysia's growing population and urbanization by modernizing its facilities and expanding its operations. This transformation enabled Leong Hup to become a leading integrated poultry producer in Southeast Asia. The acquisition of Baker's Cottage allowed Leong Hup to further diversify its target market by obtaining halal certification and tapping into the Muslim market. Baker's Cottage, originally focused on local bakery products, leveraged its halal certification post-acquisition to appeal to a broader demographic.

Besfomec and Hei Hwang, both started by catering to the Chinese community with traditional Chinese medicine and herbal drinks. As these companies grew, they expanded their target markets to include non-Chinese consumers interested in traditional remedies. This strategic move to broaden their market reach reflects the growing global interest in alternative medicine and traditional remedies, allowing them to cater to a more diverse audience. Kam Lun Tai's market expansion trajectory is similar to that of other food industry players. Initially, the company focused on the local Chinese community with its dim sum and mooncakes. Over time, Kam Lun Tai diversified its product offerings and expanded its market reach to include broader Malaysian and international audiences. This growth strategy mirrors the general trend observed among Chinese family businesses, which involves starting with a local focus and progressively expanding to capture a wider market.

The target markets of LH Plus, SKP Resources, Kemajuan, Top Glove, Fung Keong, and Aerofoam reflect diverse strategies tailored to their respective industries—plastics and rubber. These companies illustrate a range of approaches from local specialization to extensive international expansion.

LH Plus Sdn. Bhd. and SKP Resources both operate within the plastic industry but target different market segments. LH Plus initially focused on the domestic market, producing a range of plastic products for local consumers and businesses. Over time, the company expanded its reach to include regional markets, leveraging Malaysia's robust plastic manufacturing capabilities. LH Plus's strategic approach involved catering to niche markets within Southeast Asia, capitalizing on regional growth and demand for high-quality plastic goods. In contrast, SKP Resources began as a domestic-focused enterprise but quickly shifted toward a broader international market. The company, which specializes in plastic components for electronics and automotive sectors, strategically targeted global clients by establishing a reputation for quality and reliability. SKP Resources' expansion was driven by increasing demand for precision plastic parts in international markets, leading to its significant presence in global supply chains. Kemajuan operates in a niche market within the plastic sector, specializing in industrial and commercial plastic products. While initially focusing on the local market, Kemajuan has gradually expanded its target market to include regional clients. The company's emphasis on industrial applications and custom solutions has positioned it as a key player in both domestic and regional markets, catering to various industrial needs.

Top Glove and Fung Keong operate in the rubber industry with distinct target markets. Top Glove, started by serving the local Malaysian market but swiftly expanded to international markets. The company's global strategy is centered on its ability to meet high-volume demands and maintain cost-efficiency, which has facilitated its entry into diverse international markets, including Europe, North America, and Asia. In contrast, Fung Keong initially focused on local markets within Malaysia, producing rubber-based products primarily for domestic use. Over time, Fung Keong's strategy evolved to include regional markets in Southeast Asia, capitalizing on its established reputation and traditional expertise in rubber production. Aerofoam also operates in the rubber industry but with a different target market focus. The company specializes in foam-based products. Aerofoam initially targeted local markets but expanded its reach to include regional and international clients. The company's emphasis on innovation and product development has allowed it to cater to specialized markets both within Malaysia and abroad.

In summary, the target market strategies of LH Plus, SKP Resources, Kemajuan, Top Glove, Fung Keong, and Aerofoam reflect their distinct industry positions and growth trajectories. While LH Plus and SKP Resources have focused on regional and international markets within the plastic sector, Kemajuan has carved out a niche in industrial plastics. Top Glove's global expansion contrasts with Fung Keong's regional focus, and Aerofoam's specialization in foam products demonstrates a strategic adaptation to diverse market needs. Each company's approach highlights the importance of aligning market strategies with industry demands and operational capabilities.

8.3.1.3 Product Evolution

The ability of these businesses to adapt their product offerings to meet changing market demands has been crucial to their sustained success. This adaptability reflects their strategic responses to economic shifts, consumer preferences, and technological advancements.

London Biscuit began as a traditional biscuit manufacturer specialized in corn flour-based snack but expanded its product line to include a wider range of snacks and confectioneries. This evolution was driven by the need to meet increasing consumer demand for variety and innovation in the food sector. The company's strategy involved investing in new production technologies and diversifying its product offerings to attract a broader customer base. By incorporating modern flavors and packaging formats, London Biscuit was able to stay competitive in a dynamic market. The decision to evolve its product line was also influenced by changing consumer preferences and the desire to capture a larger share of the snack food market.

King's Confectionery started with traditional Chinese pastries and cakes but evolved to include modern variations and new confectionery innovations. This product evolution was driven by the need to appeal to both traditional and contemporary consumer tastes. King's Confectionery leveraged its deep understanding of cultural preferences and invested in product development to create a blend of traditional and modern offerings. The company's ability to adapt and innovate was essential for maintaining its market position and attracting new customers.

Leong Hup International initially focused on poultry products but evolved by acquiring **Baker's Cottage** and expanding into the bakery sector. This strategic diversification was driven by the desire to capture new market segments and cater to consumer preferences. By obtaining halal certification, Baker's Cottage was able to tap into Malaysia's Muslim market, demonstrating the strategic importance of aligning product offerings with demographic and cultural shifts. The company's focus on modernization and diversification, for instance, introduced "farm to plate" concept was crucial for addressing the growing demand for convenience and variety in food products.

Besfomec and **Hei Hwang** began with TCM and traditional Chinese herbal remedies but evolved their product lines to include modern health and wellness products. This evolution was driven by increasing consumer interest in holistic health solutions and the desire to capture a broader market for wellness products. By expanding their offerings, these companies responded to changing health trends and positioned themselves as leaders in the modern wellness market.

Kam Lun Tai evolved from producing fusion style dim sum, mooncakes to offering a broader range of ready to eat food products. This expansion was driven by the need to meet growing consumer demand in different era for diverse and high-quality food products. The company's product evolution involved maintaining authenticity while introducing new product lines to appeal to a wider audience.

LH Plus started with basic housewares plastic products but evolved to include specialized items for the automotive and electronics sectors. This product evolution was driven by technological advancements and increasing demand for high-quality, precision-engineered products. LH Plus invested in new technologies and expanded its product portfolio to meet the needs of more sophisticated markets. The company's focus on innovation and specialization allowed it to maintain a competitive edge and capture new market opportunities. **SKP Resources** began with household plastic products but shifted to producing precision components for high-tech industries. This evolution was driven by the need to address growing demand for specialized plastic parts and leverage technological advancements. SKP's investment in precision engineering and high-quality manufacturing enabled it to position itself as a key player in global supply chains. **Kemajuan** evolved its product offerings from basic industrial plastics to one-stop solution of packaging for various sectors. This evolution was influenced by the need to cater to specialized market needs and offer tailored solutions. Kemajuan's focus on customization and high-performance products allowed it to respond to market demands and maintain a competitive position.

Top Glove began with basic rubber gloves and evolved to include a wide range of medical and industrial gloves, including advanced nitrile and latex gloves. This product evolution was driven by the need to meet global health and safety standards and address increasing demand for specialized gloves. Top Glove's focus on innovation and quality allowed it to expand its product line and capture a significant share of the global market. **Fung Keong** transitioned from producing affordable canvas shoes to offering a diverse range of goods for motorcycle. This evolution was driven by technological advancements and changing market needs. Fung Keong's investment in new technologies and product development enabled it to adapt to industry trends and expand its market reach. **Aerofoam** initially focused on latex foam mattress but expanded its product line to include various bedding accessories and OEM of bedding products. This evolution was influenced by growing market demands and technological advancements in foam manufacturing. Aerofoam's commitment to innovation and adaptation allowed it to capture new market opportunities and diversify its product offerings.

In summary, the product evolution strategies of these companies reflect their adaptive responses to changing market conditions, technological advancements, and consumer preferences. While food industry firms have expanded their product lines to include modern variations and new product categories, plastic and rubber companies have evolved their offerings to meet the demands of high-tech and industrial markets. This comparative analysis highlights the importance of innovation and adaptation in sustaining competitive advantage and meeting market needs.

8.3.1.4 Business Identity

The development of a strong business identity and brand has been a key factor in the success of these CFBs. Establishing a unique identity not only helps differentiate a business in a competitive market but also fosters customer loyalty and trust.

London Biscuit has cultivated a strong business identity rooted in its heritage as a biscuit maker, emphasizes quality and local flavors. London Biscuit's identity is built on its long-standing reputation for quality and reliability in the snack industry, which has been reinforced by its ability to adapt to changing market preferences while maintaining traditional values. **King's Confectionery** has established its identity around its specialization in Chinese pastries and cakes. The brand identity focuses on authenticity and tradition, appealing to customers seeking genuine Chinese confections. Over time, King's Confectionery has evolved by incorporating modern twists into traditional recipes, thus broadening its appeal while maintaining its core identity of cultural authenticity. **Leong Hup International** is known for its strong business identity in the poultry industry, characterized by its commitment to quality and innovation. The company's identity evolved from a local poultry supplier to a leading integrated producer, emphasizing modernization and efficiency. The acquisition of **Baker's Cottage** and entry into the bakery sector further diversified its identity, combining its core poultry expertise with new product lines and catering to different market segments. **Besfomec** and **Hei Hwang** have developed their business identities around traditional Chinese herbal remedies and health products. Both companies emphasize authenticity and the use of traditional knowledge in their products, which resonates strongly with customers seeking trusted herbal solutions. Their identities are anchored in their cultural heritage and commitment to maintaining traditional practices while adapting to modern health trends. **Kam Lun Tai** has created an identity centered on its expertise in mooncakes and dim sum. The company's identity emphasizes quality and authenticity, which is deeply rooted in its cultural heritage. Kam Lun Tai's focus on maintaining its recipes while expanding its product range has allowed it to establish a strong market presence and appeal to both local and international customers.

The acquisition of halal certification marked a significant shift in the business identity of these CFBs, transforming them from ethnic or niche producers into versatile brands with broader market appeal. By adopting halal practices, all six CFBs gained access to new markets while also enhancing consumer trust and quality assurance, enabling them to remain competitive in a multicultural environment. As they grew, their identities evolved from catering primarily to specific ethnic communities to becoming inclusive brands capable of attracting a diverse demographic, reinforcing their relevance and market reach.

LH Plus has built its business identity around precision and innovation in the plastic manufacturing sector. The company's identity is defined by its specialization in high-quality, precision-engineered plastic products, catering to advanced industries. LH Plus emphasizes technological advancement and customization, which distinguishes it in a competitive market. **SKP Resources** has established its identity through its focus on precision plastic components for high-tech industries.

The company's identity centers on its capability to deliver high-quality, specialized products that meet stringent industry standards. **Kemajuan** is recognized for its focus on customized industrial plastics. Its identity is built on the ability to provide tailored solutions for various industries, reflecting a commitment to addressing specific customer needs and market demands. Kemajuan's identity is defined by its adaptability and focus on delivering high-performance, customized plastic solutions.

Top Glove has developed a strong identity as a leading global manufacturer of rubber gloves. The company's identity revolves around its extensive product range, high-quality standards, and innovation in glove technology. Top Glove's brand is synonymous with reliability and global reach, highlighted by its significant presence in the medical and industrial glove markets. **Fung Keong** has established its identity in the production of affordable canvas shoes before transitioning to manufacturing bicycle and motorcycle products. The company's identity is characterized by its ability to adapt its product range to meet changing market demands, reflecting a focus on providing practical, cost-effective solutions for diverse consumer needs. **Aerofoam** has built its business identity around its specialization in latex foam products. The company's identity is characterized by its focus on technological innovation and customization. Aerofoam's commitment to advancing foam technology and meeting diverse customer needs supports its position as a leading provider in the foam manufacturing sector.

Across the food, plastic, and rubber industries, business identities are shaped by a combination of historical legacy, specialization, and innovation. In food industry, the CFBs emphasize cultural authenticity and tradition, while also adapting to modern trends. In plastic and rubber industry, they build their identities around technological advancement and specialization, catering to specific market needs and maintaining a competitive edge. This comparative analysis highlights how business identities are crafted through a blend of heritage, innovation, and market positioning, reflecting each company's unique approach to sustaining and evolving their brand presence.

8.3.2 Commodifying Ethnicity and International Business Expansion

8.3.2.1 Commodifying Ethnicity

In the food industry, commodifying ethnicity has been a crucial strategy for Chinese family businesses to build brand identity and appeal to culturally specific markets. For London Biscuit, King's Confectionery, and Kam Lun Tai, their products prominently feature elements of Chinese cultural heritage, allowing them to differentiate in a competitive market by emphasizing authenticity and tradition. London Biscuit incorporated flavors and designs, appealing to nostalgia and heritage among Chinese consumers. Similarly, King's Confectionery leveraged traditional Chinese pastries and cakes as its primary offerings, creating a sense of continuity with the past while reaching modern audiences. Kam Lun Tai, known for its mooncakes and dim sum, has used its deep-rooted Cantonese culinary identity to market itself as a symbol of authentic Chinese culture, especially during festive seasons. These brands utilized their ethnic roots not only as a cultural touchstone but as a marketing tool that bridges tradition and modern consumer demands. Besfomec and Hei Hwang focused on ethnic-based products like herbal drinks and traditional medicine, tapping into cultural practices and remedies passed down through generations. Their branding emphasized the value of traditional wisdom in modern wellness trends, commodifying Chinese heritage to expand market share within and beyond Chinese communities. Leong Hup and Baker's Cottage initially targeted the Chinese market with familiar poultry and baked goods but later incorporated a broader ethnic appeal, combining traditional Chinese flavors with a modern, halal-certified identity.

In the plastic and rubber industry, commodifying ethnicity takes a more nuanced approach due to the nature of products. While companies like LH Plus, Kemajuan, and Top Glove do not overtly market their ethnic identity, they embed Chinese values such as diligence, resilience, and community support in their organizational culture and business operations. However, SKP Resources purposely distinguishes itself by downplaying its Chinese identity to avoid reinforcing the stereotypical negative perceptions associated with Chinese businessmen, such as being overly profit-driven. By projecting a more neutral and professional image, SKP aims to appeal to a broader range of clients, especially in global markets, where such stereotypes could hinder growth. This strategic positioning helps the company navigate a multicultural business environment while still benefiting from its inherent cultural strengths. Meanwhile, Fung Keong and Aerofoam incorporate elements of cultural values into their commitment to quality and customer satisfaction, though they do not explicitly market these as ethnic traits.

Overall, while food-related businesses more directly commodify their ethnic identity to create a sense of cultural authenticity, the CFBs plastic and rubber industry focus on leveraging traditional values more subtly. This approach reinforces their reputation for reliability and quality, with companies like SKP choosing to strategically manage their identity in ways that mitigate potential biases and broaden their appeal.

8.3.2.2 International Business Expansion

International business expansion plays a critical role in the growth trajectories of CFBs, with strategies varying significantly across industries and firms. London Biscuit, King's Confectionery, Leong Hup, Baker's Cottage, Besfomec, Hei Hwang, and Kam Lun Tai have adopted diverse approaches to internationalization based on their product offerings and target markets. London Biscuit and King's Confectionery pursued international expansion by exporting packaged food products and confectionery items to neighboring countries in Southeast Asia and beyond. The ability to produce cost-effective goods while maintaining quality standards enabled them to penetrate global markets, although London Biscuit's aggressive expansion led to financial strains, demonstrating the risks of rapid internationalization. Kam Lun Tai leveraged the global popularity of mooncakes, exporting to

Chinese communities across Asia and targeting festive seasons for increased sales. In contrast, Leong Hup and Baker's Cottage focused on regional expansion within Southeast Asia. Leong Hup's growth into one of the largest integrated poultry producers in the region was achieved through strategic acquisitions and joint ventures, complemented by Baker's Cottage's expansion into Muslim-majority markets. Besfomec and Hei Hwang, while more niche in product lines like herbal drinks and health supplements, also expanded internationally through targeted exports to countries with consumers that appreciate TCM knowledge and related products.

In the plastic and rubber industry, international expansion strategies are more heavily driven by production scalability and global supply chains. LH Plus, SKP Resources, and Kemajuan expanded internationally by leveraging Malaysia's position as a manufacturing hub, focusing on contract manufacturing and serving multinational corporations. Their ability to produce at scale and meet international standards attracted clients globally, with SKP Resources specializing in plastics for global electronics brands. Top Glove's expansion strategy exemplifies aggressive growth, focusing on global dominance in the rubber glove industry. By establishing multiple manufacturing facilities and distribution networks worldwide, Top Glove grew into a significant global player. Fung Keong and Aerofoam's internationalization is more limited but focused on specific market niches. Fung Keong's shift from producing canvas shoes to motorcycle related products allowed it to target niche markets in Southeast Asia, while Aerofoam focused on expanding its reach in the bedding and cushion market within Asia.

In summary, while CFBs in food industry prioritize cultural connections and ethnic markets in their internationalization, CFBs in plastics and rubber industry focus on scaling production for global markets. The diversity in approaches highlights how these CFBs balance cultural heritage with the practical demands of international growth, each adapting their strategies according to product type, market conditions, and business identity.

8.3.3 Tacit Knowledge and Knowledge Transfer

Tacit knowledge and its transfer across generations play a crucial role in sustaining the longevity and competitive edge of Chinese family businesses (CFBs). For companies like London Biscuit, King's Confectionery, Leong Hup, Baker's Cottage, Besfomec, Hei Hwang, and Kam Lun Tai, the continuity of business values, skills, and practices is largely dependent on the seamless handover of tacit knowledge from one generation to the next. London Biscuit, for instance, saw the gradual transfer of operational expertise and strategic decision-making from its founders to the next generation, who adapted these insights to navigate new market challenges and expand product lines. King's Confectionery also effectively passed on its knowledge of traditional Chinese pastries while integrating modern bakery management practices, allowing subsequent generations to scale operations. In family-run food businesses like Leong Hup and Baker's Cottage, the knowledge transfer included not only operational expertise but also strategic diversification decisions, leading to the acquisition of halal certification and subsequent expansion into broader markets. Besfomec and Hei Hwang, rooted in traditional herbal remedies, maintained a strong reliance on the founder's expertise in Chinese medicine. This knowledge was adapted by younger generations, who enhanced it with modern marketing techniques and product innovation, enabling these businesses to evolve while preserving their core identity.

For CFBs like LH Plus, SKP Resources, Kemajuan, Top Glove, Fung Keong, and Aerofoam, the transfer of tacit knowledge is essential for maintaining operational efficiency and ensuring technological advancements are sustained across generations. LH Plus and SKP Resources, both involved in contract manufacturing, relied heavily on the founder's deep industry connections and production techniques, which were passed down and modernized by the next generation to meet evolving industry standards. The second and third generations introduced professional management and innovation-driven practices while maintaining the core knowledge that made these businesses successful in the first place. Top Glove's success is also attributed to effective knowledge transfer, where operational excellence and strategic risk management were passed down, enabling the company to navigate the complexities of global expansion. Fung Keong's journey from canvas shoe production to tire manufacturing highlights how knowledge transfer across generations allowed the business to shift focus and adapt to changing market demands while retaining its core manufacturing competencies. Similarly, Aerofoam sustained its competitive advantage in the bedding industry by transferring specialized production techniques and market insights across generations, blending traditional craftsmanship with modern business practices.

When examining tacit knowledge transfer across generations in these CFBs, several key similarities and differences emerge that highlight both shared practices and industry-specific variations.

One of the most prominent similarities across all the CFBs is the preservation of core business values and operational expertise. From London Biscuit's emphasis on maintaining the quality of its baked goods to Leong Hup's expertise in poultry farming and Fung Keong's manufacturing techniques, each business prioritizes the transmission of fundamental knowledge from the founding generation to their successors. This knowledge transfer often takes place within close family networks, where younger members are mentored and trained by senior relatives. This mentorship is crucial to sustaining business continuity and ensuring that industry-specific insights are passed down effectively. Additionally, all these businesses share a commitment to adapting inherited knowledge to fit the contemporary business environment. CFBs like Kam Lun Tai and Baker's Cottage, the younger generation has modernized traditional practices by introducing professional management strategies, integrating advanced technology, and expanding product offerings to tap into new markets. This blending of traditional wisdom with modern innovations is a common feature across the food and manufacturing sectors.

However, differences emerge when considering the approach to professionalization. CFBs in food industry such as King's Confectionery and Kam Lun Tai, knowledge transfer remains more informal and family-centric, with a focus on preserving recipes and cultural traditions. In contrast, large tech-based manufacturing firms like LH Plus and Top Glove adopt more structured approaches, incorporating formal training programs and professional management alongside the family's tacit knowledge. These businesses often invest more heavily in research and development, reflecting a different scale and complexity in knowledge transfer.

Another key difference lies in the scope of knowledge being transferred. Food businesses like London Biscuit Besfomec and Hei Hwang prioritize product-specific knowledge, such as traditional recipes and production techniques, while also focusing on customer relationships and brand heritage. On the other hand, firms like SKP Resources and Aerofoam transfer more technical knowledge related to production processes, supply chain management, and global market expansion, emphasizing operational efficiency and technological advancement.

Generational involvement also varies across these CFBs. In traditional businesses like Hei Hwang and Besfomec, the younger generation is deeply integrated into daily operations from an early age, ensuring a seamless transfer of both business acumen and cultural values. Conversely, in larger corporations like Top Glove and LH Plus, the introduction of professional managers complements the family's expertise, creating a hybrid model where tacit knowledge from the family is enhanced by external professional inputs. This balance between family legacy and professional management often dictates how successfully these businesses scale and innovate.

The process of transferring tacit knowledge across generations varies across industries but remains fundamental to the success and sustainability of these CFBs. Food-based businesses emphasize more on the preservation of cultural heritage and product authenticity, while CFBs in plastic and rubber industry focus on the operational expertise and innovation needed to remain competitive. Tacit knowledge encompasses the skills, experiences, and insights gained through direct involvement in business operations. Unlike explicit knowledge, which can be easily documented and transmitted, tacit knowledge is deeply embedded in individual experiences and often shared through direct interaction and apprenticeship. In Chinese family businesses, tacit knowledge includes business acumen, market intuition, and cultural understanding passed down from founders to successive generations. This knowledge is crucial for making informed decisions, innovating processes, and navigating market dynamics.

The process of transferring tacit knowledge within family businesses is multifaceted and involves direct mentorship, on-the-job training, and fostering a culture of open communication. Founders often play a pivotal role in this process, personally mentoring their successors and embedding core values and business principles. This transfer is not merely a transactional exchange but a relational and contextual process that shapes the successors' understanding and application of the knowledge. In the cases, the founder's children were actively involved in the business from a young age, learning the nuances of product development, customer service, and operational efficiency. This hands-on approach ensured that the core competencies and business ethos were preserved, enabling the family business to evolve and expand its market presence while maintaining a strong connection to its roots. The ability to adapt inherited knowledge to changing market conditions, introduce professional management, and integrate new technologies has been key to the long-term resilience of these businesses.

8.3.4 Summary

The comparative analysis underscores the strategic prowess of successful Chinese family businesses in Malaysia, adeptly navigating local market dynamics and leveraging ethnic enclaves to forge robust community support. By commodifying their ethnic heritage, these businesses established distinctive brand identities and expanded into international markets through commitment to product quality and strategic government partnerships. Crucially, the effective transfer of tacit knowledge across generations ensured business continuity and adaptability amidst evolving market conditions, underpinning their sustained growth and market prominence.

Initially capitalizing on ethnic enclaves, these businesses gained initial market traction and fortified their foundations. Evolving their market strategies and product portfolios allowed them to maintain competitiveness and appeal across diverse consumer bases. By leveraging their cultural heritage, they crafted unique selling propositions that resonated both locally and internationally, cementing their market positions.

The role of tacit knowledge and its intergenerational transfer emerges as pivotal. It facilitated consistent product quality, spurred innovation, and safeguarded operational efficiency. The featured case studies illustrate varied facets of tacit knowledge transfer, emphasizing its role in sustaining high standards and market agility. As these CFBs navigate contemporary market complexities, the ongoing emphasis on tacit knowledge and its transmission across generations remains indispensable.

The comparative analysis of these themes highlights the dynamic and adaptive nature of Chinese family businesses in Malaysia. From their origins within ethnic enclaves to their transformation into global enterprises, these businesses have navigated complex challenges through strategic product evolution, the commodification of ethnicity, and the careful transfer of tacit knowledge across generations. The intersection of tradition and modernity is evident in their ability to maintain cultural identity while pursuing global ambitions, ensuring their continued relevance and success in an increasingly competitive market.

9 Innovating Tradition of Excellence in Chinese Family Businesses in Malaysia

Previous studies suggest that younger family members are often reluctant to join small-scale SMEs, including those in Malaysia, due to challenges in fostering information and knowledge sharing through top-down management, which discourages succession. Chinese family businesses, typically small at startup, face constraints that hinder their growth into large, well-established corporations. Nevertheless, this study of 12 Chinese family businesses in the food, plastics, and rubber industries underscores the importance of tacit knowledge innovation introduced by the next generation. In these cases, the development of the founder's tacit knowledge was crucial to the enterprises' growth. This chapter highlights the shift from a traditional family-managed structure to a more formal organizational system. The second and third generations, often educated abroad, spearhead these transformations by focusing on R&D and expanding the business through subsidiaries and increased sales volumes. Senior family members, usually siblings of the founder, often remain shareholders without direct involvement in management. These businesses increasingly prioritized production innovation and R&D, aided by professional management, to produce marketable products. As they transitioned from small to large enterprises, these Chinese family businesses consistently upgraded their technology, keeping pace with advancements to build trusted brands in both domestic and international markets. They also established overseas manufacturing plants or offices to tap into Asian and non-Asian markets. Some even leveraged their heritage, promoting traditional food products, signature Malaysian rubber goods, and Malaysia's role as a key hub in the semiconductor industry, to maintain competitiveness and market distinction.

9.1 The Evolution of Nanyang Brands Through Tacit Knowledge and Modernization

This historical analysis of the longitudinal case studies show that these Chinese family businesses had undergone generational shifts and retained a prominent place in their respective industries, particularly in terms of tacit knowledge transformation. The study of different dialect groups reveals that immigration patterns and

DOI: 10.4324/9781032705842-9

traditional skills were pivotal in shaping the industries they dominated. During the first generation, tacit knowledge was acquired from their origins through hands-on experience and repetitive practice. It was found that early Chinese immigrants established strong business foundations using skills and networks from their origins.

The generations that follow strive to adapt to market changes and simultaneously preserve cultural values, make efforts to instill a culture of candidness, and regard situational leadership as important. These brands embodied good management practices without neglecting traditional Chinese cultural knowledge or values such as family consultation, frugality, and honesty. In terms of professional and educational backgrounds, the newer generations typically attain university education in the appropriate fields and have the necessary skills and qualifications to manage businesses more efficiently.

Chinese culture is an important element to these CFBs to market their products and created their brand name. SKP Resources stands out among the 12 CFBs, who diminishing their Chinese identity to embrace the professionalization. However, its business is still based on Chinese cultural core foundation, which is *"jia"* (family). The Gan family work together to prune their family tree to retain the power of autonomy in SKP Resources. Unlike Chinese in Indonesia, Thailand, or other Southeast Asia countries who integrated into the main society through assimilation and diminishing their Chinese identity in early stage, the Chinese in Malaysia are divided by the Chinese sub-ethnic identity and retain the use of cultural values in business practices today. The unique blend of Chinese culture and contemporary business practice continuously transform the family tacit knowledge, is one of the reasons they able to sustain a prominent position in respective industry. CFBs in Malaysia have shown their cultural values and strategic approaches to business. Their ability to leverage traditional knowledge while embracing innovation has enabled them to thrive across generations.

Over time, CFBs sustained their market positions and family legacies through various strategies. The case studies illustrate this well: London Biscuit developed through their acquisition strategy, King's Confectionery leveraged culinary skills of the Hainanese, Leong Hup and Baker's Cottage proved the expert of Teochews in livestock farming. The case study on Besfomec demonstrated how leveraged Hakka TCM knowledge, Hei Hwang, known for its longevity and healthy life with black foods, Kum Lun Tai commemorated Chinese reunion culture through their products. The study on LH Plus shows how it evolved from basic transportation services dominated by Henghuas to advanced manufacturing, SKP Resources began as a plastic injection workshop transform into a public listed plastics manufacturing company, Kemajuan leveraged the metal smiting knowledge of the Hakka and Cantonese Chinese. The case study on Top Glove revealed how the business acumen of the Hokkiens family, Fung Keong, demonstrated adaptability in manufacturing, and Aerofoam demonstrates the innovation and implication of Hakka's metal smiting knowledge in latex foam mattresses manufacturing. All these case studies successfully produced quality Nanyang branded products during generational change.

9.2 Challenges in Converting Tacit Knowledge into Formal R&D

Based on the case studies, several factors contribute to the limited emphasis on converting tacit knowledge into R&D in Malaysian Chinese SMEs. These factors often vary by industry but can include cultural factors, tacit knowledge integration issues, resource constraints, and insufficient government and institutional support.

Cultural preferences for stability and risk aversion can also deter investments in R&D. Therefore, risky investments aimed at accumulating intangibles could be restrained. Traditional business practices often value continuity and incremental improvements. For example, Hei Hwang, known for promoting longevity and healthy living with black foods in powder form, relies on traditional health practices and acquired manufacturing knowledge rather than developing new manufacturing skills through R&D. This approach emphasizes cultural continuity and consumer trust in time-tested methods.

Integrating tacit knowledge into formal R&D processes is often challenging. Tacit knowledge is highly contextual and specific to individuals, making it difficult to codify and transfer into a structured R&D framework. This difficulty can hinder its conversion into structured research and development efforts. Especially in highly competitive markets, there may be a stronger emphasis on cost control and immediate market responsiveness rather than on investing in long-term R&D.

Besfomec, for instance, leverages Hakka Traditional Chinese Medicine (TCM) knowledge but faces difficulties in codifying this tacit knowledge into structured R&D efforts. The specialized and context-specific nature of TCM knowledge makes it challenging to formalize and use to develop innovation.

SMEs are typically at a disadvantage when it comes to getting access to resources and capabilities. As a result, many SMEs face financial constraints that limit their ability to invest in R&D, considering that allocating resources to R&D may not be seen as a priority compared to other immediate business needs. A shortage of skilled personnel to undertake R&D activities can hinder the conversion of tacit knowledge into formal research initiatives.

Insufficient access to government grants, subsidies, or institutional support for R&D can be a barrier. A lack of supportive policies and infrastructure for R&D in certain industries can impede the conversion of tacit knowledge into formal research efforts. Through the case studies, we observe that CFBs actively strive to align with government policies rather than relying solely on policies aimed at benefiting them. The Malaysian government has historically focused on the redistribution of economy and core industries which are crucial for Malaysia‘s economic growth. However, the case studies highlight a perceived lack of sufficient support and attention from the government toward CFBs, in terms of inequity of business obligations and their family business characteristics.

9.3 Inter-Ethnic Collaborations: Pathways to Internationalization

Based on the insights gathered from our discussions, Malaysian Chinese family businesses (CFBs) have made use of various strategies beyond traditional factors like class, ethnic resources, and Chinese networks to expand and enhance their enterprises. One significant avenue explored by these businesses involves strategic partnerships and joint ventures with multinational companies (MNCs), facilitated by government policies aimed at technology transfer and capability development.

Joint ventures with MNCs have proven instrumental for Malaysian CFBs, allowing them to acquire advanced technologies and know-how to enhance their production capabilities and competitiveness in specific industries. This approach not only boosts their expertise but also elevates their reputation within their respective sectors. By tapping into MNC partnerships, these CFBs can mitigate risks associated with innovation and market entry, thereby fostering a more positive outlook toward evolving into producers of branded products or enhancing value-added production.

Furthermore, inter-ethnic collaborations emerge as another pivotal strategy for Malaysian CFBs. Establishing ties with larger shareholders and multinational partners not only enriches their internationalization process but also provides deeper insights into foreign markets. This collaborative approach helps in reducing uncertainty and perceived risks, enabling CFBs to navigate global markets more effectively. Such collaborations foster a conducive environment for knowledge exchange and capacity building, critical for sustaining long-term growth and competitiveness.

In the context of specific industries like plastics manufacturing, Malaysian CFBs face challenges and opportunities shaped by global economic dynamics. The sector, largely dominated by subcontracting for MNCs in industries such as semiconductors, electronics, automotive, and consumer goods, has traditionally seen Malaysian firms operating as OEM suppliers rather than embracing higher-value roles like Original Design Manufacturing (ODM) or Original Brand Manufacturing (OBM). This trend reflects barriers such as scale-up requirements, limited R&D investments, and workforce capabilities.

However, recent shifts driven by competitive pressures from lower-cost economies like China and Vietnam have prompted Malaysian plastics manufacturers to rethink their strategies. There's a growing inclination toward transitioning from mere OEM roles toward more competitive, value-added manufacturing processes. This strategic pivot involves investments in technology, innovation, and workforce development to enhance product quality and design capabilities, thereby ensuring sustainable growth amidst global competition.

In conclusion, the success and evolution of Malaysian Chinese family businesses hinge not only on traditional strengths like ethnic resources and networks but also on strategic collaborations with MNCs and adaptive responses to global industry trends. Embracing these strategies empowers CFBs to navigate complex market landscapes, innovate continuously, and sustain their competitive edge in an increasingly interconnected global economy.

9.4 Transforming Tacit Knowledge into Innovation and Business Growth

This study investigates how generational changes in Chinese family businesses (CFBs) in Malaysia have influenced organizational cultural characteristics, networks, and innovation capacity. It analyzes how the distinct behaviors of the first, second, and third generations have impacted business nature, strategic management, and growth, transitioning from China to innovative practices in Nanyang.

Key findings indicate that each generation exhibits different managerial styles. Generational shifts led to changes in company objectives, network utilization, and innovation strategies, significantly influencing organizational evolution. Unlike founders, newer generations minimized risks, maintained family harmony, and recruited professional staff to foster innovation. This research extends beyond governance structures to explore how tacit knowledge transforms into products, services, solutions, and systems. Subsequent generations upgraded technologies, establishing reputable brands in domestic and international markets. Commercializing the founders' tacit knowledge was crucial for the longevity of these enterprises. Enhanced production processes and product diversification gained momentum under second and third generation leadership.

The study highlights that business development was influenced by organizational cultural characteristics of a CFBs and how newer generations managed market shifts and strategies. Prominent features included diversification, improved networking, and the adoption of professional managers. Educated second and third generations actively participated in R&D, promoting professional management and product development. They favored a transparent organizational approach. However, maintaining consistent business development modes proved challenging due to the pressure to meet family expectations. This cultural challenge highlights the need for innovation.

The study suggests that founders granting autonomy to the next generation enhances innovation capacity, providing a competitive edge. Generational transitions brought changes in internal goals, structures, family responsibilities, and new business initiatives. External factors, like governmental regulations and export-focused policies, influenced R&D scope and strategies. These policies led to transformations in organizational frameworks, investment in new facilities, niche markets, and new business ventures. Building corporate identity through branding was emphasized.

In conclusion, innovation capacity depends on the characteristics of each family business and their approach to innovation. The different business behaviors of the second and third generations affect strategy implementation and shape business development.

9.5 The Role of Tacit Knowledge in Different Industries

Chandler's 3M theory emphasizes three critical elements for organizational growth and sustainability: Markets, Management, and Manufacturing. In the context of Chinese family businesses in Malaysia, these elements are adapted and evolved through successive generations who bring new knowledge and innovations while retaining the core values and tacit expertise of their forebears.

1. Food Industry:

In the food industry, the sustainability of Chinese family businesses hinges on the delicate balance between preserving traditional culinary methods and incorporating modern manufacturing practices. Founders of these enterprises often relied on deeply embedded tacit knowledge of recipes, techniques, and cultural flavors. This tacit knowledge, accumulated over decades, provides a unique value proposition that distinguishes their products in the market.

As the second and third generations take over, they introduce structured knowledge gained through formal education in business, food science, and marketing. They modernize operations by implementing quality control systems, adopting advanced packaging techniques, and expanding distribution channels. However, the core of their products remains rooted in the tacit knowledge of traditional methods and tastes. For example, family businesses in the confectionery and snack food sectors maintain the essence of traditional recipes while upgrading production lines to meet contemporary health standards and consumer demands. This balance between tradition and innovation enables these businesses to maintain brand loyalty while attracting new customers.

2. Plastics Industry:

The plastics industry exemplifies a different approach to tacit knowledge innovation, where the focus is on adapting to rapid technological advancements. Founders of these businesses often began with basic manufacturing capabilities and limited market reach. Their tacit knowledge included hands-on skills in molding techniques, material handling, and production workflows.

Second and third-generation successors, educated in engineering and business management, introduced structured knowledge to enhance operations. They adopted state-of-the-art machinery, automated production processes, and implemented quality assurance protocols that met global standards. This infusion of new knowledge enabled these businesses to diversify their product lines, improve efficiency, and reduce production costs. Furthermore, successors expanded market reach by forming strategic partnerships with international clients, positioning their firms as reliable suppliers in the global supply chain. By innovating in manufacturing while retaining the foundational tacit knowledge, these businesses achieved scalability and long-term sustainability.

3. Rubber Industry:

In the rubber industry, the combination of tacit knowledge and structured knowledge is crucial for maintaining competitiveness in a global market. Founders' tacit knowledge included expertise in rubber tapping, processing, and product development. This foundational knowledge provided a competitive edge in producing high-quality rubber goods, ranging from footwear to industrial components.

Successors brought structured knowledge in the family businesses and introduced innovations in product design, quality control, and supply chain management. Some family businesses in this sector established overseas manufacturing plants to be closer to key markets, thereby reducing logistics costs and increasing responsiveness to customer needs. In addition, these businesses leveraged their heritage to promote Malaysian rubber products as premium goods. By combining traditional craftsmanship with modern production techniques, they carved out niche markets and solidified Malaysia's reputation as a hub for quality rubber products. This strategic adaptation ensured that the businesses remained relevant and competitive across generations.

Effective management and marketing practices also play a critical role. Founders often managed businesses through intuitive decision-making, community relationships, and hands-on involvement. This tacit approach fostered trust, loyalty, and a strong organizational culture. As successors take over, they integrate formal management practices, such as strategic planning, financial analysis, and human resource management. This combination of tacit and structured knowledge results in a hybrid management style that maintains the core values of the business while enhancing efficiency and scalability. In marketing, younger generations leverage digital platforms, branding strategies, and global market insights to expand the reach of their products. However, they remain grounded in the tacit knowledge of local market preferences, cultural nuances, and customer relationships.

9.6 Overcoming the Myth of Tacit Knowledge vs. Structured Knowledge

A common misconception among aspiring entrepreneurs is that tacit knowledge and structured knowledge are mutually exclusive. Some may believe that formal education and professional theories are sufficient for business success, while others may overly rely on hands-on experience and traditional methods.

However, the case studies of successful Chinese family businesses in Malaysia reveal that the most sustainable enterprises are those that innovate by combining both forms of knowledge. The second and third generations, often educated abroad, bring new perspectives and capabilities to the business. They formalize management structures, introduce R&D initiatives, and expand into new markets. At the same time, they respect and build upon the tacit knowledge accumulated by the founders. The integration of structured knowledge from professional education and the wisdom of hands-on experience creates a powerful formula for long-term success.

For younger family members considering joining or starting their own businesses, the key takeaway is the importance of balancing tacit knowledge with structured knowledge. While it is essential to acquire professional skills and theoretical knowledge, hands-on experience and the wisdom of previous generations provide a foundation that cannot be replicated through education alone. The businesses that have sustained themselves across generations are those that actively adapt to new knowledge while preserving the essence of their inherited tacit knowledge. This dual approach ensures not only survive but thrive, contributing to Malaysia's economic and beyond.

References

Au, Y. P. (1991). *Chinese book on Singapore traditional work*. Singapore: Seng Yew Book Store. 21–27. 区如柏. (1991).《出门行路要找兴化人》，载《祖先的行业》，新加坡：胜友书局. 21–27.

Abdul Rahman, R. (2006). *Effective corporate governance* (1st ed.). Malaysia: University Publication Centre (UPENA), UiTM.

Adizes, I. (1989). *Corporate lifecycles: How and why corporations grow and die and what to do about it.* Englewood Cliffs. NJ: Prentice Hall.

Adler, P. S., & Kwon, S. W. (2002). Social capital: Prospects for a new concept. *The Academy of Management Review*, *27*(1), 17–40.

Afandi, E., Kermani, M., & Mammadov, F. (2017). Social capital and entrepreneurial process. *International Entrepreneurship and Management Journal, 13*(3), 685–716.

Ainsworth, S., & Wolfram Cox, J. (2003). Families divided: Culture and control in small family business. *Organization Studies, 24*(9), 1463–1485.

Aldrich, H. (1999). *Organizations evolving*. Newbury Park, CA: Sage Publications.

Aldrich, H., Jones, T., & McEvoy, D. (1984). Ethnic advantage and minority business development. In R. Ward & R. Jenkins (Eds.), *Ethnic communities in business: Strategies for economic survival* (pp. 189–210). Cambridge, UK: Cambridge University Press.

Alshenqeeti, H. (2014). Interviewing as a data collection method: A critical review. *English Linguistics Research*, *3*(1), 39–45.

Amran, N. A., & Ahmad, C. A. C. (2010). Family succession and firm performance among Malaysian companies. *International Journal of Business and Social Science, 1*(2), 193–203.

Amrith, S. S. (2015). Connecting diaspora histories: Indians and Chinese in colonial Malaya. In J. Bhattacharya & C. Kripalani (Eds.), *Indian and Chinese immigrant communities: Comparative perspectives* (pp. 13–24). London & New York: Anthem Press.

Amsden, A. (1989). *Asia's next giant: South Korea and late industrialisation.* New York: Oxford University Press.

Andriesse, E. (2011). Laos: A state coordinated frontier economy. *ISS Working Paper Series/ General Series*, *522*(522), 1–20.

Aoki, M. (2001). *Toward a comparative institutional analysis*. The MIT Press.

Arasaratnam, S. (1969). Some notes on the Dutch in Malacca and the Indo-Malayan Trade 1641–1670. *Journal of Southeast Asian History*, *10*(3), 480–490.

Aronoff, C. E., & Ward, J. L. (1995). Family-owned businesses: A thing of the past or a model for the future? *Family Business Review*, *8*(2), 121–130.

Asgari, M., Ahmad, S. Z., & Gurrib, I. (2010). Explaining the internationalization process of Malaysian service firms. *International Journal of Trade, Economics and Finance, 1*(1), 68–73.

Astrachan, J. H., & Shanker, M. C. (2003). Family businesses' contribution to the US economy: A closer look. *Family Business Review, 16*(3), 211–219.

Atieno, R. (2009). *Linkages, access to finance and the performace of small-scale enterprises in Kenya* (No. 2009.06). Research Paper/UNU-WIDER.

Atkinson, J., & Storey, D. (Eds.). (1994). *Employment, the small firm and the labour market*. London: Routledge.

Auansakul, P. (1995). Chinese traders and Thai groups in the rice business. *Southeast Asian Journal of Social Science, 23*(1), 29–42.

Backman, M. (2001). *Asian eclipse: Exposing the dark side of business in Asia*. Singapore: John Wiley.

Bala, B. K., Alias, E. F., Arshad, F. M., Noh, K. M., & Hadi, A. H. A. (2014). Modelling of food security in Malaysia. *Simulation Modelling Practice and Theory, 47*, 152–164.

Bany-Ariffin, A. N., Nor, F. M., & McGowan Jr, C. B. (2010). Pyramidal structure, firm capital structure exploitation and ultimate owners' dominance. *International Review of Financial Analysis, 19*(3), 151–164.

Barbosa, H., Barthelemy, M., Ghoshal, G., James, C. R., Lenormand, M., Louail, T., ... & Tomasini, M. (2018). Human mobility: Models and applications. *Physics Reports, 734*, 1–74.

Barbour, R. (2008). *Introducing qualitative research: A student guide to the craft of doing qualitative research.* California: Sage Publications.

Barney, J. (1991). Firm resources and sustained competitive advantage. *Journal of Management, 17*(1), 99–120.

Barrett, C. B., Barbier, E. B., & Reardon, T. (2001). Agroindustrialization, globalization, and international development: The environmental implications. *Environment and Development Economics, 6*(4), 419–433.

Barro, R. J. (1998). The East Asian Tigers have plenty to roar about. *Business Week, 27*, 24.

Barth, F. (1969). *Ethnic groups and boundaries*. Boston: Little, Brown and Company.

Bashford, A. (2014). Immigration restriction: Rethinking period and place from settler colonies to postcolonial nations. *Journal of Global History*, 9(1), 26–48.

Basu, A. (2011). From 'break out' to 'breakthrough': Successful market strategies of immigrant entrepreneurs in the UK. *International Journal of Entrepreneurship, 15*, 1.

Basu, A. (1998). An exploration of entrepreneurial activity among Asian small businesses in Britain. *Small Business Economics, 10*, 313–326.

Bates, T. (1994). Social resources generated by group support networks may not be beneficial to Asian immigrant-owned small businesses. *Social Forces, 72*(3), 671–689.

Bates, T., & Robb, A. (2013). Greater access to capital is needed to unleash the local economic development potential of minority-owned businesses. *Economic Development Quarterly, 27*(3), 250–259.

Bell, R., & Pham, T. T. (2021). Modelling the knowledge transfer process between founder and successor in Vietnamese family businesses succession. *Journal of Family Business Management, 11*(4), 479–495.

Benton, G., & Gomez, E. T. (2000). Chinatown and transnationalism. *Paper Presented at "International Conference on Immigrant Societies and Modern Age Education," 31 August - 3 September, 2000*, Entrepreneurship, Education, and Immigrant Societies.

Benton, G., & Gomez, E. T. (2008). *The Chinese in Britain, 1800-present: Transnationalism, economy and identity.* Basingstoke: Palgrave Macmillan.

Benton, G., & Gomez, E. T. (2014). Belonging to the nation: Generational change, identity and the Chinese diaspora. *Ethnic and Racial Studies, 37*(7), 1157–1171.

Benton, G., Liu, H., & Zhang, H. (Eds.). (2018). *The qiaopi trade and transnational networks in the Chinese diaspora*. London: Routledge.

Berou Jr, A. (2012). Employment or entrepreneurship: A theoretical analysis on decision-making process and economic outcomes. *International Journal of Information Technology and Business Management, 22*(1), 8–20.

Berry, J. W. (2005). Acculturation: Living successfully in two cultures. *International Journal of Intercultural Relations, 29*(6), 697–712.

Bissinger, J. (2014). Myanmar's economic institutions in transition. *Journal of Southeast Asian Economies, 31*(2), 241–255.

Blythe, W. L. (1947). Historical sketch of Chinese labour in Malaya. *Journal of the Malayan Branch of the Royal Asiatic Society, 20*(1), 64–114.

Bonacich, E. (1973). A theory of middleman minorities. *American Sociological Review, 38*, 583–594.

Bourdieu, P. (2018). The forms of capital. In Granovetter M. & Swedberg R. (Eds.), *The sociology of economic life* (pp. 78–92). London: Routledge.

Bowring, P. (2018). *Empire of the winds: The global role of Asia's great archipelago*. London: Bloomsbury Publishing.

Bravo, M. R. (2017). Urbanization in the Philippines and its influence on agriculture. In Yokohari, M., Murakami, A., Hara, Y., Tsuchiya, K. (Eds.), *Sustainable landscape planning in selected urban regions. Science for sustainable societies*. Tokyo: Springer.

Brown, R. A. (1994). *Capital and entrepreneurship in South-east Asia*. Macmillan.

Brown, R. A. (2000). *Chinese big business and the wealth of Asian nations*. Palgrave.

Brush, C. G., & Manolova, T. S. (2004). Women, age, and money: International entrepreneurship theory in the work of Candida G. Brush. In Dana L.-P. & Wright R. W. (Eds.), *Handbook of research on international entrepreneurship* (pp. 41–57). Cheltenham, op. cit: Edward Elgar.

Burch, D. (1996). Globalized agriculture and agri-food restructuring in Southeast Asia: The Thai experience. In Burch, D., Rickson, R. E. & Lawrence, G. (Eds.), *Globalization and agri-food restructuring: Perspectives from the Australasia region* (pp. 323–344). Hampshire: Ashgate Publishing.

Burke, A., Williams, N., Barron, P., Jolliffe, K., & Carr, T. (2017). *The contested areas of Myanmar. Subnational conflict, aid and development*. San Francisco: The Asia Foundation.

Burns, T., & Stalker, G. M. (1994). *The management of innovation*. United Kingdom: Oxford University Press.

Busenitz, L. W., & Lau, C. M. (1996). A cross-cultural cognitive model of new venture creation. *Entrepreneurship: Theory and Practice, 20*(4), 25–40.

Butcher, J. (1993). Loke Yew. In J. Butcher & H. Dick (Eds.), *The rise and fall of revenue farming: Business elites and the emergence of the modern state in Southeast Asia* (pp. 255–261). New York: St Martin's Press.

Calhoun, C. (2020). The class consciousness of frequent travellers: Toward a critique of actually existing cosmopolitanism. In C. Calhoun & S. J. Kahn (Eds.), *Enchantments of modernity* (pp. 310–340). India: Routledge.

Camarota, S. A. (2000). *Reconsidering immigrant entrepreneurship: An examination of self-employment among natives and the foreign-born*. Washington, D.C.: Center for Immigration Studies.

Camba, A. J., & Lung, S. (2021). Chinese capital as a cultural object: Self identification and Filipino-Chinese discourses on Sinicization, Brokerage, and Distinction. *Translocal Chinese: East Asian Perspectives, 15*(2), 186–213.

Campbell, G. (1912). Origin and migration of the Hakkas. *Chinese Recorder, 43*(8), 473–480.

Campbell, P. C. (1970). *Chinese coolie emigration to countries within the British Empire.* Taipei: Ch'eng-wen Pub. Co.

Carlock, R. S., & Ward, J. L. (2001). *Strategic planning for the family business: Parallel planning to unify the family and business.* New York: Palgrave.

Carney, M., & Gedajlovic, E. (2002). The co-evolution of institutional environments and organizational strategies: The rise of family business groups in the ASEAN region. *Organization Studies, 23*, 11–29.

Carstens, S. (1988). From myth to history: Yap Ah Loy and the Heroic past of Chinese Malaysians. *Journal of Southeast Asian Studies, 19*(2), 185–208.

Chaganti, R., & Greene, P. G. (2002). Who are ethnic entrepreneurs? A study of entrepreneursapos; ethnic involvement and business characteristics. *Journal of Small Business Management, 40*(2), 126–143.

Chan, A. B. (1980). The myth of the Chinese sojourner in Canada. In K. V. Ujimoto & G. Hirabayashi (Eds.), *Visible minorities and multiculturalism: Asians in Canada* (pp. 30–40). Toronto: Butterworths Press.

Chandler, A. D. (1962). *Strategy and structure.* Cambridge, MA: MIT Press.

Chandler, A. D., Jr. (1977). *The visible hand: The managerial revolution in American Business.* Cambridge: Harvard University Press.

Chandler, A. D., Jr. (1990). *Strategy and structure: Chapters in the history of the industrial enterprise.* Cambridge, MA: MIT Press.

Chandler, A. D., Jr. (1997). *The United States: Engines of economic growth in the capital-intensive and knowledge-intensive industries* (pp. 63–101). Cambridge: Cambridge University Press.

Chandler, A. D., Jr., Amatori, F., & Hikino, T. (1999). *Big business and the wealth of nations.* Cambridge: Cambridge University Press.

Chang, S. C., Wu, W. Y., & Wong, Y. J. (2010). Family control and stock market reactions to innovation announcements. *British Journal of Management, 21*(1), 152–170.

Chee-Beng, Tan. (1997). Chinese identities in Malaysia. *Asian Journal of Social Science, 25*(2), 103–116.

Chen, H. L., & Hsu, W. T. (2009). Family ownership, board independence, and R&D investment. *Family Business Review, 22*(4), 347–362.

Chen, J. (2022). *Study on overseas Chinese and ethnic Chinese of Yunnan Origin in Southeast Asia.* New York, United States of America: Peter Lang Verlag.

Chen, K. C. (1987). *China's War with Vietnam, 1979: Issues, Decisions, and Implications.* Stanford: Hoover Institution Press, (pp. 50–51, 53).

Chin, J. K. (2010). Junk trade, business networks and Sojourning communities: Hokkien merchants in early Maritime Asia. *Journal of Chinese Overseas, 6*(2), 157–215.

Chin, T. S., & Jusoh, A. D. N. A. N. (2021). Cabaran Peniaga Cina Dalam Sektor Penghasilan Makanan Di Butterworth, 1900–2000. *Jebat: Malaysian Journal of History, Politics & Strategy, 48*(2), 240–255.

Chin, Y. W. (2008). The evolution of Chinese Malaysian entrepreneurship: From British Colonial rule to post-new economic policy. *Journal of Chinese Overseas, 4*(2), 203–237.

Chin, Y. W., & Lim, E.-S. (2018). *SME policies and performance in Malaysia. 3*, 1–41.

Chua, C. (2004). Defining Indonesian Chineseness under the new order. *Journal of Contemporary Asia, 34*(4), 465.

Chua, J. H., Chrisman, J. J., & Sharma, P. (1999). Defining the family business by behavior. *Entrepreneurship Theory & Practice, 23*(4), 19–39.

Chung, S. P. Y. (2002). *A Southeast Asian tycoon and his movie dream: Loke Wan Tho and MP&GI.* In A. Wong (Ed.), The Cathay Story (pp. 36–51). Hong Kong: Hong Kong Film Archive.

Ciorîia, Ş. (2018). The "Bamboo network" of Southeast-Asia and its socio-philosophical grounds. *Revista Universitară de Sociologie, 14*(2), 41–65.

Claessens, S., Djankov, S., & Lang, L. H. P. (2000). The separation of ownership and control in East Asian corporations. *Journal of Financial Economics, 58*(1–2), 81–112.

Clark, K., & Drinkwater, S. (2010). Recent trends in minority ethnic entrepreneurship in Britain. *International Small Business Journal, 28*(2), 136–46.

Claver, E., Rienda, L., & Quer, D. (2009). Family firms' international commitment: The influence of family-related factors. *Family Business Review, 22*(2), 125–135.

Cohen, M. L. (1968). The Hakka or "guest people": Dialect as a sociocultural variable in southeastern China. *Ethnohistory, 15*(3), 237–292.

Cole, P. M. (1997). Women in family business. *Family Business Review, 10*(4), 353–37.

Collins, J. (2003). Australia: Cosmopolitan capitalists down under. In Kloosterman, R., & Rath, J. (Eds.), *Immigrant entrepreneurs: Venturing abroad in the age of globalisation* (pp. 61–78). New York: New York University Press, and Oxford: Berg Publishing.

Coppel, C. A. (2013). Diaspora and hybridity: Peranakan Chinese culture in Indonesia. In C. B. Tan (Ed.), *Routledge handbook of the Chinese Diaspora* (pp. 345–358). New York: Routledge.

Corbetta, G. (1999). The company values and business familiars. In D. Mele (Ed.), *Considerations on entrepreneurship and family business* (pp. 157–172). Pamplona: Ediciones Universidad de Navarra.

Cortes, M., Berry, A., & Ishaq, A. (1987). *Success in small and medium scale enterprises: The evidence from Colombia.* United Kingdom: Oxford University Press.

Crabtree, B., & Miller, W. (1992). A template approach to text analysis: Developing and using codebooks. In B. Crabtree, & W. Miller (Eds.), *Doing Qualitative Research* (vol. 3, pp. 93–109). California: Sage Publications.

Craig, J. B., Cassar, G., & Moores, K. (2006). A ten-year investigation of strategy, systems, and environment upon innovation in family firms. *Family Business Review, 19*(1), 1–10.

Craig, J., & Dibrell, C. (2006). The natural environment, innovation, and firm performance: A comparative study. *Family Business Review, 19*(4), 275–288.

Curdt-Christiansen, X. L. (2014). Planning for development or decline? Education policy for Chinese language in Singapore. *Critical Inquiry in Language Studies, 11*(1), 1–26.

Daft, R. (1982). Bureaucratic versus non-bureaucratic structure of the process of innovation and change. In S. B. Bacharach (Ed.), *Research in the sociology of organizations* (pp. 129–166). Greenwich, CT: JAI Press.

Damanpour, F. (1991). Organizational innovation: A meta-analysis of effects of determinants and moderators. *Academy of Management Journal, 34*(3), 555–590.

David, Y. H. W., & Chee-beng, T. (2001). *Changing Chinese foodways in Asia* (p. 304). Hong Kong: The Chinese University Press.

David, C. (2003). Agriculture. In A. Balisacan & H. Hill (Eds.), *The Philippine economy: Development, policies, and challenges.* Quezon City: Ateneo de Manila University Press.

Davis, P. S., & Harveston, P. D. (2000). Internationalization and organizational growth: The impact of internet usage and technology involvement among entrepreneurled family businesses. *Family Business Review*, *13*(2), 107–120.

De Vienne, M. S. (2011). The Chinese in Brunei: From ceramics to oil rent. *Archipel*, *82*(1), 25–48.

Decrop, A. (1999). Triangulation in qualitative tourism research. *Tourism Management*, *20*(1), 157–161.

den Butter, F. A., Masurel, E., & Mosch, R. H. (2004). The economics of co-ethnic employment. In L.-P. Dana (Ed.), *Handbook of research on ethnic minority entrepreneurship* (pp. 79–90). Cheltenham, UK: Edward Elgar Publishing.

Del Tufo, M. V. (Ed.). (1949). *Malaya, comprising the Federation of Malaya and the Colony of Singapore: A report on the 1947 census of population* (p. 76). London: Crown Agents for the Colonies.

Desai, D. S. (1969). The Portuguese administration in Malacca, 1511–1641. *Journal of Southeast Asian History*, *10*(3), 501–512.

Dhaliwal, S. (2000). Entrepreneurship-A learning process: The experiences of Asian women entrepreneurs and women in business. *Journal of Education and Training*, *42*(8), 445–452.

Dhoraisingham & Samuel. (1992). Tan Tock Seng, 27; Singapore Days of Old, Hong Kong. *Illustrated Magazine*, 51.

Dinçer, H., Yüksel, S., Eti, S., & Tula, A. (2019). Effects of demographic characteristics on business success: An evidence from Turkish banking sector. In J. Leitão, H. Alves, & J. J. Ferreira (Eds.), *Handbook of research on business models in modern competitive scenarios* (pp. 304–324). Pennsylvania: IGI Global.

Dosi, G., Teece, D. J., & Winter, S. G. (1992). Toward a theory of corporate coherence. In G. Dosi (Ed.), *Technology and enterprise* (pp. 185–211). Oxford: Clarendon Press.

Douglas, C. (1899). Extent of the Amoy vernacular, and its sub-division into dialects. In Thomas Barclay (Ed.), *Chinese-English dictionary of the vernacular or spoken language of Amoy* (in English & Amoy Hokkien). (p. 610). London: Presbyterian Church of England.

Douw, L., & Post, P. (1996). *South China: State, culture and social change during the 20th century* (p. 25). North-Holland.

Drabble, J. H. (2003). Technology transfer in Singapore/Malaya during the colonial period: Some further comments. *Journal of the Malaysian Branch of the Royal Asiatic Society*, *76*(2), 81–85.

Draim, A. (2001). Highlighting the crucial role of family business. *Business Times*, 7625776-1.

Drozdow, N. (1989). Thinking that is intuitive to the boss must be charted for the next generation. *Business Week Newsletter for Family-Owned Business*, *1*(19), 31–39.

Dunstan, S., Boyd, S., & Crichton, S. (2004). *Migrants' experiences in New Zealand: Pilot survey report.* Wellington: Department of Labour.

Dyer, W. G. (1986). *Cultural change in family firms: Anticipating and managing business and family transitions.* San Francisco, CA, London: Jossey-Bass.

Egreteau, R., & Jagan, L. (2013). *Soldiers and diplomacy in Burma: Understanding the foreign relations of the Burmese Praetorian state* (pp. 271–273). Singapore: National University of Singapore Press.

Eisenhardt, K. (1989). Building theories from case study research. *Academy of Management: The Academy of Management Review*, *14*(4), 532–550.

Elbaum, B., & Lazonick, W. (1987). *The decline of the British economy* (pp. 1–17). Oxford: Oxford University Press.

Ember, M., Ember, C. R., & Skoggard, I. (2004). *Encyclopedia of diasporas: Immigrant and refugee cultures around the world. Volume I: Overviews and Topics; Volume II: Diaspora Communities*. New York: Springer Science & Business Media.

Engelen, E. (2001). 'Breaking in' and 'breaking out': A Weberian approach to entrepreneurial opportunities. *Journal of Ethnic and Migration Studies, 27*(2), 203–223.

Ernst, D. (2004). Global production networks in East Asia's electronics industry and upgrading prospects in Malaysia. *Global Production Networking and Technological Change in East Asia, 476*(2), 89–157.

Fee, L. K., & We, K. K.. (2004). Chinese enterprise in colonial Malaya: The case of Eu Tong Sen. *Journal of Southeast Asian Studies, 35*(3), 415–432.

Felker, G. B. (2003). Southeast Asian industrialisation and the changing global production system. *Third World Quarterly, 24*(2), 255–282.

Fernández, Z., & Nieto, M. J. (2005). Internationalization strategy of small and medium-sized family businesses: Some influential factors. *Family Business Review, 18*(1), 77–89.

Finlay, L. (2009). Ambiguous encounters: A relational approach to phenomenological research. *Indo-Pacific Journal of Phenomenology, 9*(1), 1–17.

Flamholtz, E. G. (1986). *Managing the transition from an entrepreneurship to a professionally manager firm.* San Francisco: Jossey-Bass.

Fletcher, D. E. (2000). Family and enterprise. In S. Carter & D. Jones-Evans (Eds.), *Enterprise and small business: Principles, practice and policy*. Harlow: Pearson Education.

Flower, R., Lim, W., & Loh, C. Y. (2006). *Tan Sri Loh Boon Siew: The life and times of a Fire Dragon*. Singapore: SNP Edition.

Freedman, A. L. (1998). *Politicization and influence in Chinese communities overseas: The United States, Indonesia, and Malaysia*. New York: New York University.

Freedman, A . L. (2001). The effect of government policy and institutions on Chinese overseas acculturation: The case of Malaysia. *Modern Asian Studies, 35*(02), 411–440.

Freedman, M. (1960). Immigrants and associations: Chinese in nineteenth-century Singapore. *Comparative Studies in Society and History, 3*(1), 25–48.

Freeman, S., Edwards, R., & Schroder, B. (2006). How smaller born-global firms use networks and alliances to overcome constraints to rapid internationalization. *Journal of International Marketing, 14*(3), 33–63.

Gallo, M. A. (1995). Family businesses in Spain: Tracks followed and outcomes reached by those among the largest thousand. *Family Business Review, 8*(4), 245–254.

Gatfield, T. J. (1997). International marketing of higher education. Unpublished doctoral thesis, Griffith University, Brisbane.

Gartner, W. B., Carter, N. M., & Reynolds, P. D. (2004). Business start-up activities. In W. B. Gartner, N. M. Carter, & P. D. Reynolds (Eds.), *Handbook of entrepreneurial dynamics: The process of business creation* (pp. 285–298). Thousand Oaks, CA: SAGE Publications.

Gersick, K., Davis, J., Hampton, M., & Lamsberg, I. (1997). *Generation to generation: Life cycles of the family business*. Boston, MA: Harvard Business School Press.

Ghauri, P. (2004). Designing and conducting case studies in international business research. In R. Piekkari & C. Welch (Eds.), *Handbook of qualitative research methods for international business* (pp. 109–124). Cheltenham: Edward Elgar Publishing Limited.

Glisby, M., & Holden, N. (2003). Contextual constraints in knowledge management theory: The cultural embeddedness of Nonaka's knowledge-creating company. *Knowledge and Process Management, 10*(1), 29–36.

Globe Asia. (2016). 100 Top Groups. *Globe Asia 10* (August), 42–79.

Goldberg, S. D. (1996). Research note: Effective successors in family-owned businesses – significant elements. *Family Business Review*, *9*, 185–197.

Gomez, E. T. (1994). *Political business: Corporate involvement of Malaysian Political Parties.* Townsville: Centre for Southeast Asian Studies, James Cook University of North Queensland.

Gomez, E. T. (1999). *Chinese business in Malaysia: Accumulation, accommodation, ascendance.* Honolulu: University of Hawaii Press.

Gomez, E. T. (2003). Introduction: Political business in East Asia. In *Political Business in East Asia* (pp. 17–49). London: Routledge.

Gomez, E. T. (2007). Family firms, transnationalism and generational change: Chinese enterprise in Britain and Malaysia. *East Asia*, *24*(2), 153–172.

Gomez, E. T. (2009). The rise and fall of capital: Corporate Malaysia in historical perspective. *Journal of Contemporary Asia*, *39*(3), 345–381.

Gomez, E. T. (2012). Targeting horizontal inequalities: Ethnicity, equity, and entrepreneurship in Malaysia. *Asian Economic Papers*, *11*(2), 31–57.

Gomez, E. T., & Hsiao, H. H. M. (2012). Chinese business research in Southeast Asia. In E. T. Gomez & H. H. M. Hsiao (Eds.), *Chinese business in Southeast Asia* (pp. 1–37). Oxon: Routledge.

Gomez, E. T., & Hsiao, H. H. M. (Eds.). (2013). *Chinese business in Southeast Asia: Contesting cultural explanations, researching entrepreneurship*. Oxon: Routledge.

Gomez, E. T., & Jomo, K. S. (1999). *Malaysia's politicial economy: Politics, patronage and profits*. Cambridge University Press.

Gomez, E. T., Loh, W. L., & Lee, K. H. (2004). Chinese business in Southeast Asia. In E. T. Gomez, W. L. Loh, & K. H. Lee. (Eds.), *Chinese business in Southeast Asia* (pp. 62–84). London and New York: Routledge Curzon.

Gomez-Mejia, L. R., Cruz, C., Berrone, P., & De Castro, J. (2011). The bind that ties: Socioemotional wealth preservation in family firms. *The Academy of Management Annals*, *5*(1), 653–707.

Gong, B. H. (2003). *The Overseas Cantonese History* [广府华侨华人史]. Guangzhou: Guangdong Higher Education Press.

Gonzales, W. D. W. (2021). Filipino, Chinese, neither, or both? The Lannang identity and its relationship with language. *Language & Communication*, *77*, 5–16.

Goodrich, B. W. F. (1959). Chinese secret societies in Malaya. *The Police Journal*, *32*(4), 238–243.

Gordon, A. (2004). Dynamics of labour transformation: Natural rubber in Southeast Asia. *Journal of Contemporary Asia*, *34*(4), 523–546.

Goudeau, S., Autin, F., Croizet, J. C. (2017). Etudier, Mesurer et Manipuler la Classe Sociale en Psychologie Sociale: Approches Economiques, Symboliques et Culturelles [Studying, Measuring and Manipulating Social Class in Social Psychology: Economic, Symbolic and Cultural Approaches]. *Revue Internationale De Psychologie Sociale-international Review of Social Psychology*, *30*(1), 1–19.

Gravers, M. (2015). Disorder as order: The ethno-nationalist struggle of the Karen in Burma/ Myanmar—A discussion of the dynamics of an ethicized civil war and its historical roots. *Journal of Burma Studies*, *19*(1), 27–78.

Graves, C., & Thomas, J. (2008). Determinants of the internationalization pathways of family firms: An examination of family influence. *Family Business Review*, *21*(2), 151–167.

Greiner, L. E. (1972). Evolution and revolution as organizations grow. *Harvard Business Review*, *50*(4), 37–46.

Greiner, L. E. (1998). Evolution and revolution as organizations grow. *Harvard Business Review, 76*(3), 55–64.

Griffin, C. (1985). Qualitative methods and female experience: Young women from school to the job market. In S. Wilkinson (Ed.), *Feminist social psychology: Developing theory and practice* (pp. 173–192). London: Open University Press.

Guang, H. M. (2012). *External and internal perceptions of the Hainanese community and identity, past and present.* (Master's thesis, National University of Singapore). ScholarBank@NUS Repository.

Habbershon, T. G., & Williams, M. L. (1999). A resource-based framework for assessing the strategic advantages of family firms. *Family Business Review, 12*(1), 1–25.

Hadjimanolis, A. (2000). An investigation of innovation antecedents in small firms in the context of a small developing country. *R&D Management, 30*(3), 235–246.

Hall, A., Melin, L., & Nordqvist, M. (2001). Entrepreneurship as radical change in the family business: Exploring the role of cultural patterns. *Family Business Review, 14*(3), 193–208.

Hall, A., Melin, L., & Nordqvist, M. (2006). Understanding strategizing in the family business context. In P. Poutziouris, K. Smyrnios, & S. Klein (Eds.), *Family business research handbook*. Cheltenham, UK and Brookfield, US: Edward Elgar.

Hall, B. H. (1992). Investment and research and development at the firm level: Does the source of financing matter? (NBER Working Paper No. 4096). National Bureau of Economic Research, Cambridge, MA.

Hall, K. R. (2010). *A history of early Southeast Asia: Maritime trade and societal development, 100–1500*. Lanham, MD: Rowman & Littlefield Publishers.

Halpern, J. (1961). The role of the Chinese in Lao society. Santa Monica: The Rand Corporation.

Hamilton, E. (2006). Whose story is it anyway? Narrative accounts of the role of women in founding and establishing family businesses. *International Small Business Journal, 24*(3), 253–271.

Handler, W. C. (1989). Methodological issues and considerations in studying family businesses. *Family Business Review, 2*(3), 257–276.

Handler, W. C., & Kram, K. E. (1988). Succession in family firms: The problem of resistance. *Family Business Review, 1*(4), 361–381.

Hanks, S. H., Watson, C. J., Jansen, E., & Chandler, G. N. (1993). Tightening the life-cycle construct: A taxonomic study of growth stage configurations in high-technology organizations. *Entrepreneurship Theory and Practice, 18*(2), 5–30.

Han, M. G. (2012). External and internal perceptions of the Hainanese community and identity, past and present (Bachelor's thesis).

Hashemi, S., Mohammed, H. J., Kiumarsi, S., Kee, D. M. H., & Anarestani, B. B. (2023). Destinations food image and food neophobia on behavioral intentions: Culinary tourist behavior in Malaysia. *Journal of International Food & Agribusiness Marketing, 35*(1), 66–87.

Hayat, H. (2017). Capital crunch plagues MSMEs. Retrieved January 1, 2024, from https://borneobulletin.com.bn/ capital-crunch-plagues-msmes/

Heng, D. (2009). *Sino–Malay trade and diplomacy from the tenth through the fourteenth century* (vol. 121). Athens, OH: Ohio University Press.

Heng, D. (2022). *Southeast Asian interconnections: Geography, networks and trade*. Cambridge: Cambridge University Press.

Heng, P. K., & Sieh, L. M. L. (2000). The Chinese business community in Peninsular Malaysia, 1957–1999. In H. Lee Kam & T. Chee Beng (Eds.), *The Chinese in Malaysia* (pp. 262–286). Shah Alam: Oxford University Press.

Herbert, U. (2007). Europe in high modernity. Reflections on a theory of the 20th century. *Journal of Modern European History*, *5*(1), 5–21.

Herrero, I. (2018). How familial is family social capital? Analyzing bonding social capital in family and nonfamily firms. *Family Business Review*, *31*(4), 441–459.

Hewison, K. (2003). Thailand's capitalism before and after the economic crisis. In K. S. Jomo (Ed.), *Politics and markets in the wake of the Asian crisis* (pp. 207–226). London: Routledge.

Hill, R. D. (2013). *Agriculture in the Malaysian region*. Singapore: NUS Press.

Hilmar, T. (2022). Class and memory activism. In J. Wüstenberg & Y. Gutman (Eds.), *Handbook of memory activism*. New York: Routledge.

Hiratsuka, D. (2016). *Production networks in Asia: A case study from the hard disk drive industry* (pp. 139–157). Springer Japan.

Hlaing, K. Y. (2006). Laos: The state of the state. *Southeast Asian Affairs*, *2006*(1), 127–147.

Ho, D. G. E., & Ho, H. M. Y. (2021). Ethnic identity and the Southeast Asian Chinese: Voices from Brunei. In C. Y. Hoon & Y. Chan (Eds.), *Contesting Chineseness. Asia in transition* (vol. 14, pp. 149–166).Singapore: Springer.

Ho, H. M. Y. (2021). Localization of Malay Muslim identity in Brunei Darussalam: A modern nation's cultural and economic goals. In H. M. Y. Ho & D. Deterding (Eds.), *Engaging modern Brunei* (pp. 127–143). Singapore: Springer.

Hock, G. L., & Suryadinata, L. (2012). *Malaysian Chinese: Recent developments and prospects*. Singapore: Institute of Southeast Asian Studies.

Hodder, R. (1996). *Merchant princes of the East: Cultural delusions, economic success, and the overseas Chinese in Southeast Asia*. John Wiley and Sons.

Hofstede, G. (1980). Culture and organizations. *International Studies of Management & Organization*, *10*(4), 15–41.

Hofstede, G. H. (2001). *Culture's consequences: Comparing values, behaviors, institutions, and organizations across nations* (2nd ed.). Thousand Oak, CA: Sage.

Hooker, M. B. (2002). *Law and the Chinese in Southeast Asia*. Singapore: Institute of Southeast Asian Studies.

Hoon, C.-Y. (2008). *Chinese identity in Post-Suharto Indonesia: Culture, politics and media*. Brighton: Sussex Academic Press.

Hsiao, H. H. (2020). The new research trends of Southeast Asian Hakka ethnic associations. In H. H. Hsiao, H. P. Chang, & W. A. Chang (Eds.), *The networks of the Hakka Ethnic Associations in Southeast Asia* (pp. 17–35). Taoyuan: National Central University Publishing Center.

Hsiao, H. H. M., & Lim, K. T. (2007). The formation and limitation of Hakka identity in Southeast Asia. *Taiwan Journal of Southeast Asian Studies*, *4*(1), 3–28.

Huff, G., & Caggiano, G. (2008). Globalization and labor market integration in late nineteenth and early twentieth-century Asia. *Research in Economic History*, *25*, 255–317.

Huff, W. G. (1995). The developmental state, government, and Singapore's economic development since 1960. *World Development*, *23*(8), 1421–1438.

Hult, G. T. M., Hurley, R. F., & Knight, G. A. (2004). Innovativeness: Its antecedents and impact on business performance. *Industrial Marketing Management, 33*, 429–438.

Hurley, R. F., & Hult, G. T. M. (1998). Innovation, market orientation, and organizational learning: An integration and empirical examination. *Journal of Marketing*, *62*(3), 42–54.

Hutchings, K., & Michailova, S. (2003). Facilitating knowledge sharing in Russian and Chinese subsidiaries: The importance of groups and personal networks. *Journal of Knowledge Management*, *7*(4), 16–28.

Indonesia Population. (2023) - Worldometer. (2023, December 11). www.worldometers.info/world-population/indonesia-population/
Jakobsen, M. (2014). *Ethnic Chinese entrepreneurship in Malaysia: On contextualisation in international business studies*. Abingdon, Oxfordshire: Routledge.
Jarness, V. (2013). Class, status, closure. The Petropolis and cultural life. New York, NY: Routledge.
Jasani, N. K. (2002). *Malaysia's family business: The family & the business international survey report*. Kuala Lumpur: Shamsir Jasani Grant Thornton & Malaysia Institute of Management.
Jesudason, J. V. (1989). *Ethnicity and the economy: The state, Chinese business, and multinationals in Malaysia*. USA: Oxford University Press.
Jesudason, J. V. (1997). Chinese business and ethnic equilibrium in Malaysia. *Development and Change*, *28*(1), 119–141.
Johannisson, B., & Huse, M. (2000). Recruiting outside board members in the small family business: An ideological challenge. *Entrepreneurship & Regional Development, 12*(4), 353–378.
Jomo, K. S. (2001). *Growth after the Asian crisis: What remains of the East Asian model?* Cambridge, MA: United Nations Conference on Trade and Development. UN.
Jomo, K. S. (2005). Malaysia's new economic policy and national unity. In *Racism and public policy* (pp. 182–214). London: Palgrave Macmillan UK.
Jomo, K. S., & Folk, B. C. (2013). *Ethnic business: Chinese capitalism in Southeast Asia*. New York: Routledge.
Jones, D. M. (2005). The politics of economic governance. In J. Higgott, G. Payne, & S. R. H. (Eds.), *Governance in the Asia-Pacific* (pp. 173–195). Routledge.
Jones, G., & Rose, M. (2013). *Family capitalism*. London: Routledge.
Jones, T., Barrett, G., & McEvoy, D. (2000). Market potential as a decisive influence on the performance of ethnic minority business. In J. Rath (Ed.), *Immigrant* businesses (pp. 37–53). Basingstoke: Macmillan.
Mulliner, K., & The-Mulliner, L. (1991). *Historical dictionary of Singapore* (p. 149). Metuchen, NJ: Scarecrow Press.
Kassim, A. (2001). Integration of foreign workers and illegal employment in Malaysia. In M. K. Jamil & L. A. Samir (Eds.), *International migration in Asia: Trends and policies* (pp. 113–135). Tokyo: Asian Development Bank Institute.
Kassim, A., & Zin, R. H. M. (2011). Policy on irregular migrants in Malaysia: An analysis of its implementation and effectiveness (No. 2011-34). PIDS Discussion Paper Series.
Kaur, A. (2004). Mobility, labour mobilisation and border controls: Indonesian labour migration to Malaysia since 1900. In *15th Biennial Conference of the Asian Studies Association of Australia, Canberra* (vol. 29, pp. 1–23).
Kaur, A. (2004). *Wage Labour in Southeast Asia since 1840*. New York, NY: Palgrave Macmillan.
Kaur, A. (2006). Indian labour, labour standards, and workers' health in Burma and Malaya, 1900–1940. *Modern Asian Studies*, *40*(2), 425–475.
Kaur, A. (2012). Labour brokers in migration: Understanding historical and contemporary transnational migration regimes in Malaya/Malaysia. *International Review of Social History, 57*(S20), 225–252.
Kazanjian, R. K. (1988). Relation of dominant problems to stages of growth in technology-based new ventures. *Academy of Management Journal*, *31*(2), 257–279.

Kelly, M. J., Schaan, J. L., & Joncas, H. (2000). Collaboration between technology entrepreneurs and large corporations: Key design and management issue. *Journal of Small Business Strategy (archive only)*, *11*(2), 60–76.

Kennedy, J. C. (2002). YTL Corporation's CEO Tan Sri Dato'Francis Yeoh on providing world-class products at third-world prices. *Academy of Management Executive*, *16*(3), 27–30.

Keong, V. P. (2007). *Pioneers, entrepreneurs, and labourers: Building the social and economic foundations of Statehood* (pp. 44–94). Malaysian Chinese and Nation-Building: Before Merdeka and Fifty Years After.

Kets de Vries, M. F. (1994). The leadership mystique. *Academy of Management Perspectives*, *8*(3), 73–89.

Khairuddin, O., & Yeoh, H. E. (1986, July 8–24). An overview of the plastics industry in Malaysia. Paper presented at the Workshop on Plastics Technology, Malaysia Industry Development Authority (MIDA), Kuala Lumpur.

Khan, I., Dongping, H., Abdullah, M., Ahmad, Z., Ahmad Ghauri, T., & Ghazanfar, S. (2017). Men's attitude and motivation toward consumption of grooming products: A comparison of Chinese and Pakistani male consumers. *Cogent Business and Management*, *4*(1), 1309783.

Khanh, T., Phuong, T. H. (1997). Ethnic Chinese in Vietnam and their identity. In L. Suryadinata (Ed.), *Ethnic Chinese as Southeast Asians*. New York: Palgrave Macmillan.

Khoo, J. E. (1996). *The straits Chinese: A cultural history* (p. 23). Amsterdam: The Pepin Press.

Khor, K. P. (1983). *The Malaysian economy: Structures and dependence*. Kuala Lumpur: Marican.

Kim, H., Kim, H., & Lee, P. M. (2008). Ownership structure and the relationship between financial slack and R&D investments: Evidence from Korean firms. *Organization Science*, *19*(3), 404–418.

Kiu, M. K. (1997). *The diffusion of Foochow settlement in Sibu-Binatang Area, Central Sarawak 1901–1970*. Sibu: Sarawak Chinese Cultural Association.

Kloosterman, R., & Rath, J. (2001). Immigrant entrepreneurs in advanced economies: Mixed embeddedness further explored. *Journal of Ethnic and Migration Studies*, *27*, 198–201.

Kloosterman, R., & Rath, J. (2003). *Immigrant entrepreneurs: Venturing abroad in the age of globalization*. Oxford and New York: Berg.

Kloosterman, R., Van Leun, J., & Rath, J. (1999). Mixed embeddedness: Immigrant entrepreneurship and informal economic activities. *International Journal of Urban and Regional Research*, *23*(2), 253–277.

Kloosterman, R. C. (2010). Matching opportunities with resources: A framework for analysing (migrant) entrepreneurship from a mixed embeddedness perspective. *Entrepreneurship and Regional Development*, *22*(1), 25–45.

Klyver, K., Evald, M. R., & Hindle, K. (2011). Social networks and new venture creation: The dark side of networks. In K. Hindle & K. Klyver (Eds.), *Handbook of research on new venture creation* (pp. 145–159). Cheltenham, UK: Edward Elgar Publishing.

Knight, J. (2015). Migrant employment in the ethnic economy: Why do some migrants become ethnic entrepreneurs and others co-ethnic workers? *Journal of International Migration and Integration*, *16*, 575–592.

Koiranen, M. (2002). Over 100 years of age but still entrepreneurially active in business: Exploring the values and family characteristics of old Finnish family firms. *Family Business Review*, *15*(3), 175–187.

Koh, J., & Ho, S. (2009). *Culture and customs of Singapore and Malaysia* (p. 3). Santa Barbara: Greenwood Press.

Koning, J. (2011). Chapter Two. Business, belief, and belonging: Small business owners and conversion to charismatic Christianity. In M. Dieleman, J. Koning, & P. Post (Eds.), *Chinese Indonesians and regime change* (pp. 21–46). Leiden: Brill.

Koning, J., & Verver, M. (2012). Historicizing the 'ethnic' in ethnic entrepreneurship: The case of the ethnic Chinese in Bangkok, *Entrepreneurship & Regional Development: An International Journal, 25*(5–6), 325–348.

Kontos, M. (2003). Self-employment policies and migrants' entrepreneurship in Germany. *Entrepreneurship and Regional Development, 15*(2), 119–35.

Koon, H. P. (1997). The new economic policy and the Chinese community in Peninsular Malaysia. *The Developing Economies, 35*(3), 262–292.

Kuhn, P. A. (2008). *Chinese among others: Emigration in modern times.* Lanham, MD: Rowman & Littlefield.

Kuhn, P., & Liu, H. (2006). *Toward an historical ecology of Chinese migration. The Chinese Overseas* (vol. 1, pp. 67–97). London and New York: Routledge.

Lai Chee Kien. (2006). Multi-ethnic enclaves around middle road: An examination of early Urban settlement in Singapore. *BiblioAsia, 2*(2), 4–11.

Lai, A. E. (2010). The Kopitiam in Singapore: An evolving story about migration and cultural diversity. Singapore: Singapore University Press.

Lall, S. (1995). Industrial strategy and policies on foreign direct investment in East Asia. *Transnational Corporations*, *4*, 1–26.

Lansberg, I. (1988). The succession conspiracy. *Family Business Review*, *1*(2), 119–143.

Laothamatas, A. (1988). Business and politics in Thailand: New patterns of influence. *Asian Survey*, *28*(4), 451–470.

Laungaramsri, P. (2019). China in Laos: Enclave spaces and the transformation of borders in the Mekong Region. *Australian Journal of Anthropology*, *30*(2), 195–211.

Laursen, K., Masciarelli, F., & Prencipe, A. (2012). Trapped or spurred by the home region? The effects of potential social capital on involvement in foreign markets for goods and technology. *Journal of International Business Studies, 43*, 783–807.

Lebdioui, A. (2022). The political economy of moving up in global value chains: How Malaysia added value to its natural resources through industrial policy. *Review of International Political Economy*, *29*(3), 870–903.

LeBlanc, L. J., Nash, R., Gallagher, D., Gonda, K., & Kakizaki, F. (1997). A comparison of US and Japanese technology management and innovation. *International Journal of Technology Management*, *13*(5–6), 601–614.

Lee, E., Wong, S. P., & Laxman, L. (2014). Language maintenance and cultural viability in the Hainanese community: A case study of the Melaka Hainanese. *Athens Journal of Humanities and Arts, 1*(2), 157–168.

Lee, H. A. (2023). Malaysia's new economic policy and affirmative action: A remedy in need of a rethink. In A. Deshpande (Ed.), *Handbook on economics of discrimination and affirmative action* (pp. 819–839). Singapore: Springer Nature Singapore.

Lee, J., & Tan, F. C. K. (2001). Growth of Chinese family enterprises in Singapore. *Family Business Review*, *14*(1), 49–74.

Lee, K. H. (2019). Chinese Diaspora and faith formation in Peninsular Malaysia: Ayer Salak, 1850–2019. *Malaysian Journal of Chinese Studies, 8*(2), 1–10.

Lee, K. H., & Tan, C. B. (Eds.). (2000). *The Chinese in Malaysia.* Kuala Lumpur: Oxford University Press.

Lee, P. P. (1978). *Chinese society in nineteenth century Singapore*. Kuala Lumpur: Oxford University Press.

Lee, R. L. (2017). Malaysian identities and mélange food cultures. *Journal of Intercultural Studies*, 38(2), 139–154.

Lee, S. K. (2008). The Peranakan Baba Nyonya culture: Resurgence or disappearance? *SARI:Jurnal Alam dan Tamadun Melayu, 26*, 161–170.

Lee, S.-Y. (1984). Financial institutions and markets in Singapore. Financial Institutions and Markets in Southeast Asia: A Study of Brunei, Indonesia, Malaysia, Philippines, Singapore and Thailand (pp. 226–295). New York, NY: Palgrave Macmillan.

Leonidou, L. C., Katsikeas, C. S., & Piercy, N. F. (1998). Identifying managerial influences on exporting: Past research and future directions. *Journal of International Marketing*, *6*(2), 74–102.

Leong, S. T., Wright, T., & Skinner, G. W. (1997). *Migration and ethnicity in Chinese history: Hakkas, Pengmin, and their neighbors*. Palo Alto, CA: Stanford University Press.

Li, X., & Liu, L. (2010). Embedded guanxi networks, market guanxi networks and entrepreneurial growth in the Chinese context. *Frontiers of Business Research in China*, *4*(3), 341–359.

Liang, H., & Lean, H. H. (2024). Fifty years of excellence and beyond: The electrical and electronic industry of Penang, Malaysia. In S. R. Tan, H. Jang, & J. Wood (Eds.), *Economic growth and development in the tropics* (pp. 30–48). London: Routledge.

Liedholm, C., & Mead, D. (1987). *Small scale industries in developing countries: Empirical evidence andpolicy implications* (Working Paper). Department ofAgricultural Economics, Michigan State University.

Light, I., & Bonacich, E. (1988). *Immigrant entrepreneurs: Koreans in Los Angeles 1965–82*. Berkley, CA: University of California Press.

Light, I., Bernard, R. B., & Kim, R. (1999). Immigrant incorporation in the garment industry of Los Angeles. *International Migration Review*, *33*(1), 5–25.

Lim, C. P. (1987). Changes in the Malaysian economy and trade trends and prospects. In C. I. Bradford Jr. & W. H. Branson (Eds.), *Trade and structural change in Pacific Asia* (pp. 435–466). Chicago, IL: University of Chicago Press.

Lim, E. N. K., Lubatkin, M. H., & Wiseman, R. M. (2010). A family firm variant of the behavioral agency theory. *Strategic Entrepreneurship Journal, 4*(3), 197–211.

Lim, G. T. (2004). *My story*. Subang Jaya: Pelanduk Publications.

Lim, L. Y. C. (1983). Chinese business, multinationals and the state: Manufacturing for export in Malaysia and Singapore. In L. Y. C. Lim & L. A. P. Goslin (Eds.), *The Chinese in Southeast Asia: Ethnicity and economic activity* (vol. 1)., Singapore: Maruzen Asia.

Lim, M. H. (1981). *Ownership and control of the one hundred largest corporations in Malaysia*. Kuala Lumpur: Oxford University Press.

Lim, S. E. (1960). Tan Cheng lock his leadership of the Malayan Chinese. *Journal of Southeast Asian History*, *1*(1), 29–55.

Lim, S. H., & Mokhtar, K. S. (2017). Migration control in Malaysia: Shifting toward internal enforcement. *Asia-Pacific Social Science Review*, *16*(3), 46–64.

Lim, T. G. (1977). *Peasants and their agricultural economy in colonial Malaya 1884–1941*. Kuala Lumpur: Oxford University Press.

Ling, C., Jian, A., Zhu, H., & Fang, H. (2021). Chinese family business in Southeast Asia. In L. Chen, J. A. Zhu, & H. Fang (Eds.), *Family business in China, Volume 2: Challenges and opportunities* (pp. 137–151). Cham, Switzerland: Palgrave Macmillan.

Ling, H. Y., & Thock, K. P. (2015). The economic activities of Foochow in Sibu: Development and transformation. *Journal of Chinese Literature and Culture*, 3(2), 20–31.
Ling, W., & Fang, L. (2003). The Chinese leadership theory. In J. Osland, M. E. Mendenhall, & L. A. Maznevski (Eds.), *Advances in global leadership* (pp. 183–204). Leeds, UK: Emerald Group Publishing Limited.
Little, I. M. D., Mazumdar, D., & Page, J. (1987). *Small manufacturing enterprises in developing countries: A comparative study of India and other countries*. United Kingdom: Oxford University Press.
Litz, R. (1997). The family firm's exclusion from business school research: Explaining the void; addressing the opportunity. *Entrepreneurship Theory and Practice*, *21*(3), 55–71.
Liu, X., Mattariganond, D., & Narasaj, B. (2019). Migration of Yunnan people into Myanmar from ancient times to the 19th century. *Journal of Mekong Societies*, *15*(1), 18–39.
Lockard, C. A. (2003). *Chinese immigration and society in Sarawak, 1868–1917* (pp. 52–53). Sarawak Chinese Cultural Association.
Lockard, C. A. (2009). *Chinese society and politics in Sarawak: Historical essays*. Sibu, Sarawak, Malaysia: Sibu Sarawak Chinese Cultural Association.
Lockard, C. A. (2013). Chinese migration and settlement in Southeast Asia before 1850: Making fields from the sea. *History Compass, 11*(9), 765–781.
Long, J. A., & Tan, D. (2011). The growth of the private wealth management industry in Singapore and Hong Kong. *Capital Markets Law Journal*, *6*(1), 104–126.
Luangthongkum, T. (2007). The position of Non-Thai languages in Thailand. In L. H. Guan & L. Suryadinata (Eds.), *Language, nation and development in Southeast Asia* (p. 191). ISEAS Publishing.
Luo, Y. (2003). Industrial dynamics and managerial networking in an emerging market: The case of China. *Strategic Management Journal, 24*(13), 1315–1327.
Lynelle Tham. (2022). Chan Sow Lin, tin mining tycoon who set KL in motion. Free Malaysia Today - 19 Oct 2022
Mackie, J. A. (1992). Overseas Chinese entrepreneurship. *Asian-Pacific Economic Literature*, *6*(1), 41–64.
Mackie, J. (2003). Thinking about the Chinese overseas. *American Asian Review*, *21*(4), 1.
Mak, L. F. (1985). *Fang-yen-quan ren-tong (Dialect Group Identity)*. Taipei: Institute of Ethnology, Academia Sinica.
Mak, L. F. (1993). *Occupation and Chinese Dialect Group in British Malaya*. Chinese Adaptation and Diversity: Essays on Society and Literature in Indonesia, Malaysia & Singapore, 8–27.
Mak, L. F., & Lai, H. M. (1992). Occupational structures of Chinese immigrants in early Malaya and North America. *Southeast Asian Journal of Social Science, 20*(1), 43–66.
Malaysia Crude Oil: Exports, 1980 – 2024 | CEIC Data. (n.d.). *Malaysia Crude Oil: Exports, 1980 – 2024 | CEIC Data*. Retrieved May 3, 2024, from www.ceicdata.com/en/indicator/malaysia/crude-oil-exports
Mangan, C. (2018). Private enterprises in fragile situations: Myanmar. International Growth Centre (IGC) country report. London: IGC.
Marshall, C., & Rossman, G. B. (2014). *Designing qualitative research*. Sage Publications.
McAmis, R. D. (2002). *Malay Muslims: The history and challenge of resurgent Islam in Southeast Asia*. Wm. B. Eerdmans Publishing.
McCollom, M. E. (1992). Organizational stories in a family-owned business. *Family Business Review*, *5*(1), 3–24.
McCoy, A. W. (1994). *An anarchy of families: State and family in the Philippines*. Quezon City: Ateneo de Manila University Press.

McPherson, M. (2019). Think non-ethnic, but act ethnic: Perspectives from South Asian entrepreneurs. *Journal of Entrepreneurship, Management and Innovation, 15*(2), 117–152.

McVey, R. T. (1992). *Southeast Asian Capitalists* (No. 9). SEAP Publications. Metuchen, NJ: Scarecrow Press, 149.

Mehmet, O. (1986). *Development in Malaysia: Poverty, wealth and trusteeship*. London: Croom Helm.

Menkhoff, T. (1993). *Trade routes, trust and trading networks: Chinese small enterprises in Singapore*. Tokyo: Maruzen Asia.

Merriam-Webster. (n.d.). Dynasty. In *Merriam-Webster.com dictionary*. Retrieved November 21, 2024, from www.merriam-webster.com/dictionary/dynasty

Michaud, J. (2013). China, Vietnam, and Laos. *Red stamps and gold stars: Fieldwork dilemmas in upland socialist Asia, 52*, 22.

Mills, L. A., Turnbull, C. M., & Bassett, D. K. (1960). British Malaya 1824-67. *Journal of the Malayan Branch of the Royal Asiatic Society, 33*(3, 191), 1–424.

Minai, M. S., & Lucky, I. O. E. (2011). Re-investigating the effect of individual determinant, external factor and firm characteristics on small firm performance during economic downturn. *African Journal of Business Management, 5*(26), 10846–10854.

Mohamed, A. F. (2009). Recycling systems in Malaysia: Case studies on industrial waste. In Kojima, M. & E. Damanhuri (Eds.), 3R policies for Southeast and East Asia (pp. 53–72). Economic Research Institute for ASEAN and East Asia (ERIA). Jakarta, Indonesia

Morck, R., & Nakamura, M. (2003). The history of corporate ownership in Japan. *Finance Working, European Corporate Governance Institute, 20*, 1–143.

Morck, R., & Yeung, B. (2003). Agency problems in large family business groups. *Entrepreneurship Theory and Practice, 27*(4), 367–382.

Morse, J. M., & Richards, L. (2002). *Readme first: For a user guide to qualitative methods*. Thousand Oaks, California: Sage Publications.

Mosbah, A., & Abd Wahab, K. (2018). Chinese family business in Malaysia: Development, culture, and the family business philosophy. *Social Sciences, 8*(5), 1013–1021.

Mulholland, K. (1997). The family enterprise and business strategies. *Work Employment and Society, 11*(4), 685–711.

Munari, F., Oriani, R., & Sobrero, M. (2010). The effects of owner identity and external governance systems on R&D investments: A study of western European firms. *Research Policy, 39*(8), 1093–1104.

Mya Than, Khin Maung Kyi. (1997). The ethnic Chinese in Myanmar and their identity. In L. Suryadinata (Ed.), *Ethnic Chinese as Southeast Asians* (pp. 115–157). New York: Palgrave Macmillan.

Myint-U, T. (2011). *Where China meets India: Burma and the new crossroads of Asia*. New York: Farrar, Straus and Giroux.

Nanyang University, Department of History (1971). Xinjiapo huazu hangye shi diaocha baogao, (4) xinhuaren yu jiaotongye (Research reports on Chinese trades in Singapore, No. 4, The Henghuas and traffic trades). Nanyang University, Department of History, Singapore, 83.

Napolitano, G. (1991). Industrial research and sources of innovation: A cross-industry analysis of Italian manufacturing firms. *Research Policy, 20*(2), 171–178.

Nathan Peng & Sock-Yong Phang. (2018). Singapore's economic development: Pro- or anti-Washington Consensus? *Economic and Political Studies, 6*(1), 30–52.

Neubauer, F. F., & Lank, A. G. (Eds.). (1998). *The family business: Its governance for sustainability*. London: Routledge.

Ng, E., & Ng, C. (2003). Women micro entrepreneurs in Hong Kong. In J. E. Butler (Ed.), *New perspectives on women entrepreneurs* (pp. 121–50). Greenwich, CT: Information Age Publishing.

Ngu, I. T. (2011). *Global trade and political continuity: The rise of timber tycoons in Sarawak, 1945–1963*. Department of Southeast Asian Studies, Humboldt-University.

Nguyen, V. H. (1993). *Nguoi Hoa tai Vietnam [The Hoa in Vietnam]*. Nha xuat ban NBC.

Nield, R. (2015). *China's foreign places: The foreign presence in China in the treaty port era, 1840–1943*. Hong Kong: Hong Kong University Press.

Niew Shong Tong. (1976). The pattern of economic activity of the modern Chinese communities in East Malaysia and Brunei. China Society (*China Society 25th Anniversary Journal)*, 40–55.

Niew, S. (1969). *The population geography of the Chinese communities in Malaysia, Singapore and Brunei* (p. 296). University of London, School of Oriental and African Studies (United Kingdom).

Nonaka, I. (1994). A dynamic theory of organizational knowledge creation. *Organization Science, 5*, 14–37

Nordqvist, M., & Melin, L. (2008). Strategic planning champions: Social craftspersons, artful interpreters, and known strangers. *Long Range Planning, 41*(3), 326–344.

Null, Null. (2021). *Laporan Banci Penduduk dan Perumahan (BPP) 2021: Ciri-ciri Demografi, Isirumah dan Perumahan*. Jabatan Perancangan Ekonomi dan Statistik Kementerian Kewangan dan Ekonomi.

Null, Null. (2021). Malaysia's food industry: A melting pot with the right ingredients. www.mida.gov.my. MIDA | Malaysian Investment Development Authority.

Okorafo, S. C. (1999). Internationalization of family businesses: Evidence from Northwest Ohio, USA. *Family Business Review, 12*, 147–158.

Omohundro, J. T. (1983). Social network and business success for the Philippine Chinese. In L. Lim & P. Gosling (Eds.), *The Chinese in South East Asia: Ethnicity and economic activity* (vol. 1, pp. 65–85). Tokyo: Maruzen Asia.

Ong, G. C. (2019). Corporate governance of innovation In *Singapore Chinese family business*.

Osman-Rani, H. (1992). Toward a Fully Developed Malaysia: Vision and Challenges. *Southeast Asian Affairs*, 202–217.

Palanca, E. (1995). *Chinese business families in the Philippines since the 1890s*. London: Routledge.

Pananond, P. (2001). The making of Thai multinationals: A comparative study of the growth and internationalization process of Thailand's Charoen Pokphand and Siam Cement Groups. *Journal of Asian Business, 17*(3), 57–76.

Pang, L. L. (2015). Minority participation in an Islamic Negara. *The Journal of Islamic Governance, 1*, 1.

Pang, L. L. (2019). No Longer 'Ali-Baba'But 'Ali Chandran' Businesses in Brunei Darussalam: An exploration. *Policy & Governance Review*, *3*(2), 107–126.

Patton, M. (1990). *Qualitative evaluation and research methods* (pp. 169–186). Beverly Hills, CA: Sage.

Peng, C. O. (2013). Chinese education in Southeast Asia. In T. Chee-Beng (Ed.), *Routledge handbook of the Chinese diaspora* (pp. 446–458). London: Routledge.

Peng, M. W., & Luo, Y. (2000). Managerial ties and firm performance in a transition economy: The nature of a micro-macro link. *Academy of Management Journal*, 43(3), 486–501.

Peng, W. T. (1977). *The origins of Chinese Kongsi with special reference to West Borneo*. The Australian National University (Australia).

Penrose, E. T. (1980). *The theory of the growth of the firm*. Oxford: Basil Blackwell.

Pham, T. T., Bell, R., & Newton, D. (2019). The father's role in supporting the son's business knowledge development process in Vietnamese family businesses. *Journal of Entrepreneurship in Emerging Economies, 11*(2), 258–276.

Pires, G., & Stanton, J. (2000). Ethnicity and acculturation in a culturally diverse country: Identifying ethnic market segments. *Journal of Multilingual and Multicultural Development, 21*(1), 42–57.

Pires, G., & Stanton, J. (2005). *Ethnic marketing: Accepting the challenge of cultural diversity*. London: Thomson Learning.

Poh-Seng, P. (1969). The Straits Chinese in Singapore: A case of local identity and socio-cultural accommodation. *Journal of Southeast Asian History, 10*(1), 95–114.

Polanyi, M. (1958). *Personal knowledge: Toward a post-critical philosophy* (2nd ed. 1962). Routledge & Kegan Paul.

Polanyi, M. (1962). Tacit knowing: Its bearing on some problems of philosophy. *Reviews of Modern Physics, 34*(4), 601.

Polanyi, M. (1966). *The tacit dimension*. Routledge and Kegan Paul.

Population in Brief 2023: Key Trends. (2023, December 10). Population in Brief 2023: Key Trends. www.population.gov.sg/media-centre/articles/population-in-brief-2023-key-trends/

Portes, A. (1995). *The economic sociology of immigration: Essays on networks, ethnicity, and entrepreneurship*. New York: Russell Sage Foundation.

Portes, A., & Zhou, M. (1992). Gaining the upper hand: Economic mobility among immigrant and domestic minorities. *Ethnic and Racial Studies, 15*(4), 491–522.

Porter, M. E. (1990). *The competitive advantage of nations*. New York: Free Press.

Porter, M. E. (2001). The value chain and competitive advantage. *Understanding Business Processes, 2*, 50–66.

Poza, E. J. (2010). Late stage entrepreneurial activity: What students should know about family-owned and family-controlled companies. In A. Stewart, G. T. Lumpkin, & J. A. Katz (Eds.), *Entrepreneurship and family business* (pp. 359–366). Bingley, UK: Emerald Group Publishing Limited.

Prajogo, D. I., & Ahmed, P. K. (2006). Relationships between innovation stimulus, innovation capacity, and innovation performance. *R&D Management, 36*(5), 499–515.

Pue, G. H. (2017). 'Our Chinese': The mixedness of Peranakan Chinese identities in Kelantan, Malaysia. In Z. L. Rocha (Ed.), *Mixed race in Asia: Past, present and future* (pp. 147–161). London: Routledge.

Purcell, V. (1947). Chinese settlement in Malacca. *Journal of the Malayan Branch of the Royal Asiatic Society, 20*(1 ,141), 115–125.

Puthucheary, J. J. (1960). *Ownership and control in the Malayan economy*. Singapore: Eastern Universities Press.

Raijman, R., & Tienda, M. (2000). Immigrants' pathways to business ownership: A comparative ethnic perspective. *International Migration Review, 34*(3), 682–706.

Ram, M. (2001). Family dynamics in a small consultancy firm: A case study. *Human Relations, 54*(4), 395–418.

Ram, M., & Smallbone, D. (2001). Ethnic Minority Enterprise: Policy in Practice, Report commissioned by the Small Business Service, June, De Montford University and the Centre for Enterprise and Economic Development.

Ram, M., & Smallbone, D. (2003). Policies to support ethnic minority enterprise: The English experience. *Entrepreneurship and Regional Development, 15*(2) 51–66.
Ram, M., Smallbone, D., Deakins, D., & Jones, T. (2003). Banking on'break-out': Finance and the development of ethnic minority businesses. *Journal of Ethnic and Migration Studies, 29*(4), 663–681.
Ramoglou, S., & Tsang, E. W. (2016). A realist perspective of entrepreneurship: Opportunities as propensities. *Academy of Management Review, 41*(3), 410–434.
Rath, J., & Kloosterman, R. (1999) Outsider's business: A critical review of research on immigrant entrepreneurship. *International Migration Review, 34*(3), 657–681.
Redding, G., & Witt, M. A. (2011). Chinese business systems and the challenges of transition. In C. Rowley (Ed.), *China's changing workplace* (pp. 34–50). London: Routledge.
Redding, S. G. (1990). *The spirit of Chinese capitalism.* New York: W. de Gruyter.
Redding, S. G. (1993). Cultural effects on the marketing process in South-east Asia. *Societal Culture and Management, 24*, 217–232.
Reid, A. (2011). Chinese on the mining frontier in Southeast Asia. In E. Tagliacozzo (Ed.), *Chinese circulations: Capital, commodities, and networks in Southeast Asia*. Durham, North Carolina: Duke University Press.
Reid, A., & Rodgers, K. A. (2001). *Sojourners and settlers: Histories of Southeast China and the Chinese*. Hawaii: University of Hawaii Press.
Reynolds, P., Storey, D. J., & Westhead, P. (1994). Cross-national comparisons of the variation in new firm formation rates. *Regional Studies, 28*(4), 443–456.
Richter, F. (1999). *Business networks in Asia: Promises, doubts, and perspectives.* Bloomsbury Publishing USA.
Rieffel, L. (2010). *Myanmar/Burma: Inside challenges, outside interests* (pp. 95–97). Washington, D.C.: Brookings Institution Press.
Rivera, J. P. R., Tullao, T. S. (2023). Estimating the impact of selected macroeconomic indicators on remittance inflows in the Philippines. *Journal of Southeast Asian Economies, 39*(3), 273–290.
Roberts, J. L. (2016). *Mapping Chinese Rangoon: Place and nation among the Sino-Burmese*. Washington, D.C.: University of Washington Press.
Robison, R., Hewison, K., & Higgott, R. (Eds.). (1987). *Southeast Asia in the 1980s: The politics of economic crisis*. London: Unwin Hyman.
Rossetti, F. (1997). Rebirth of the Laotian Chinese community as peace returns to Indochina: The Chinese in Laos. *China Perspectives, 13*, 26–40. SAGE.
Rudolph, J. (1998). *Reconstructing identities: A social history of the Babas in Singapore* (pp. 43–44, 66–67). Singapore: Ashgate.
Ryan, C., Deane, R. H., & Ellington, N. P. (2001). Quality management training in small to midsized manufacturing firms. *Quality Management Journal, 8*(2), 44–52.
Saah, P. (2022). The impact of education and training on the success of small and medium-sized enterprises. *Journal of Economics Education and Entrepreneurship, 3*(2), 32–46.
Sahakijpicharn, K. (2007). Guanxi network and business performance of Sino-Thai SMEs (PhD thesis, University of Wollongong).
Sai, S. M. (2021). Benevolent technocracy: The Chinese Protectorate, migration control and racialised governmentality in colonised Malaya. *Journal of Southeast Asian Studies, 52*(3), 441–463.
Saleh, A. S., & Ndubisi, N. O. (2006). *SME development in Malaysia: Domestic and global challenges*. (Economics Working Papers wp06-03). School of Economics, University of Wollongong.

Salobir, C. L. (2011). *Food culture in Colonial Asia. A taste of empire*. Milton Park Abingdon Oxon: Routledge Press.

Salvato, C., & Moores, K. (2010). Research on accounting in family firms: Past accomplishments and future challenges. *Family Business Review, 23*(2), 193–215.

Sam, D. L., & Berry, J. W. (2010). Acculturation: When individuals and groups of different cultural backgrounds meet. *Perspectives on Psychological Science, 5*(4), 472–481.

Sanders, J., & Nee, V. (1996). Immigrant self-employment: The family as social capital and the value of human capital. *American Sociological Review, 61*(2), 231–249.

Savage, V. R., & Yeoh, B. (2013, June 15). *Singapore Street Names: A Study of Toponymics*. Singapore: Marshall Cavendish International Asia Pte Ltd.

Saw, S. H. (1988). The population of peninsular Malaysia. NUS Press. *Science, 25*(2), 103–116.

Schumpeter, J. (1934). *The theory of economic development*. Homewood, Illinois, USA: Irwin University Books..

Scranton, P. (1997). *Endless novelty: Specialty production and American industrialization, 1865–1925*. Princeton, New Jersey, USA: Princeton University Press.

Seng, L. T. (2015). Coolies, triads and pimps: Chinatown in former times. BiblioAsia. Available at: https://biblioasia.nlb.gov.sg/vol-11/issue-3/oct-dec-2015/coolies.

Sequeira, J. M., & Rasheed, A. A. (2006). Start-up and growth of immigrant small businesses: The impact of social and human capital. *Journal of Developmental Entrepreneurship*, *11*(04), 357–375.

Shane, S. A. (2003). *A general theory of entrepreneurship: The individual-opportunity nexus*. Princeton, New Jersey, USA: Edward Elgar Publishing.

Share, M. (1994). The Chinese Community in South Vietnam during the Second Indochina War. *Journal of Third World Studies. Association of Third World Studies Inc.*, *11*(2), 240–265.

Siddique, S., & Suryadinata, L. (1982). Bumiputra and Pribumi: Economic nationalism (Indiginism) in Malaysia and Indonesia. *Pacific Affairs*, 54(4), 662–687.

Siddiqui, K. (2012). Malaysia's socio-economic transformation in historical perspective. *International Journal of Business and General Management, 1*(2), 21–50.

Sidel, J. T. (2012). The fate of nationalism in the new states: Southeast Asia in comparative historical perspective. *Comparative Studies in Society and History, 54*(1), 114–144.

Sieh, L. M. L. (1982). *Ownership and control of Malaysian manufacturing corporations*. Kuala Lumpur: UMCB Publications.

Siguaw, J. A., Simpson, P. M., & Enz, C. A. (2006). Conceptualizing innovation orientation: A framework for study and integration of innovation research. *Journal of Product Innovation Management, 23*(6), 556–574.

Simons, H. (2009). *Case study research in practice*. London: Sage.

Singh, B. (2008). Growing coffers: Aggregate wealth of Malaysia's 40 richest. *Malaysian Business*, February 16–29, 18.

Sirmon, D. G., & Hitt, M. A. (2003). Managing resources: Linking unique resources, management, and wealth creation in family firms. *Entrepreneurship Theory and Practice, 27*(4), 339–358.

Skinner, G. W. (1951). *Report on the Chinese in Southeast Asia*, December 1950 (No. 1). Southeast Asia Program, Department of Far Eastern Studies.

Skinner, G. W. (1957). *Chinese society in Thailand: An analytical history*. New York: Cornell University Press.

SME Corporation Malaysia. (2022a). SME definations. www.smecorp.gov. my/index.php/en/policies/2020-02-11-08-01-24/sme-definition

SME Corporation Malaysia. (2022b). MSME statistics. www.smecorp.gov. my/index.php/en/policies/2020-02-11-08-01-24/sme-statistics

Smith, M., & Allsebrook, A. (1994). *Ethnic groups in Burma*. Anti-Slavery International. London, UK.

Song, O. S. (1984). *One hundred years of history of the Chinese in Singapore*. Singapore: Oxford University Press.

Soriano, E. (2016). Inspiring Filipino-Chinese entrepreneurs. *Asian Journal*. https://asianjournal.com/business/consumer-columnists/inspiring-filipino-chinese-entrepreneurs/

Southiseng, N., Ty, M., Walsh, J., & Anurit, P. (2008). Development of excellent entrepreneurs in small and medium enterprises in Laos and Cambodia. *GMSARN International Journal, 2*(4), 147–156.

Spence, J. D. (1996). *God's Chinese son: The Taiping Heavenly Kingdom of Hong Xiuguan*. New York: W. W. Norton & Company.

Stamp, L. D. (1930). Burma: An undeveloped monsoon country. *Geographical Review. American Geographical Society, 20*(1), 107–109.

Steier, L. (2001). Next-generation entrepreneurs and succession: An exploratory study of modes and means of managing social capital. *Family Business Review, 14*(3), 259–276.

Steier, L. (2007). New venture creation and organization: A familial sub-narrative. *Journal of Business Research, 60*(10), 1099–1107.

Storey, D. J. (1994). *Understanding the small business sector.* London: Routledge.

Strobl, A., Peters, M., & Raich, M. (2014). Entrepreneurial networks: Exploring the role of social capital. *International Review of Entrepreneurship, 12*(3), 37–60.

Stuart-Fox, M. (1979). Factors influencing relations between the Communist parties of Thailand and Laos. *Asian Survey, 19*(4), 333–352.

Suddaby, R., & Jaskiewicz, P. (2020). Managing traditions: A critical capability for family business success. *Family Business Review, 33*(3), 234–243.

Suehiro, A. (1992). Capitalist development in postwar Thailand: Commercial bankers, industrial elite, and agribusiness groups. *Southeast Asian Capitalists, 21,* 1960–1975.

Sugihara, K. (2004). The East Asian path of economic development: A long-term perspective. In G. Arrighi, T. Hamashita, & M. Selden (Eds.), *The resurgence of East Asia* (pp. 92–137). London: Routledge.

Suryadinata, L. (1978). *Pribumi Indonesians, the Chinese Minority, and China: A study of perceptions and policies*. Singapore: Heinemann Educational Books.

Suryadinata, L. (1993). Patterns of Chinese political participation in four ASEAN states. *Contemporary Southeast Asia, 15*(3), 292–308.

Suryadinata, L. (1997). *Ethnic Chinese As Southeast Asians* (p. 288). Singapore: Institute of Southeast Asian Studies.

Suryadinata, L. (2012). *Southeast Asian personalities of Chinese descent: A biographical dictionary, Volume I & II*. Singapore: Institute of Southeast Asian Studies.

Suryadinata, L., Arifin, E. N., & Ananta, A. (2003). The Ethnic Chinese: A Declining Percentage. In *Indonesia's Population: Ethnicity and Religion in a Changing Political Landscape, Indonesia's Population Series* (pp. 73–102). Singapore: Institute of Southeast Asian Studies.

Susilo, D., & Sugihartati, R. (2020). *Indonesian nationalism discourse on YouTube video produced by Young Chinese-Indonesians*. Plaridel: Advance On.

T'ien J. (1983). The Chinese of Sarawak: Thirty Years of Change. *Southeast Asean Studies, 21*(3), 275–287.

Tagiuri, R., & Davis, J. (1996). Bivalent attributes of the family firm. *Family Business Review, 9*(2), 199–208.

Tan, C. B. (1988). Nation-building and being Chinese in a Southeast Asian state: Malaysia. In J. W. Cushman & W. Gungwu (Eds.), *Changing identities of the Southeast Asian Chinese since World War II* (p. 139). Hong Kong: Hong Kong University Press.

Tan, C. B. (1988). *Chinese Peranakan Heritage in Malaysia and Singapore.* Kuala Lumpur: Fajar Bakti.

Tan, Danielle. (2012). "Small is beautiful": Lessons from Laos for the study of Chinese overseas. *Journal of Current Chinese Affairs*, *41*(2), 61–94.

Tan, E. A. (2001). Philippine – The 1997–1999 Philippine Economic Downturn: A Preventable One. Quezon City, Philippines: University of the Philippines Press.

Tan, E. K. (2001). From sojourners to citizens: Managing the ethnic Chinese minority in Indonesia and Malaysia. *Ethnic and Racial Studies*, *24*(6), 949–978.

Tan, E. L. (1953). The Chinese banks incorporated in Singapore and the Federation of Malaya. *Journal of the Malayan Branch of the Royal Asiatic Society, 26*(1), 113–139.

Tan, G. L. (2018). *An introduction to the culture and history of the Teochews in Singapore*. Singapore: World Scientific Publishing Co Pte Ltd.

Tan, H. W., & Batra, G. (1995). *Enterprise training in developing countries: Incidence, productivity effects, and policy implications*. Washington, D.C.: World Bank.

Tan, K. H. (1990). *Chinese dialect groups: Traits and trades*. Singapore: Opinion Books.

Tan, K. H. (1997). 甲必丹时代的华人社会 [The Chinese community during the Kapitan Cina Era]. In Y. L. Lee (Ed.), 甲必丹叶亚来的一生 [The Life Journey of Capitan Yap Ah Loy]. Kuala Lumpur: Malaysian Chinese Research Centre.

Tan, L. H. (2011). Family-owned firms in Singapore: Legal strategies for constraining self-dealing in concentrated ownership structures. *Singapore Academy of Law Journal,* 23, 890–931.

Tan, M. L. (2021). *Social boundaries and the mental health of the Lannang: Ethnic Chinese in the Philippines* (pp. 197–209). Cham, Switzerland: Springer International Publishing.

Tan, S. K., & Tan, S. H. (2024). A story of food and place: Constructing Chinese identities in a multicultural Malaysian society. *Identities*, *31*(4), 1–24.

Tan, T. W. (1982). *Income distribution and determination in West Malaysia.* Kuala Lumpur: Oxford University Press.

Tanaka, S., & Kenney, M. (1996). US and Japanese electronics industries in Malaysia: A comparative analysis. *Journal of International Cooperation Studies*, *4*(1), 59–72.

Teik-Cheok Loy, J. (2012). Overseas Chinese family business research: A comparative analysis. *Journal of Family Business Management*, *2*(1), 31–39.

Tharenou, P., Donohue, R., & Cooper, B. (2007). *Management Research Methods.* New York: Cambridge University Press.

Thien, R. (2012, October 29). Waring against misuse of licences: Don't be passive partners, Bruneians told. *The Brunei Times*.

Thomas, A. S., & Mueller, S. L. (2000). A case for comparative entrepreneurship: Assessing the relevance of culture. *Journal of International Business Studies, 31*(2), 287–301.

Thornton, P. H. (1999). The sociology of entrepreneurship. *Annual Review of Sociology, 25*, 19–46.

Thung Ju Lan. (2012). Heterogenitas Orang Keturunan Cina (Tionghoa) di Indonesia Dalam Perspektif Sosial-Budaya. *Paradigma: Jurnal Kajian Budaya, 3*(1), 42–53.

Tienda, M. (2001). Comparative perspectives on ethnic and immigrant entrepreneurship and business development in Chicago. *Paper prepared for the Illinois Coalition for Immigrant and Refugee Rights*. Retrieved September 2024 from www.roosevelt.edu/ima/pdfs/ethnic-immigrant-entrepreneurship.pdf

Tim Doling. (1972). *The annals of Philippine Chinese historical association, issues 3-7*. Philippine Chinese Historical Association.

Tong, C. K., & Yong, P. K. (2014). Guanxi bases, xinyong and Chinese business networks. In Chee-Kiong Tong (ed.), *Chinese business: Rethinking guanxi and trust in Chinese business networks* (pp. 41–61). Singapore: Springer Singapore.

Townsend, R. (2005). Networks and finance in poor neighborhoods. In P. Bolton & H. Rosenthal (Eds.), *Credit markets for the poor* (pp. 178–202). New York, NY: Russell Sage Foundation.

Tregonning, K. C. (1963). Straits Tin: A brief account of the first seventy-five years of The Straits Trading Company, Limited. *Journal of the Malayan Branch of the Royal Asiatic Society, 36*(1)(201), 102.

Tregonning, K. G. (1979). Tan Cheng Lock: A Malayan Nationalist. *Journal of Southeast Asian Studies, 10*(1), 25–76.

Trisha, N. (2021, April 1). Final salute to well-known coffee brand owner. *The Star.*

Trocki, C. A. (2006). *Singapore: Wealth, power and the culture of control*. New York: Routledge.

Trocki, C. A. (2012). *Opium, empire and the global political economy: A study of the Asian opium trade 1750–1950*. London: Routledge.

Trocki, C. A. (2019). *Opium and empire: Chinese society in colonial Singapore, 1800–1910*. Ithaca, NY: Cornell University Press.

Trung Vu Nguyen. (2009). Marginalizing Practices: Bureaucracy, Ethnography and Becoming Chinese in Colonial Vietnam (Ph.D. diss., University of Wisconsin-Madison), 89–92.

Tsao, F. W. K. (1993). *Succession and succession: Lessons from the Chinese cultural tradition*. Central, Hong Kong: Frank W. K. Tsao.

Turnell, S. (2009). *Fiery dragons: Banks, moneylenders and microfinance in Burma* (p. 261). Copenhagen, Denmark: NIAS Press.

Van Delft, H., Gorter, C., & Nijkamp, P. (2000). In search of ethnic entrepreneurship opportunities in the city: A comparative policy study. *Environment and Planning C: Government and Policy, 18*(4), 429–451.

Van Trang, T. (2015). Chinese identity negotiation by Chinese Vietnamese women in Cho Lon community, Ho Chi Minh city, Vietnam through the use of Chinese at home. *Journal of Mekong Societies, 11*(1), 55–87.

Vatikiotis, M. R. (2003). Catching the Dragon's Tail: China and Southeast Asia in the 21 st Century. *Contemporary Southeast Asia, 25*(1), 65–78.

Victor, Z., & Wong, S. L. (2016). Competing for leadership and ownership: The Li & Fung Group's legendary and strategy. *Journal of Entrepreneurship in Emerging Economies, 8*(3), 304–320.

Vietor, R. H., & White, H. (2016). *Singapore's "Midlife Crisis"?* (pp. 7–48) Singapore: World Scientific Book Chapters.

Volery, T. (2007). Ethnic entrepreneurship: A theoretical framework. *Handbook of Research on Ethnic Minority Entrepreneurship, 1*, 30–41.

Vu, T. (2013). Southeast Asia's New Nationalism: Causes and significance. *TRaNS: Trans-Regional and-National Studies of Southeast Asia, 1*(2), 259–279.

Wade, R. (1990). *Governing the market: Economic theory and the role of government in East Asian industrialization*. New Jersey: Princeton University Press.

Waldinger, R. (1986). *Through the eye of the needle: Immigrants and enterprise in New York's garment trades*. New York: New York University Press.

Waldinger, R. (1989). Structural opportunity or ethnic advantage? Immigrant business development in New York. *International Migration Review, 23*(1), 48–72.

Waldinger, R. (1995). The 'other side'of embedded ness: A case-study of the interplay of economy and ethnicity. *Ethnic and Racial Studies, 18*(3), 555–580.

Waldinger, R., Aldrich, H., & Ward, R. (1990). *Ethnic entrepreneurs: Immigrant business in industrial societies.* Newbury Park, CA: Sage Publications.

Walford, G. (2007). Classification and framing of interviews in ethnographic interviewing. *Ethnography and Education, 2(2),* 145–157.

Walsh, J. (2011). Challenges of economic stress on Chinese entrepreneurs and their families in Laos. *Journal of Social and Development Sciences*, *2*(1), 31–37.

Wang Gungwu. (1993). Secret societies and overseas Chinese. *The China Quarterly*, *47*, 553–560.

Wang Gungwu. (1996). Sojourning: The Chinese experience in Southeast Asia. In A. Reid (Ed.), *Sojourners and settlers: Histories of Southeast Asia and the Chinese* (pp. 1–9). Honolulu: University of Hawai'i Press.

Wang Gungwu. (2009). Chinese history paradigms. *Asian Ethnicity, 10*(3), 201–216.

Wang Zhenwu. (1988). Singapore Sanhe Association and Bobai. Bagui qiaokan, (2), 21–27. 王贞武. (1988). 新加坡"三和会馆"与博白乡贤. *八桂侨刊*, (1), 21–27.

Ward, J. (1987). *Keeping the family business healthy: How to plan for continuing growth, profitability and family leadership*. San Francisco, CA: Jossey-Bass.

Ward, J. (1999). *Values synthesize familiarizes companies.* In D. Meat Mele (Ed.), *Ethical considerations on entrepreneurship and family business* (pp. 149–155). Pamplona: Ediciones Universidad de Navarra.

Ward, J. L (2008). *Introduction in Tapies J. and J.L. Ward, family values and value creation. The fostering of enduring values within family-owned business* (pp. 1–6). New York: Palgrave Macmillan.

Ward, R. (1991). Economic development and ethnic business. In J. Curran, & R. A. Blackburn (Eds.), *Paths of Enterprise: The future of the small business*. London: Routledge.

Ward, R., & Jenkins, R. (1984). *Ethnic communities in business, strategies for economical survival.* Cambridge: Cambridge University Press.

Weber, M., & Kalberg, S. (2013). *The Protestant ethic and the spirit of capitalism.* London: Routledge.

Webster, T. J. (2014). Malaysian economic development, leading industries and industrial clusters. *The Singapore Economic Review*, *59*(05), 1450044.

Wee, L. (2014). The minoritization of languages in Singapore. In P. Sercombe & R. Tupas (Eds.), *Language, education and nation-building: Assimilation and shift in Southeast Asia* (pp. 181–199). London: Palgrave Macmillan UK.

Wee Liang Tan, & Siew Tong Fock. (2001). Coping with growth transitions: The case of Chinese family businesses in Singapore. *Family Business Review, 14*(2), 123–139.

Weidenbaum, M., & Hughes, S. (1996). *The bamboo network: How expatriate Chinese entrepreneurs are creating a new economic superpower in Asia*. New York: Martin Kessler Books and The Free Press.

Wen, W. Wong, & Wong, T. K. D. (2020). The Development of Cantonese Chinese Community in the Klang Valley, 1860–1941. *Journal of Chinese Literature and Culture, 8*(1), 1–24.

Weidenbaum, M. (1996). The Chinese family business enterprise. *California Management Review, 38*(4), 141–156.

Wertz, F. J. (2005). Phenomenological research methods for counseling psychology. *Journal of Counseling Psychology*, *52*(2), 167.

Whah, C. Y. (2007). From tin to Ali Baba's gold: The evolution of Chinese entrepreneurship in Malaysia. *IIAS Newsletter*, *45*, 18.

Whah, C. Y. (2008). The evolution of Chinese Malaysian entrepreneurship: From British Colonial Rule to Post-New Economic Policy. *Journal of Chinese Overseas, 4*(2), 203–237.

Whah, C. Y. (2017). The state and Malaysian Chinese Business: Past, present and future. *Malaysia Journal of Chinese Studies, 6*(1–2), 1–30.

Whah, C. Y., & Lim, E.-S. (2018). SME policies and performance in Malaysia. 3, 1–41.

Wickberg, E. (1964). The Chinese mestizo in Philippine history. *Journal of Southeast Asian History, 5*(1), 62–100.

Wijaya, T. (2019). Chinese business in Indonesia and capital conversion: Breaking the chain of patronage. *Southeast Asian Studies, 8*(2), 295–329.

Wong, C. Y., Sheu, J., & Lee, K. (2023). Dynamics or dilemma: Assessing the innovation systems of three satellite platform regions (Singapore, Dublin and Penang). *Eurasian Geography and Economics, 64*(5), 589–628.

Wong, H. W., & Chau, K. L. F. (2019). *Tradition and transformation in a Chinese family business*. New York: Routledge.

Wong Sin Kiong黄賢強. (2000).〈客籍領事梁碧如與檳城華人社會的幫權政治〉。收錄于徐正光主編《第四屆國際客家學研討會論文集：歷史與社會經濟》. 台北：中研院民族所, 401–426.

Wong Sin Kiong黄賢強.(2007). 客家領袖與檳城的社會文化. 周雪香主編《多學科視野中的客家文化》. 福州：福建人民出版社, 216–231.

Wong, S. L. (1985). The Chinese family firm: A model. *British Journal of Sociology, 36*(1), 58–72.

Wong, W. C. (2009). The Connotation of "Hakka" In *Southeast Asia: The Classification Process of Chinese in British Malaya*. 國立中央大學. 碩士論文.

Woo-Cumings, M. (Ed.). (2019). *The developmental state*. Cornell University Press.

Woo, W. T., Koh, H. L., & Teh, S. Y. (2020). Achieving excellence in sustainable development goals in Sunway University Malaysia. In K. L. Ho (Ed.), *Universities as living labs for sustainable development: Supporting the implementation of the sustainable development goals* (pp. 265–282). Cham, Switzerland: Springer.

Woon, T. K. (1989). Privatization in Malaysia: Restructuring or Efficiency? *ASEAN Economic Bulletin, 5*(3), 242–258.

Wu, X. A. (2009). China meets Southeast Asia: A long-term historical review. In K. L. Ho (Ed.), *Connecting and distancing: Southeast Asia and China* (pp. 3–30). Singapore: Institute of Southeast Asian Studies.

Xavier, J. A., Feranita, F., Jambulingam, M., & Singh, M. K. G. (2021). Assessing ethnic business sustainability in transgenerational succession. *Asia-Pacific Journal of Business Administration, 13*(4), 477–496.

Xavier, J. A., & Gomez, E. T. (2018). Still an ethnic enterprise after a generational change? Indian-owned SMEs in Malaysia. *Journal of Southeast Asian Studies*, *49*(2), 297–322.

Yang, Y-D. (2003). The Burmese Chinese of the early Qing Dynasty (1662–1795). *Overseas Chinese History Studies*, *4*, 44–53.

Yap, J. T., Cuenca, J. S., & Reyes, C. M. (2009). Impact of the global financial and economic crisis on the Philippines. Research Papers in Economics.

Yen, C. H. (1991). *History of Chinese Society of Singapore and Malaysia* (p. 33). Beijing: Zhongguo Huaqiao Chuban Gongsi. 颜清湟. (1991). *新马华人社会史*. 中国华侨出版公司, 33.

Yen, C. H. (1995). Early Fukienese Migration and Social Organization in Singapore and Malaya Before 1900. In C. H. Yen (Ed.), *Community and politics: The Chinese in Colonial Singapore and Malaysia* (pp. 75–77). Singapore: Times Academic Press.

Yen, C.-H. (1986). A Social History of the Chinese in Singapore and Malaya, 1800–1911. *Journal of Asian Studies, 47*(3), 721.
Yen, C.-H. (2002). *The ethnic Chinese in East and Southeast Asia: Business, culture and politics*. Singapore: Times Academic Press.
Yen, C.-H. (2006). The role of Hokkien Chinese in the history of Malaysia and Singapore. *Journal of Malaysian Chinese Studies, 9*, 79–104.
Yew, J. L. K. (2019). Ghee Hiang heritage: The Chinese innovating perseverance of tacit knowledge last few generations in Malaysia. *International Communication of Chinese Culture, 6*, 247–264.
Yew, J. L. K. (2020). Tacit knowledge and generational change: The China factor, enterprise development and Malaysian Chinese family SMEs in traditional food production. *China Report, 56*(1), 103–128.
Yew, J. L. K. (2021). Still a Chinese family business?: The role of tacit knowledge and innovation in Malaysian food industry. *Journal of Chinese Overseas, 17*(2), 399–418.
Yew, J. L. K. (2023). A conceptual framework for tacit knowledge transformation in family business: A case study of plastic family firm in Malaysia. *Vision*, 0(0).
Yew, J. L. K., & Gomez, E. T. (2014). Advancing tacit knowledge: Malaysian family SMEs in manufacturing. *Asian Economic Papers, 13*(2), 1–24.
Yew, J. L. K., & Tan, J. D. (2022). Adapting to local markets and political changes: Chinese businesses in Malaysia and Indonesia. *South East Asia Research, 30*(4), 452–471.
Yeo, A., & Gloria, E. (2022). National identity and the limits of Chinese public diplomacy in the Philippines. *Journal of Contemporary China, 32*(139), 1–19.
Yeoh, E. K. K. (2008). China's regional policy, poverty and the ethnic question. *The Copenhagen Journal of Asian Studies, 26*(2), 26–59.
Yeung, H. W. C. (1999). The internationalization of ethnic Chinese business firms from Southeast Asia: Strategies, processes and competitive advantage. *International Journal of Urban and Regional Research, 23*(1), 88–102.
Yeung, H. W. C. (2004). *Chinese capitalism in a global era: Toward hybrid capitalism*. London: Routledge.
Yeung, H. W. C. (2006). Change and continuity in Southeast Asian ethnic Chinese business. *Asia Pacific Journal of Management, 23*, 229–254.
Yi Li. (2015). *Yunnanese Chinese in Myanmar: Past and present*. Singapore: ISEAS Publishing.
Yin, R. K. (2003). *Case study research: Design and methods* (3rd ed.). Thousand Oaks, California: Sage Publications.
Yin, R. K. (2009). *Case study research: Design and methods* (vol. 5). Thousand Oaks, California: Sage Publications.
Yong, C. Y. (2015). Loke Yew. Singapore Infopedia, National Library Board Singapore. Updated November, 26.
Yoshihara, K. (1988). *The Rise of Ersatz Capitalism in South-East Asia*. Singapore: Oxford University Press.
Zahra, S. A. (2005). Entrepreneurial risk taking in family firms. *Family Business Review, 18*(1), 23–40.
Zahra, S. A., & Covin, J. G. (1995). Contextual influences on the corporate entrepreneurship-performance relationship: A longitudinal analysis. *Journal of Business Venturing, 10*(1), 43–58.
Zahra, S. A., Klein, S. B., & Astrachan, J. H. (2006). Theory building and the survival of family firms: Four promising research directions. In P. Z. Poutziouris, K. X. Smyrnios, &

S. B. Klein (Eds.), *Handbook of research on family business* (pp. 614–617). Cheltenham, UK: Edward Elgar.

Zahra, S. A., & Sharma, P. (2004). Family business research: A Strategic reflection. *Family Business Review, 17*(4), 331–346.

Zainal, A., Zali, A. N., & Kassim, M. N. (2010). Malaysian gastronomy routes as a tourist destination. *Journal of Tourism, Hospitality and Culinary Arts (JTHCA)*, *2*(1), 1–10.

Zhou, M. (2004). Revisiting ethnic entrepreneurship: Convergencies, controversies, and conceptual advancements, *International Migration Review, 38*(3), 1040–1074.

Zhou, M., & Bankston III, C. L. (2016). *The rise of the new second generation*. Hoboken, NJ: John Wiley & Sons.

Zhuang, G. (2008). On the Four Waves: History of Chinese Migration into Southeast Asia. *Southeast Asian Affairs (Xiamen)*, *1*(133), 69–81.

Zin, R. H. M. (1999). Malaysian reverse investments: Trends and strategies. *Asia Pacific Journal of Management*, *16*, 469–496.

陈昌榜. Chen. C. B. (1987). 马来西亚文冬的广西籍华侨华人. *八桂侨刊*, (1), 35–36.

陈平润. (1989). 广西籍华侨华人社团简介. 八桂侨刊, (2), 21–27.

陈吴泉. (1983). 月港的兴起与闽南华侨. 载《月港研究论文集》(第203页). 中共龙溪地委宣传部, 福建省历史学会厦门分会编。

陈自强. (1983). 论明代漳州月港. 载《月港研究论文集》(第90-97页). 中共龙溪地委宣传部, 福建省历史学会厦门分会编。

林伍光. (1989). <战后马来西亚华侨，华人经济的发展与现状>. 东南亚华人经济，福州：福建人民出版社 (Lin Wuguang. (1989). The Chinese in post-war Malaysia, economic development and current conditions. *The Economy of the Chinese in Southeast Asia* , Fuzhou: Fujian People's Press).

符国华 & 韩明定. Fu & Han. (2001). 海南人在新加坡的历史与现状. *海南档案*, *3*, 43–46.

赵和曼. (1996). *广西籍华侨华人研究*. 中国华侨出版社. *24*, 768–769.

赵麟斌. Zhao. L.B. (2016). 略述福州华人华侨对马来西亚经济发展的影响. *闽江学院学报, 37*(*3*), 1–6.

郑莉. (2009).《跨越国界的文化网络：新加坡兴化人的庙宇与仪式传统》，厦门大学博士学位论文。

郑莉. (2014). 东南亚华人的同乡同业传统——以马来西亚芙蓉坡兴化人为例. 开放时代, (*1*), 210–223.

郭慧. Guo. H. (2012).一代名商王绍经. *新东方*,(06),85.

Index

For Product Safety Concerns and Information please contact our EU representative GPSR@taylorandfrancis.com
Taylor & Francis Verlag GmbH, Kaufingerstraße 24, 80331 München, Germany

www.ingramcontent.com/pod-product-compliance
Ingram Content Group UK Ltd.
Pitfield, Milton Keynes, MK11 3LW, UK
UKHW020010200926
475702UK00015B/2571
9781032705866